STEPHANIE ALEXANDER was the creative force behind Stephanie's Restaurant before its closure on New Year's Eve in 1997. The restaurant was the recipient of many national and international awards and accolades, and was regarded as an essential Melbourne experience. In partnership with her daughter Lisa Montague, longtime friend Angela Clemens and cheese expert Will Studd, Stephanie opened the Richmond Hill Cafe & Larder in the autumn of 1997. She was awarded an Order of Australia in 1994 and in 1995 received an Australian Achiever award, presented to her by the prime minister.

Stephanie is a regular contributor to various national food publications. Her previous books include *Stephanie's Menus for Food Lovers*, *Stephanie's Feasts and Stories*, *Stephanie's Australia*, *Stephanie's Seasons*, *The Cook's Companion*, *Recipes My Mother Gave Me*, and *Stephanie Alexander and Maggie Beer's Tuscan Cookbook*. Stephanie is currently at work producing a television series for the ABC about food in Australia.

Stephanie's Journal

stephanie
alexander

Stephanie's Journal

VIKING

Viking
Penguin Books Australia Ltd
487 Maroondah Highway, PO Box 257
Ringwood, Victoria 3134, Australia
Penguin Books Ltd
Harmondsworth, Middlesex, England
Penguin Putnam Inc.
375 Hudson Street, New York, New York 10014, USA
Penguin Books Canada Limited
10 Alcorn Avenue, Toronto, Ontario, Canada M4V 3B2
Penguin Books (NZ) Ltd
Cnr Rosedale and Airborne Roads, Albany, Auckland, New Zealand
Penguin Books (South Africa) (Pty) Ltd
4 Pallinghurst Road, Parktown 2193, South Africa

First published by Penguin Books Australia Ltd, 1999

10 9 8 7 6 5 4 3 2 1

Design by Sandy Cull, Penguin Design Studio
Photography by Neil Lorimer
Author photograph by Simon Griffiths
Illustrations for all plates except September by Rosanna Vecchio
Typeset in Weiss by J&M Typesetting, Victoria
Printed and bound in Australia by Australian Book Connection, Victoria

National Library of Australia
Cataloguing-in-Publication data:

Alexander, Stephanie, 1940– .
   Stephanie's journal.

   Includes index.
   ISBN 0 670 86376 9.

   1. Alexander, Stephanie, 1940– – Diaries. 2. Cooks –
   Australia – Diaries. 3. Restaurateurs – Australia –
   Diaries. I. Title.

641.5092

*The author and publisher wish to thank copyright owners for the use of
extracted material in this book.*

CONTENTS

ACKNOWLEDGEMENTS

Overwhelmingly thanks to my family and friends who gave me loving support through the thick and the thin of 1997. And thanks once again to the talented team at Penguin, both design and editorial staff, and especially to Executive Publisher Julie Gibbs, and to Rosanna Vecchio who was responsible for the photographic illustrations. My mother bought her Spode teaset with her first earnings as a food writer and it is especially significant that it appears on the cover of this book – a symbol of achievement and commitment. I am also grateful to all the authors whose works are listed in the bibliography, for their inspiration.

INTRODUCTION

When I started to write this journal I had no inkling that 1997 would be

such a momentous year. Or that my life would be changed so dramatically.

Or that Stephanie's Restaurant would close forever. *Stephanie's Journal*

records the end of an era, and includes my own thoughts about

these things.

I had expected, rather, to explore my recurring preoccupations: how

one is connected through people and places to the past, which then

influences the present and the future. How one's personal philosophy

influences all aspects of one's life. And how out of step I sometimes feel

with a world that judges most enterprise by its profitability first of all,

whereas I am stuck with an obsession to do things well and hang the

expense. I am also constantly amazed at how chance happenings – or

fate – can catch one's imagination, or change one's direction, or fire

one's creativity.

The book includes stories about people and places and artistic

endeavour. It includes an account of the two months I spent in Tuscany

with my friend Maggie Beer, since published in a different form as

Stephanie Alexander and Maggie Beer's Tuscan Cookbook. It details the

establishment of Richmond Hill Cafe & Larder. And it includes much

about friendship and about growing old and about loss.

Inevitably there is plenty about good food – about finding it, cooking

it and enjoying it. As always, my joy in my vocation is all-pervading.

Good food and fellowship sustain me when I feel low, and delight me

when I want to celebrate. I am always optimistic that the next meal will

be wonderful. I feel full of energy, and life seems to get more satisfying

as it progresses. I am excited and curious about the future.

January

2 JANUARY

I have decided to keep a journal as I did in 1992, which was later published as *Stephanie's Seasons*. It is intriguing to ponder whether a new year will just reflect more of the same, or whether there will be genuine change.

In scrolling through the files on my computer today I came across this sad little piece that I wrote on 25 January last year. I certainly don't feel as black as this twelve months on.

Despair and black thoughts haunt me. I lie in my polished cherry wood bed between smooth sheets and feel panicky, yet just outside my open window is the early morning reassurance of an enduring tree trunk. I feel closer to the more short-lived damp leaves. Inner reassurance eludes me.

The world is in pairs like animals in Noah's Ark. A goes with B, and B finds C, and D fights with E, and then F leaves G. Where does it leave me? Me and my shadow . . . To seek my own destiny, to make my own decisions, to find satisfaction in solitude, and to cope with the wasp nest by the pool.

Proofs of my new book mount in piles. They are actually a pleasure to handle. Smooth sheets, just like my bed sheets. Clean type, no more brutal red lines, or redirection signs, or cramped additional words, or mysterious editorial marks. Now I read again my original thoughts shed of their dross and am pleased. Very pleased. My editor, Caroline, has done an excellent job. Where does she get the patience to maintain her meticulous march through this mountain of prose, with appreciation and good humour and an astounding memory?

I am fearful that my father's black cloud has drifted from him to me. A sticky enveloping and crushing sense of pointlessness.

Self-obsession that cannot be moved and that pushes friends away. No one can cope with the truly depressed. Their pain is so inward, and seemingly so trivial. Why should *she* feel bad? She should snap out of it. Lovely children, pleasant house, delightful garden, adoring dog, status and success (apparently), interesting friends (but where are they? locked into their own pleasures and pain, I suppose). My obsessions and worries are real enough, though.

I can push away the blackness by working hard at something practical – today it will be a new pigeon dish with sticky chestnuts and French nutty lentils. And making dainty heart-shaped raspberry-filled sponge cakes as a test for Valentine's Day. A restaurant full of lovers is a very odd thought.

As in 1992, New Year's Eve was spent with my closest friends. Jean, Helen, Kathy and I have been close since university days when we shared three eventful years at University Women's College. Extraordinary to think that nearly forty years have passed. Our daughters have long since graduated themselves, at least one having spent time in the same hall of residence as her mother.

Jean and her husband, John, were to leave the next day for a six-month posting in Frankfurt. We had heard that Frankfurt airport was closed because of ice, that northern Italy was experiencing temperatures so low that the lagoon in Venice had frozen. Meanwhile in Melbourne, we sat in the garden and sipped champagne, admiring a glorious vista of breeze-stirred blue salvia, agapanthus and plumbago. The temperature was about 23°C. My Julia roses are the colour of thick cream stirred into port wine, and the Sparrieshoop roses are wide open and fading from rose to palest pink. The terracotta pots overflow with scarlet petunias.

It was a good dinner and the conversation was fun. Can the present be utterly fulfilling without thought of the future or the past? How can we feel engaged in a world where governments seem to have no room for ethics and all decision-making is pragmatic?

This year does not open before me as a blank sheet. Already some chapters are partly written.

The proofs of a year ago are now a thing of the past. *The Cook's Companion* was published in early October and is selling like mad. It is a personal triumph, not just because it will earn me a new car, and then some, but because its message, that everyone can cook well with a bit of help from a friend, has been embraced wholeheartedly. The evidence is that there are a whole lot of Australians out there who have taken up their wooden spoons, opened their copies and are cooking!

My business partner in Stephanie's Restaurant, Dur-é Dara, and I made a momentous decision in mid-October and called for Expressions of Interest, but so far we have had nothing serious to consider. The immediate result was and continues to be an amazing upturn of business as every Melburnian who has ever enjoyed a meal at Stephanie's rushes to book a farewell experience. We have taken a calculated risk and gone for maximum publicity. Although few have understood our subtle message – if we do not attract a suitable offer, we will have no alternative but to continue. I know it is the correct moment for me to move on from this extraordinary and magnificent business, but of course it cannot be abandoned. Without a realistic offer, we will continue as we are and we will show we are still a force to be reckoned with.

Another major project on the horizon is a series of residential cooking schools that Maggie Beer and I are to hold in Tuscany in September and October of this year. This plan was hatched during a blissful holiday we shared in Umbria over a year ago. At the time I had expected that there would be no more Stephanie's Restaurant and that I would actually need to think of income-producing ventures. This is apparently not going to be the case, so Italy will have to be fitted in with a year that offers 'more of the same'. Already we have more than twenty firm commitments and can only accommodate thirty-six. Peter Bevan and Tony Phillips, our costumier friends, are to be our 'apprentices'. This project still needs lots of attention and Maggie and I have set aside a week in March to attend to it.

On the last day of 1996 I saw the film *Stealing Beauty* with my elder daughter, Lisa Montague. It was a languorous and loving pastorale by Bertoldo Bertolucci looking in on a family and friends, living, loving and holidaying in a stone house set in the hills near Siena and not too far from Villa di Corsano, where we will be. The heat of the Tuscan landscape was palpable in this film, but so was the joy of al fresco dining, tables lit by lamplight and people in loose clothes – or no clothes – and wild bacchanals in stone-walled gardens. I wonder whether we will manage these too?

My new project, Richmond Hill Cafe & Larder, will open in late April. This is the culmination of a long-held wish to create a foodie destination. A place that offers produce as well as cafe-style meals; a place that can host such diversified activities as wine tastings and book signings, and be a home to a cheese club; and above all a place that is friendly and relaxed, yet serious about its aims and its pursuit of quality.

One afternoon I just happened to drive down Bridge Road, Richmond, one of our most crowded retail shopping strips, and there it was – the perfect shop – and it was for lease. Of course, it wasn't quite as easy as that. The securing of the lease, the negotiations with all relevant bodies and the conceptual planning filled every spare minute late last year. Not to mention persuading cheese expert Will Studd to join in the project and convincing him that this was the right spot.

The team is made up of me, Will, my former personal assistant, Angela Clemens (and her husband, Duffy), and my daughter Lisa. We are now plotting and pushing to keep to our target. The design stage has been very involved. The tendering will probably be equally frustrating. We just want to get the construction started as we are paying rent every week on large premises.

To close this first entry, I should perhaps fill in faithful readers with a few more personal details. My younger daughter, Holly Alexander, is returning to France later in the year to complete her Arts degree at Jean Moulin University in Lyon. Lisa will be leaving her job as an event publicist to take up the managing of the new cafe. Angela has resigned as personal assistant to the partners at the Restaurant to concentrate on managing our new business.

Lisa, Angie and I confess to the night-time horrors of 'Can we do this?', 'Will we fail?'. We feel quite confident in the mornings!

9 JANUARY

*T*oday I walked to a fitness class (a routine I have embraced for the past two years) and admired the newly exposed, desert-red trunk of my favourite gum tree, its bark peeled and discarded. It still smells as wonderful as when I described it in 1992 and provides a moment of joy whenever I pass by.

Stephanie's Restaurant commenced the New Year to much tumult and shouting. Full house for the first two nights and the numbers have been steady since. Melbourne seems to value its institutions in an interesting manner. It appears that the general public finds it reassuring that this asset or institution exists, should one wish to use it, but there is not much understanding that a consistent level of support is needed to keep it viable. All seems fine at the moment.

Dur-é and I have set limits for ourselves this year, partly to acknowledge and accommodate our other projects, but also partly because we feel we have a great team of people who are able to manage the day-to-day routines very well and who are getting better and better at solving crises. The reality is that we will trial each working three days only. This is Week One.

Apart from projects already mentioned, I intend to overcome my reluctance to discover the Internet, or at least to use e-mail. Like everyone else I have to acknowledge that I am living through a period of momentous change. I can choose not to participate in this revolution but I must not pretend to have chosen when I am merely fearful of dealing with the technology. Probably one chooses not to participate at one's peril. As John reminded me before he flew away to Frankfurt, 'It will be so important to us when we are old and frail to be able to communicate widely'. A thought that is altogether too terrible to examine closely. (My father, who is eighty-eight, is reluctant to take on the challenge of the electronic keyboard, although he is comfortable with the electric typewriter I have given him.) John sent us an e-mail yesterday just to touch base and show us how easy it is.

Holly has been entertaining a fifteen-year-old Brisbane girl she got to know through chat sessions on the Internet. I must say I think it is odd that such a young girl is permitted to travel across the continent to stay with an unknown family. Does her family not become anxious? I think I would have when Holly was fifteen. What if I were an alcoholic or a child molester?

10 JANUARY

*D*ur-é and I dined in the Restaurant tonight. The salmon sampler was especially delicious – a small shaved fennel salad alongside the slice of seared salmon fillet in a gentle fish jelly, a spoonful of handmade mayonnaise (wooden spoon, not whisk), a pile of tartare dressed at the last minute with ginger and soy, and a slice of just-cut smoked salmon with a scattering of salmon roe. Dur-é had a salad of sweetbreads, dressed with orange juice, walnut oil and the reduced juices from the sweetbread braising, tossed with saffron pasta and pistachios and nestled among tender leaves.

Main courses were the sensational milk-fed veal chop topped with crisped sage leaves in browned butter and a smoky eggplant purée, and for Dur-é the buttery loin of lamb with fat lima beans tossed with pesto and grilled mushrooms. Vince Garreffa's White Rocks veal from Mondo di Carne (literally 'world of meat'!) in Perth offers exceptionally tender, well-flavoured meat, the carcass larger than we are used to in other Australian veal.

We shared a half-bottle of 1994 Horrocks Chardonnay, a sensational wine and perfect with the veal. We could not fault the food or the wine or the service. An excellent omen for 1997.

11 JANUARY

*T*his is the first Saturday in years that I have not worked (unless I've been far away). I have read the newspaper thoroughly, including a fascinating article by educationalist Neil Postman, reprinted from *The Guardian*. Postman is currently Professor of Communication Arts and Sciences at New York University. He suggests that we must establish a new storyline to convince the young of the relevance of education. Postman believes that not so long ago children were offered 'narratives', such as that education provided the surest path to self-improvement and the means to connect with society's sacred symbols, or, alternatively, the Protestant ethic with its claim that hard work and delayed gratification would result in satisfaction and society's approval. He postulates that these narratives are no longer convincing and have been replaced by more materialistic messages. The main point has become how to instruct and mould the young so that they can hope to make a living, not how to make a life. Allied to this is the rampant pursuit of consumerism, summed up neatly in a slogan he quotes: 'Whoever dies with the most toys wins'. And then there are those who suggest that the sole end of education is to accommodate oneself to technological change.

Postman rejects all these narratives as failing to motivate the young and instead proposes two alternative narratives: that of 'Spaceship Earth' and 'the Fallen Angel'. Spaceship Earth is the story of 'human beings as stewards of the Earth, caretakers of a vulnerable space capsule'. It stresses the interdependence of all people on the planet and the need for global cooperation. It is a story that will appeal, he believes, to the idealism of young people. It makes racism both irrelevant and ridiculous, and underlines the need to support and work for responsible public policy that cares for Spaceship Earth. The Fallen Angel narrative reassures each one of us that we all make mistakes and that it is by learning how to correct a mistake that meaningful progress occurs in all areas of human endeavour. To err is not merely human, it is essential in order to proceed. A hopeful and encouraging message.

This was an uplifting start to the day. On my return from the supermarket I climbed from my car in my trellised carport and felt I was not alone. Two round, brown eyes gazed down at me. A small ringtail possum has adopted an abandoned bird's nest as home, its white-tipped tail curled neatly around the nest, which is shaded from the sun by the riotous growth of a Lamarque rose. A rather good spot. I hope he/she has not spied my ripening peaches.

Maggie Beer gave me a miniature peach tree in a tub late last year. I was rather cynical about its prospects but I have had to recant as it now has about ten fruit that are daily becoming rosier and larger. The possums demolish my persimmons every year, very precisely hollowing the fruit on the side furthest away from the windows so that the damage is unnoticeable for a day or two. Still, a tree in fruit is so beautiful that I have decided not to net the peach but to take my chances.

17–20 JANUARY

We are experiencing a heatwave. Today it is to reach 40°C. The last four days have all been more than 35°C. Yesterday tennis star Steffi Graf collapsed with heat exhaustion after losing her match at the Australian Open.

I have just returned from an idyllic four-day retreat in the spa centre of Victoria. I stayed at Daylesford at one of our most delightful country houses, Lake House. Lisa joined me for the weekend, and together we walked, talked of new projects, enjoyed a mineral spa bath and massage at nearby Hepburn Springs, and visited old friends.

Under the shimmering heat the paddocks were pink-gold, hay bales were tightly curled sculptures seemingly placed at random ('our answer to Stonehenge', said my friend Noel Giacometti), the roadside was edged with flowering and shivering grasses, and the trunks of the gums were newly peeled of their bark. I chose the more rural route, all the better to enjoy the modest and appropriate timber homes with their weathered iron-roofed verandahs and mature fruiting trees. In some of the old goldmining towns these cottages have a new lease of life as bed-and-breakfast places, many also offering massages and spas. The reputation of the mineral springs in the area, once only visited by our post-war European migrants accustomed to spa centres in Europe, is on the rise.

My last visit to the mineral baths was twenty years ago and I had found the atmosphere quite creepy. The baths themselves were then of rough stone. Comatose bodies reclined in a long silent row, all heavily wrapped in towels, and the air was steamy and sulphurous. It had put me in mind of the notorious disappearance of Agatha Christie (the movie made of this story was set in a very alarming spa). I hurry to add that today's Hepburn Springs spa resort is nothing like this, nor does it resemble the place I visited so long ago.

Lisa and I chose essential oils for our baths, marvelling at the claims made for each 'flavour'. I chose rose otto, said to be excellent for dehydrated skin, and geranium, for those suffering from dermatitis. The bath surface was smooth, with just the right amount of water; I had a comfortable neck pillow and lay in the warm water gazing straight out of a large window onto a bank of mature and leafy gums that stirred with the slight breeze. After the massage my neck and shoulders had a new feeling of ease.

In the 1850s, Daylesford was the choice for many Swiss–Italian families who migrated to Australia in search of gold. My friend Noel is descended from one such family. His original family home is slowly settling further and further into the land, being loved to death by ever-growing and crushing trees. Noel has built a modern home a few metres away and took us on a guided tour of the estate. His trees bear chestnuts, walnuts, mulberries, crabapples, a yellow plum (could this be a gage? – it is one of the original trees planted long ago), apricots, medlars and many more. We discussed wrapping fresh white cheeses in chestnut leaves as is done with Banon cheese in France. This could be an interesting idea. (A few days following my return to Melbourne, Noel wrote to share a delightful image he had discovered in Elizabeth David's *French Provincial Cooking*: 'Perhaps a sheep farmer's wife will come down the hill with rabbits to sell, and the ewe's milk cheeses called *Banons*, wrapped in chestnut leaves'.)

Noel gave me a jar of his medlar jelly and cooked the most delicious currant cake for afternoon tea. The recipe is from *West Country Cooking* by Moyra Babington, a book Noel says he bought on the sixpenny table at Myer! The cake is somewhere between a fruit cake and a rich plum pudding. I have converted the imperial measures to metric.

STOUT OR PORTER CAKE

250 g butter
250 g sugar
300 ml stout or porter
2 large eggs

375 g plain flour
1 heaped teaspoon bicarbonate of soda
1 teaspoon mixed spice
750 g currants

Melt butter in a strong pan (a heavy-based saucepan) but do not allow it to boil. Then add the sugar, the stout which has been made warm (but not to the point of frothing) and the beaten eggs. When all are mixed, add the flour a little at a time and then the bicarbonate of soda, the mixed spice and then the currants. Mix well together for about 5 minutes.

Butter and line with paper a round deep cake tin, about 20 cm in diameter and 6 cm deep. Put in the cake mixture and bake at 170°C for 2–3 hours (Noel's cake took a little over 2 hours) until a skewer tests clean. Cool. This cake keeps well for at least two weeks.
Serves 8

Back at Lake House we sat on the shaded terrace and watched the sun sink over the lake, gilding the treetops and casting a bronze sheen on the water.

As night descended, lamps were lit and we dined where we sat, too enervated to move. We had our own *son-et-lumière* spectacle as the light caught the translucent wings of the thousands of Christmas beetles that danced near the lamps. As they swooped, swerved and soared they left streaks and loops of brilliant light, like a shorthand message or, alternatively, like the projected slide of very active sperm I remember from biology classes!

Next morning I rose early to enjoy the coolest part of the day. The trees barely stirred. Ducks were already gliding on the lake and cockatoos screeched on the opposite bank. There was a small scarlet-tipped feather on my balcony. I set out for a long walk.

A pad of pink waterlilies as pretty as a page from my long-ago *Peg's Fairy Book* spread on the water around the very first bend. Among stands of willow and slender gums were hawthorn and apple trees. This walk would be enchanting in the springtime.

Blackberries are a menace to native vegetation, crushing it and preventing access to waterways as well as spreading with wild abandon. Most are sprayed rigorously to check their growth. Sometimes a few escape and here was a fine stand of them, with the new berries hard and green, but reminding me of one of my favourite recipes, Grandma's bramble cake. The recipe is in at least two of my books.

A bit further on were sloping banks thick with fallen pine needles. A great spot for pine-forest mushrooms in a few months. At strategic spots around the lake were seats and tables, for picnicking or just for duck-gazing. On the shaded side of the lake the air was quite cold and then in ten paces it was hot and strongly eucalypt-scented. I felt wrapped in stillness and warmth with just the slightest rustle from the gorse pods. The far-off boatshed sparkled in the sunshine, the lake reflecting a million sun-diamonds.

Dutifully I tasted the water from the first three springs. Oh, how horrible it is. Like water infused with rusty nails. I have just finished Robert Drewe's fine book *The Drowner*. It has an early scene set in the Pump Room at Bath and he describes the water as being like warm flat-irons. I also tasted that water in the Pump Room and found it repellent. Warm flat-irons or rusty nails, I may choose to bathe in it but I will not drink it!

In Kerry Bolton's Lake Daylesford Book Barn, an extensive second-hand bookshop, I found a copy of my mother's book, *Through My Kitchen Door*, published in 1960. I bought it and also Norman Douglas's *South Wind* and *Venus in the Kitchen*. Douglas led a life purportedly dedicated to decadence and one enlivened by successive scandals. I am unsure how serious his *Venus in the Kitchen* will turn out to be (the subtitle is 'Love's cookery book'!).

After twenty years as a restaurateur, I have spent time with some wonderfully talented cooks in my kitchens. One of the best was Anne Smithers, who came to Daylesford several years ago to head up the kitchen at Lake House after some years in charge of at least two bustling city bistros post-Stephanie's. Now Annie has done a complete *volte-face* and is leasing perhaps the smallest restaurant in the country, having just five or six tables, from the present owners of a lavender farm.

In 1851 the Tinettis, a Swiss–Italian family, established a farm at Shepherd's Flat, five kilometres from Daylesford. Their cluster of European-style stone and slab buildings erected around a cobbled courtyard is now Lavandula, a successful recreation of a rural past. Its main industry is the growing, harvesting and selling of lavenders, and the manufacture and sale of related products.

Lavandula was a delightful retreat for us on this hot afternoon. With memories of visits to Grasse, the Provençal capital of the perfume industry, I adjusted my vision to an Australian backdrop. No cypress pines edging the property here but instead tall gum trees and blond grasses. The first lavender we encountered grew luxuriantly and waist-high just near the entrance, so that our nostrils were filled with its gloriously pungent perfume. The bushes were thick with bees a-buzzing and fluttering white butterflies.

The present owner, Carol White, has laid out a patchwork field of lavender that was in full bloom when we arrived: lavender, purple, pink, white. Elsewhere some of the lavender had already been cut, leaving springy green cushions. The cut lavender is stripped and bundled and hung to dry from 120-year-old beams in a dark, cool barn. She also has a lavender still that produces lavender oil for her range of skin-care products.

Carol has planted a joyous garden that happily mixes culinary plants with more lavender and old-fashioned favourites such as nigella, aquilegia, heart's ease and linaria. There are espaliered fruit trees and vegetable beds displaying bronze, end-of-season artichokes, gone to thistle but too magnificent to cut down, lettuces, rosemary and much more. Wandering

13

among the plants were peacocks and a chick (known by the residents as the chick pea), some geese and, far away, sensibly resting under a tree, two donkeys.

In a recent piece in a magazine journalist David Dale wrote of his visit to Grasse and of viewing the maceration of the flower petals in 'a warm soup of pork and beef fat', which is later distilled to produce the essence that forms the base of a perfume. Lavender and animal fats started my culinary imagination working. Lavender is usually included in small quantities along with thyme and rosemary in the mixture sold everywhere in Provence as *herbes de Provence*, so there is a precedent for adding lavender to meats. I discussed this with Annie, who said she has been happy using lavender judiciously with lamb. And I can imagine that it might be delicious rubbed into a loin of pork with rosemary.

Annie's eponymously named trattoria sets a handful of tables under a vine-shaded verandah, and is open from mid-morning until late afternoon. This is a one-woman operation, keeping her busy making bread, baking lavender-scented scones, wrapping sardines or quail in lush vine leaves, and stirring up great quantities of lemon barley water or making jam for the aforementioned scones. 'It is so satisfying and so personal', she told us. 'I have the time, there is always plenty to do, but I am never pushed over the limit as happens regularly in most commercial kitchens.'

And in such an idyllic situation – the stillness and the languor, the coolness of stone and shade, the light filtering through huge vine leaves – my spirits lifted and all seemed right with the world.

CAROL'S LAVENDER SCONES
(WITH ANNIE'S TRANSLATIONS)

1 jug (5 cups) self-raising flour   *1 teacup (1 cup) cream*
½ silver ladle (¼ cup) icing sugar   *1⅓ teacups (1⅓ cups) milk*
½ teaspoon dried lavender

Preheat oven to 240°C. Mix dry ingredients in bowl. Cut cream in with broad-bladed knife. Mix in milk quickly. Turn onto floured board. Pat into a rectangle. Cut into 12 squares. Separate and place on floured

baking sheet. Bake for 5 minutes until browned on top. Reduce oven to 180°C and bake for 10 minutes. Turn into a deep bowl lined with a clean, dry tea towel. Cover loosely to stop scones becoming too hard. Split and serve with the best jam and farm cream.
Makes 12

21–22 JANUARY

Searing heat again, and bushfires are devastating the Dandenong Ranges and Arthur's Seat on the Mornington Peninsula. By nightfall we hear that three people have died sheltering in the basement of their home at Ferny Creek, and that the police believe that the fires have been deliberately lit.

At last the rain came. Thirty-three homes destroyed, many more damaged and hundreds of people without any possessions. A colleague, John Dunham, has lost his house along with his collection of Indian art treasures, gathered over twenty years of travelling. Impossible to find words of comfort. Nothing can be brought back. One can only hope for the resilience and determination to move onwards, remembering the past and what once was, but accepting that the future will be different.

23 JANUARY

The design and planning process is finished for Richmond Hill Cafe & Larder. Now we wait for the builders to quote and commence work as soon as possible.

One of the dishes I want to have on the menu is a plate of beautiful prawns simply grilled in the shell and on a bed of very hot rock salt. The inspiration came from an exhibition of the work of Matisse shown in Melbourne in 1995. I remembered a simple and satisfying composition of pink shells, yellow lemon and a crisp cloth. When I contacted the gallery to check on the name of the painting, they queried my memory and suggested I was thinking of a work called *Tulips and Oysters on a Black Background*. Most generously, they sent me the catalogue of the exhibition. And I found it!

Number 85 was entitled *Pink Shrimp* and was just as I remembered – the small pink shrimp one finds on the Atlantic coast, salt in a scallop shell, a halved lemon, bread and a bottle of wine. I also found the small notebook I had at the exhibition and re-read my own delight in the fresh vision of Matisse, especially his bold colours, his obvious delight in patterns and curves and arabesques, and his mastery of line in his miraculous drawings that float on and animate a white background. (*Pink Shrimp*, or *Les Crevettes roses*, as Matisse called it in 1920, hangs in the Everhart Museum in Scranton, Pennsylvania.)

24 JANUARY

$\mathcal{A}$ good day in the kitchen at Stephanie's Restaurant.

I worked with the lunch team to improve the cooking of a small chicken, stressing the importance of smooth and dry skin and of being gentle when slipping tarragon-worked butter under the breast skin (to avoid tearing over the thigh). The flattened chicken is roasted in a small pan resting on a slice of baguette. I talked about leaving the neck skin long, so that it does not shrink when cooking to expose and therefore dry the breast meat, and about adjusting the timing so that the cooked chicken can rest for a few minutes on its slice of baguette now soaked with its cooling juices and delicious to eat. Above all I talked about respecting the chicken, about basting and turning it with care, and presenting it proudly, puffed, golden and perfumed, surrounded by just a few spoonfuls of buttery cooking juices, lengthened to a sauce with a little good stock.

Next I tested a confit of squab and made a croquette of chestnuts, bacon, parsley and crushed potato that sat alongside a salad dressed with walnut oil, red-wine vinegar and meltingly soft cloves of garlic that had cooked in the pork fat with the squab. I split the bird and wondered how many customers would enjoy the neck and the head, or whether I would have to remove them. The crunchy beak of a roasted pigeon is a delicacy in Hong Kong, but in Melbourne? A decision that can be deferred until we actually make the change to the autumn menu in March.

The last experiment for the day was an individual rice pudding studded with raisins and candied citron and baked in a caramel-lined mould. This needs to be modified. The pudding was very solid.

Dur-é and I are back to four days each. Our three-day week didn't last long.

26 JANUARY

*A*ustralia Day. Dur-é has received an Order of Australia for 'services to the community and in recognition of her fundraising efforts for the women of Victoria'. She is in India on vacation, staying, I believe, in silken tents in Rajasthan. We will celebrate on her return.

Once more this important day passes without progress being made or leadership being shown regarding reconciliation with indigenous Australians. In fact, the passions stirred by the High Court decision on the Wik case have elicited many ugly statements. Those who believe that negotiation between pastoralists and Aboriginal communities can be fruitful and clarifying are hard to find, compared with the clamourings of those who seem to believe that the only acceptable solution is to allow their own interests to prevail. Here and there one reads heartening evidence that many in the mining industry believe that negotiation is the best way forward. Internationally, questions have been raised about Australia's human rights record – raised, it should be said, by the American representative at the United Nations, Madeleine Albright. While it is appropriate that the inequalities in our society should be monitored and condemned, the lesson of the Los Angeles riots in 1992 showed that inequality is an entrenched American phenomenon, also needing to be addressed effectively.

27–29 JANUARY

*M*ore recipe testing in the kitchen.

I have been sent a sample of Greenwheat Freekeh, an 'old' grain that is being grown in South Australia and will soon be launched onto the market. Its producers are hoping to convince the public to add this new texture and taste to the range of cereals and pulses already available to them. With health authorities pronouncing daily on the need to increase our cereal, grain and carbohydrate intake, the producers have a good chance.

Greenwheat Freekeh is wheat harvested while still green and then roasted and smoked to become a nutty-tasting cereal. In flavour it is somewhere between brown rice and barley with a reminder of bulgur (or burghul). Which, of course, suggests how to use it – in hearty soups, as an accompaniment to meat and poultry dishes, or soaked and added to salads.

The roasted leg of lamb with Middle Eastern overtones I was planning for the Restaurant's autumn menu gave me the perfect opportunity to serve a pilaf of Greenwheat Freekeh on the side. The meat was to be flavoured with minced onion and saffron and sprinkled with finely chopped mint and powdered sumac. (Another interesting ingredient, sumac is ground from a seed and is a popular flavouring in the cooking of the Middle East, adding sour and tart notes in much the same way tamarind does in Indian and South-East Asian cookery.)

I included a few pine nuts in the pilaf. The dish was delicious, the cereal very, very filling. Probably a small bowlful would sustain one adult for a whole day. We must be careful to serve a very small portion along with the sliced lamb, its juices and some softly stewed spinach leaves.

GREENWHEAT FREEKEH WITH PINE NUTS

1 tablespoon olive oil	*½ teaspoon salt*
1 cup Greenwheat Freekeh	*¼ cup toasted pine nuts*
2½ cups light chicken stock or *water*	*2 tablespoons freshly chopped flat-leaf parsley*

Heat the oil in a heavy-based saucepan, then add the grain and stir to coat well.

Add the stock and salt. Bring to a boil over a moderate heat, then reduce the heat to low. Cover the saucepan tightly and cook until all moisture has been absorbed and the grain is tender, about 20 minutes. Stir the pine nuts and parsley through the pilaf and serve immediately.

(The grain can also be cooked ahead of time and then steamed in a
covered container or reheated in a microwave oven.)
Serves 6

Another sample of produce arrived today, this time ginger shoots from a
farmer in Queensland. They turned out to be knobs of very young ginger
with tender skin. The ginger was so delicate it could be enjoyed as a
vegetable, its hot spiciness blending well with a roasted duckling to be
served with braised turnips. The only problem with this dish is that the
young ginger will only be in season for another few weeks. We will still offer
the duck dish, but will instead use blanched sticks of the freshest ginger we
can find once the supply of young ginger ceases.

The third test dish for this week was most successful. For years now
I have offered snails farmed by Irena Votavova in her suburban Melbourne
home, but the original dish needed a new look. We worked on a sauté of
assorted mushrooms to which the snails, previously simmered in a herby
court-bouillon, were added. The dish was bound with a generous dollop
of a green herb butter. We spooned this lovely tumble of buttery green and
brown around our delicate and very popular goat's cheese soufflé (much
copied all over town), which stood in the centre of the plate. (As soon as
there are convincing autumn rains we will find pine-forest mushrooms to
add to our selection of cultivated Swiss browns, oyster mushrooms and little
white buttons.)

30 JANUARY

*I*t is impossible to keep track of all the elements in my life at the moment.
Richmond Hill Cafe & Larder absorbs a great deal of my thinking time. Each
detail has to be considered, producers contacted, samples tested, partners
consulted. I have posted in the window the notice advertising our intention
to seek a general licence and we will have to wait and see if there is any local
objection. In Victoria a general licence permits the entire area of the Cafe to
be used by anyone wishing to have a glass of wine but not necessarily a meal.

I have planned the menus, possible senior staff have been contacted and offered employment, a wine list is in progress, a brief is being drawn up for the graphic designer, Guy Mirabella, a staff manual is being written by Lisa and her assistant Jane. Budgets have been calculated and a roster drawn up. Angie has had two weeks' holiday at the beach (stunning weather every day). We will be aiming for full-steam ahead in the next few days. Miracles have to be achieved in February and March.

And of course there is also the autumn menu change to be effected at Stephanie's Restaurant, and one or possibly two new senior cooks to be recruited. My plan is to test-cook and discuss the changes early so that the changeover will be very smooth, given that we will be nearing panic stations at the Cafe in the first week of March.

This morning Jane and David Driver arrived, eager to show me a video of David's brilliant cherry-red rhubarb. The pair are rhubarb growers from South Australia, and we have been communicating since David pointed out that I had been wrong in suggesting in the first printing of *The Cook's Companion* that rhubarb is ever 'forced' in hot-houses during the winter in Australia, unlike it is in the United Kingdom. I was very grateful for the information and hope that other farmers and growers will continue to question my work. Such information was devilishly hard to find when I was researching the book. These quiet experts are no doubt hidden away all over the country.

Holly and I will take my father to the Botanic Gardens today for afternoon tea. He is increasingly unsteady and needs a walking frame. It becomes more and more difficult to think of outings where one can walk on smooth ground, have protection from the sun, be able to rest after a short while and park the car near enough so that he does not have to walk too far. He is, as ever, unfailingly good company.

I have recently found a collection of letters written by my parents and sent home during their extensive travels in Europe and Asia. I don't understand how this important reference escaped me when I was writing an account of my trip to Japan last year and needed to know as much as I could regarding Mum's own travels there. These letters are unpolished observations, often written on trains and buses and planes, sometimes with unconfirmed place names and infuriating gaps. Still, they are another resource as I try to piece together how and where my life paths have intersected those of my mother and how we have each drawn understanding from the experience.

I wonder about my motives in wanting to set down my thoughts and activities. Do I do it from some overdeveloped sense of self-importance? I hope not. Do I do it in order to better understand myself? Maybe. I do it to look for connections, connections with my own past, with my parents, and with others I hear or read about or meet.

The last few days I have been reading Norman Douglas's works, as I'd promised myself on my return from Daylesford. But first I read Elizabeth David's words on the man, his life and his work in her book *An Omelette and a Glass of Wine*. David met Norman Douglas when she was twenty-four and he was seventy-two. One cannot begin to paraphrase what are two moving and exquisite essays recording an exceptional friendship. David describes an opinionated, erudite and outrageous man, whom she loved dearly nonetheless.

'Always do as you please, and send everybody to Hell, and take the consequences. Damned good Rule of Life. N', wrote Norman in David's copy of his book *Old Calabria.*

Norman Douglas's own writing is that of a well-educated Englishman, classically literate and full of recondite references, occasionally pompous, much more often knowing and wicked, and with a special interest in the salacious and a way of exposing the weaknesses of his characters that is seductive to his readers but no doubt was horrifying to his contemporaries.

South Wind describes a life of indolence on the island of Capri (disguised as Nepenthe). The island is peopled by Russian emigrés, drop-outs, shady aristocrats, even shadier millionaires and other colourful characters all wholly occupied in the pursuit of pleasure and in minding each other's business at a time when most of Europe was engaged in the Great War. (The book was first published in 1917.)

Venus in the Kitchen was reviewed by Elizabeth David in 1952, the year of its publication. The book offers a mixture of standard Mediterranean dishes and some others mainly concerned with establishing the author's credentials as a classics scholar and indirectly with the lineage and authenticity of certain preparations, compiled, one suspects, with a desire to startle and shock. The more outlandish preparations are outlined in a light and amused tone, daring one to proceed with filleting a skink, of which 'Tristram speaks well', or 'to clean and truss a young crane' (no instructions offered).

Elizabeth David returned to Capri six months after the death of Norman Douglas and made her own private farewell by placing a pot of basil on his grave.

> In the shade of the lemon grove I break off a hunch of bread, sprinkle it with the delicious fruity olive oil, empty my glass of sour white Capri wine; and remember that Norman Douglas once wrote that whoever has helped us to a larger understanding is entitled to our gratitude for all time. Remember too that other saying of his, the one upon which all his life he acted, the one which does much to account for the uncommonly large number of men and women of all ages, classes and nationalities who took Norman Douglas to their hearts, and will hold him there so long as they live. 'I like to taste my friends, not eat them.'

Referring again to the wisdom of Norman Douglas as remembered by Elizabeth David – 'whoever has helped us to a larger understanding is entitled to our gratitude for all time' – my eternal gratitude goes to both my mother and Elizabeth David herself.

February

3 FEBRUARY

*I*t has been suggested that perhaps Mum's only published book, *Through My Kitchen Door*, could be reprinted in facsimile. I am nervous about this and very protective. I don't want the critical eyes of the late 1990s to pour scorn on the enthusiasms and tentative experiments of 1960. The slender volume with its striking monotypes (what does this mean? – I always thought the illustrations were woodcuts) by Mum's friend Christine Aldor has been such a comfort to me through the years. It has my mother's voice exactly and since her death it is even more precious. I am the teenager mentioned and shown leaning on the kitchen table on the cover. But maybe my sister, Diana, thinks it is her? And how do I know it's me? Perhaps it's Mum's friend Cele who often visited through her kitchen door? Or Phyllis? Or Molly?

Through My Kitchen Door was the work of a passionate cook who was also a keen armchair traveller. Her means did not permit travel at this time but she read avidly and practised on her family every day!

Australia in the late 1950s was a very different country from the one in which we now live. In major cities there were a few Dutch and German delicatessens, known as 'Continental' delicatessens, where one bought coffee, sausages, pickles and rye bread. Greek cakes had appeared in Lonsdale Street, Melbourne, by this time. By 1960 there were Italian food shops in major cities and those who were interested could buy olive oil, dried fish and pasta in varieties other than Kookaburra. Myer Melbourne had a gourmet food section in its Lonsdale Street store and I know that Mum used to pore over the shelves and bring home exotic ingredients such as nori sheets, poppyseeds, rice paper and soy sauce.

Chinatown existed but I do not recall the Asian supermarkets with which we are familiar today. Maybe the goods were all there but the shops seemed too mysterious for a timid Occidental lady to investigate. But in almost all of Mum's recipes that have a faintly Oriental heritage she has substituted ingredients and hazarded a guess at technique. The cooking times are far too long and the liquid far too much.

Elizabeth Chong, the Australian-born doyenne of Chinese cooking teachers, remembers my mother attending one of her classes long ago – I would guess it to be when my mother left the seaside township of Rosebud and moved to East Melbourne in 1968, already eight years after *Through My Kitchen Door* had been published. In a city that positively drips with fresh coriander, lemongrass and Chinese vegetables today, we must remember that the availability of (or, perhaps more correctly, familiarity with) such ingredients is a relatively recent phenomenon.

Mum was sometimes hazy when writing about ethnic specialities, which can be quite embarrassing to read. But only when she was imagining how it would be or might taste. Wherever a recipe is a genuine hand-me-down from a European friend it has been accurately and appreciatively recorded. Many of the recipes were donated by friends who had enjoyed Mum's hospitality around our table. The indulgent reader is won over by her enthusiasm, by the charming introductions to each section, by her intrepid march across continents, and by her catholic tastes. In fact I now feel eager to embark on a reissue of my family heirloom. We must keep its authentic voice, no up-to-date conversions, and maybe I can add comments from a 1990s perspective.

This first volume is an interesting contrast to her later unpublished writing, which records adventures in Europe and Asia. At last instead of being an armchair traveller, she actually saw and tasted for herself. Her eyes were opened wide and although the charm remains as strong the recipes and food advice are much more reliable.

4 – 5 FEBRUARY

I am tired of eating overcontrived, overgarnished, confused food. Recently I wrote a short article in a weekend magazine noting what I had found in the publicity tour for *The Cook's Companion*, which took me to every capital city and several major towns on the east coast, to Western Australia and across the Tasman to Auckland.

It had been a long time since I had eaten so many restaurant meals in such a concentrated time and it led me to reflect on the experience.

At the Brisbane Food and Wine Masterclass last year restaurateur Gay Bilson and journalist Cherry Ripe both commented on the practice of food borrowing. Gay suggested that cooks should courteously and carefully appropriate from other cultures and be aware of the pitfalls of allowing one's food to be decided by fashion or fad. Cherry reminded us that no cuisine has exclusivity of ingredients and that being derivative is no hindrance to establishing a cuisine. I agree with both statements but what seems to be happening in the restaurants of this country and of New Zealand, and in London and probably in the United States, is that we now have a global cuisine, with the only differences being the appearance of an occasional indigenous ingredient not yet bottled, preserved, dried or canned.

I believe that this is largely the result of the plethora of seductive food writing and food photography in both books and magazines, which is studied as closely as some study the fashion statements that issue from Paris, Milan and New York. The menus are uncannily similar. Do not misunderstand me. Much of the food tastes and looks delicious. What is a young cook to do? Where can one find fresh inspiration? Are there perhaps new ways to beat an egg? What new bit of the animal can be cooked? Is spinal marrow on toast really going to take off? Is it possible to set a cafe table *without* offering pools of extra-virgin olive oil in which to puddle one's bread?

The luckiest cooks are those who have Turkish, Greek, Chinese or Italian mothers or grandmothers, and a vivid taste memory of the foods they ate as children. Almost an unfair advantage, really. I read John Newton's *Wogfood* during my travels, a new chapter every night in a new town, and I responded warmly to the stories but also to the recipes for mussels cooked with garlic, oil and wine vinegar, or wild fennel salad, or sausage and tomato casserole. John has collected the stories of sixteen 'New Australians', all involved in the food industry at some time in some capacity and whose combined stories are compelling reading. Many who arrived as young children found the local attitude to food mystifying and the food itself supremely unappetising. My own experience is that it is remarkably difficult to convince the average restaurant patron to accept simple, unadorned, directly flavoured food and yet at the same time travellers often long for home-cooked food – a result of overstimulation, airconditioned hotels and general weariness. So as a newly returned traveller might I make a few suggestions:

~ We do not need TALL food. I do not wish to deconstruct my food before I can eat it. Apart from being silly it also gets cold very rapidly.

~ If you are going to serve something on salad leaves, can you please check the leaves for yellow ones and for grit, and go easy on the vinegar.

~ What can be done about the phallic pepper grinder? I thought it was as laughable as garlic bread when it appeared on the scene, but almost without exception on my recent tour I was approached by a waiter waving one and asking whether I wanted cracked pepper, always before I had even tasted a morsel. *Why* does this happen? It is not expensive to supply pepper grinders for every table, and the notion that every restaurant diner is just waiting to pocket the grinder is ludicrous.

~ Worst of all is the latest fad of sprinkling the rim of the plate with parmesan, or paprika, or breadcrumbs, or herbs, or cocoa powder or icing sugar. Wherever I went on this trip I carefully used the napkin to wipe my plate clean of these culinary measles. Or was I intended to pick up the plate and lick it? I first saw a sprinkled plate four years ago in New Orleans and thought it was a bit of nonsense, but now – lo and behold – we have it here. Cocoa powder is hell on a white shirt!

~ A final point. Olive oil is sprinkled on bread in Tuscany and probably other oil-producing regions in order to assess and appreciate the new oil. In oil-producing countries olive oil is a vital and delicious part of the diet, frequently drizzled over simply cooked and still-warm vegetables, or salads, crostini, shellfish or grilled fish. It is not drunk in quantities with bread before eating a meal and yet we have more or less instituted this as the norm in local restaurants. One is led to believe that a restaurant is not modern if it does not observe this practice.

These are bold words for one who is to offer a cafe menu in a few months. No doubt I, too, will find I am subliminally influenced by the magazines, but I am going to make a determined effort to offer straightforward food that is not tall, or surrounded by sprinkles, and there will be a pepper grinder on each table. I am still struggling with the olive oil/butter issue.

I had quite a few phone calls of exasperated agreement after this article appeared. I also had a letter from a reader who disagreed with my statements regarding dipping of bread into olive oil. I acknowledge that it is not unusual to enjoy bread with oil in oil-producing countries, but just not in the quantities one is offered here as a preliminary to a full meal.

Having recently read a review full of superlatives about a local restaurant I hurried to visit it, swept away by the promise of an extraordinary culinary experience. We were presented with a procession of dishes, their Japanese character overlaid with European touches, and no doubt influenced by the well-deserved success and subtle brilliance of Sydney's Tetsuya Wakuda. What a disappointment. The reviewer had especially loved the grand dessert of at least twelve tastes – presented together in a rainbow of colours and textures, custards, cakes, melting sorbets and fresh fruits. To my mind and palate it makes no sense to tumble colours, textures and cultures together unless the whole creates something more than the original parts. It takes a cook of breathtaking originality to succeed at doing this.

What a contrast to dine at Melbourne's Flower Drum the next evening, where Gilbert Lau presides over one of the great restaurants of the world. Again a procession of small courses, but of such refinement. Two scallops bubbled in the shell in creamy juices; a baby abalone (a new experiment in aquaculture in Tasmania) no bigger than a child's ear, steamed in its iridescent shell and sauced with a whisper of light soy; a delicate soup with watercress and prawn dumplings. The peppery watercress was absolutely perfect on this night of steaming heat! A portion of rare Murray cod, quivering and gelatinous, alongside some steamed and brilliantly green choi sum; some sticky rice with sliced spicy Chinese sausage; and to finish, a mango, its cheek smooth and its flesh deeply flavoured, the texture dense and satisfying. With all this a 1981 Mt Pleasant Riesling, its old-gold colour and character suitably rare and precious for this lovely food.

6 FEBRUARY

*E*ncouraging words from my friend and publisher Julie Gibbs at the first pages of this journal. I will press on.

At Stephanie's Restaurant Dur-é and I have worked at our partnership. The most difficult issue has always been the personal effort required to truly acknowledge each other's differences, to accept the validity of another way of viewing the same business matter, and to remember continually that we are both working towards the same goal. With a new project and new partners inevitably come new problems. Learning to interact with people is challenging. I want to be someone who is flexible and able to adapt. I have to learn to present my case more persuasively and not to feel personally threatened when it is disputed, but to listen to the opposing point of view fully and openly. And then to re-present my case if it still seems valid, incorporating or answering the objections raised. The ideal situation would be if both parties were prepared to listen, validate and evaluate the merits in each case.

My miniature standard peach has produced eight perfect fruit, each of them fully tree-ripened and picked warm, even hot, and enjoyed in the garden – by us, not our ringtail possum!

7 FEBRUARY

*O*ne of the interesting and difficult challenges of my new business will be to understand the world of food retailing. Only the very best suburban specialist food shops will survive the onslaught of the 'gourmet' supermarket. For years the supermarkets have watched a percentage of their customers pass them over for more interesting food outlets and now they are fighting back. This has to be good for the food supply in general if it challenges mediocrity and the 'cheese-slice' mentality. The supermarkets have on their side the undoubted appeal of one-stop shopping. The parent chain selects a few stores in appropriate upwardly mobile suburbs and special counters or 'shops within a shop' are being planned or are actually trading. Existing departments such as fruit and vegetables or the deli counter are transformed so that they more closely approximate what the store buyers believe the customer wants. However, there are no second chances. If a producer is interested in being represented a good deal of money must change hands, and the product must prove itself in a very short time or out it goes. Supermarkets have the buying power to scoop up the total production of small firms or individual growers. And once they have one successful product all their marketing training tells them it must be possible to do the same again, in a different flavour. The principles might be sound but in practice it doesn't always work without hitches.

When I was in Myrtleford in north-eastern Victoria late last year, judging at the biennial Ovens Valley International Festival, I heard stories of the diversification attempts of some local tobacco farmers. One story was of a contract given to growers to produce cauliflowers for the supermarket. But the catch was that the supermarket only wanted them if they were a certain number of centimetres across the head. Too small or too large – forget it! Apparently the lush local soil produced some monster caulis and there was much hilarity as the farmers told me of the various ways they attempted to use up and finally get rid of the cauliflowers. It reminded me of ten years ago, when the first enterprising and food-loving salad growers demonstrated that there was a need for a variety of greens, and that they should be picked young and rushed to the customer. It wasn't long before the mainstream growers produced an approximation of the same product. Some little guys went out of business but mixed leaves and exotic salads became universally available. I for one miss Daniel Romaneix's understanding of the importance of perfect leaves (he was one of the first to grow, pick and deliver outstanding product), and it is fair to say that some of the bags of mixed leaves currently available are no advance at all.

What the supermarket has so far not managed to lift from the best of the specialist stores is passion, expertise and service.

So why am I determined to bash my head against a brick wall? I suppose because the brick wall is there and also because I believe I can do it well and have the enthusiasm to encourage the public to try things for the first time. I know my business partner, Will Studd, feels the same way about quality cheese, although he is also keen to support better cheese being offered in the supermarkets.

8 FEBRUARY

What can I make of this? Subliminal messages are in the air. This morning I opened the paper's colour magazine, to which I contribute a monthly piece, to read today's offering by colleague Gay Bilson. Her topic – Norman Douglas! And then the phone rang. It was my editor calling to say how last week she had been re-reading Elizabeth David's *An Omelette and a Glass of*

Wine and had made a mental note to look for a copy of Norman Douglas's *Venus in the Kitchen* and then she opened this morning's paper and read Gay's article. How extraordinary. Few contemporaries would have ever heard of him and yet in the space of a few weeks his shade seems to have hovered over a few foodies.

Gay offers her readers Norman's recipe for a marmalade of carnations. Her edition of *Venus in the Kitchen* has an introduction by Jonathan Keates. The introduction to my copy is by Stephen Fry, who concludes with this paragraph:

> It is certain, however, that in this age the literature of the kitchen has swollen to its greatest ever proportions; new recipe books arrive in our bookshops daily. For any collector or enthusiastic amateur a book that reminds us of the virtues of ancient cuisine, that offers the hope of more than merely gustatory stimulation and that transports us out of the world of the non-stick pan, the wok and the food-processor and into the world of the lemon-grove, the Ischian grotto and the Heliconian hillside, any book that is free of unattainably lavish and opulent photographs and irksome measurement conversion tables, any book in this hysterically patronising, predictable and bourgeois genre that has the courage to be idiosyncratic, idiotic and inconsistent, any book that is written with such style, grace and comic sensuality, any book, in short, that dares to be so different and so direct, can only be welcomed, reverenced and adored.

I think Norman Douglas could be in for a comeback!

13 FEBRUARY

*T*he first test session at home for our Cafe menu went well today. Late last year I had my kitchen completely rebuilt – and just as well, as it has turned out. I had a double oven installed and a moveable central trolley with a chopping block of suitable proportions so that two cooks can chop at the same time. The kitchen coped well with three cooks, twelve cooked dishes and mountains of ingredients. I must say, though, I wish I had a commercial dishwasher. At Stephanie's Restaurant the cycle on the machine is three minutes. The fastest cycle on my very smart German dishwasher at home is about thirty minutes.

We were testing breakfast, vegetable and cheese dishes. Several fruity things were all presented at the same time, and then the vegetable and cheese and egg dishes came at a pretty fast pace, one or two at a time. Nothing to the fast pace that we hope will be necessary once we open the doors at the Cafe.

The rhubarb with rose-geranium was wonderful. I had the idea after meeting a Turkish woman who said that she always added a few drops of rosewater to rhubarb. My rose-geranium plant is very healthy and three leaves gave a most distinct flavour.

RHUBARB AND ROSE-SCENTED GERANIUM

400 g rhubarb, washed and cut
    into 1 cm slices
⅓ cup water

½ cup sugar
3 rose-geranium leaves

Cook ingredients together very gently in a tightly closed saucepan, stirring once or twice until rhubarb is tender. This will only take about 10 minutes. Tip into a bowl to cool and then remove the leaves.
Serves 4–6

The house muesli was felt to have too much dried fruit and next time we will roast the hazelnuts. I am not really a muesli person but I do like Swiss-style *bircher muesli*. Oatmeal is soaked with lots of grated apple, including the peel, almonds and honey. For the test session I spooned it into martini glasses, surrounding each portion with pointed slices of dark-red strawberries.

BIRCHER MUESLI

500 g rolled oats	300 g chopped or slivered almonds
juice of 4 lemons	1 cup cream, softly whipped
4 juicy apples, unpeeled and grated	2 punnets ripe strawberries, sliced or
¼ cup honey	blueberries, whole
½ cup raisins or sultanas	

Mix first six ingredients together and refrigerate overnight. Just before serving fold in the whipped cream and the berries.
Serves 10

As I was grating the new season's Gravenstein apples for this dish I remembered a childhood treat that I must have again very soon. Coarsely grated apple mixed with some granulated sugar and plenty of ground cinnamon and then piled onto very crunchy hot buttered toast. When we were children we all developed favourite toast toppings. I loved sliced tomatoes (still do), and the apple just described. My father's favourite was squashed ripe banana topped with shredded coconut.

I digress. Other successful trials today included free-range eggs baked in buttered Spanish terracotta dishes with a little balsamic vinegar added.

Labna cheese balls will be a house speciality. Offered both as an alternative to butter to spread on toast or on baked potatoes and instead of a sauce to enjoy with a plate of grilled vegetables. For one who dislikes yoghurt it has been a revelation to me to discover how I adore these soft little shapes that are simply drained and seasoned yoghurt. Mostly we marinate them with rosemary, garlic and good olive oil, but one can also enjoy them with honey and cinnamon.

We also made sweetcorn and polenta fritters, which were crunchy and quite substantial. We will serve these on their own or with fine smoked bacon, or maybe with fried green tomatoes.

I intend to offer chicken congee on our breakfast menu. Late last year I visited Malaysia with my friend Tony Tan and a group of food enthusiasts. One of the fascinating aspects of this country is how the cuisines of the various ethnic groups are still quite distinct yet at the same time one is advised to be sure to experience the unique blended cuisine of the Straits Chinese or the Nonya people. At one of the hotels where we stayed, breakfast ran the gamut of Western cereals, eggs, noodle dishes, and my favourite, chicken congee. This soupy porridge of round-grained rice cooked to a mush in chicken stock is wonderfully soothing. One can spice it with all manner of things – crisp shallots, fine slices of fresh chilli, a thread of dark rice vinegar, garlic oil, preserved duck eggs and so on. The challenge is to achieve the right degree of soupiness and not to use a reduced chicken stock, which becomes too intrusive in what should be a gentle dish, its mood spiced up by the condiments.

Another triumph was an American pancake recipe that incorporates a chunky fruit purée. I used pear but hope to use quince by the time the Cafe opens in mid-autumn. Jeff, my American chef, and I have discussed the merits of Australian and American baking powder. We both find the aftertaste of Australian baking powder unpleasant and for me it makes most scones unpalatable. It leaves a nasty chemical taste, deriving from its phosphate aerator, that lingers and sets my teeth on edge. Apparently this ingredient is not present in American baking powder. My solution is to substitute McAlpine's self-raising flour (in the green packet) for the flour in this American recipe and omit the baking powder. The raising agent in McAlpine's self-raising flour is cream of tartar and it leaves no aftertaste.

PEAR OR QUINCE PANCAKES WITH CINNAMON SUGAR

2 firm pears, peeled, cored and cut into 2 cm chunks	¼ teaspoon ground cinnamon
¼ cup sugar	¼ teaspoon salt
½ cup water	1½ cups milk
1 cup cream of tartar self-raising flour	40 g butter, melted and cooled
¼ teaspoon ground ginger	1 egg
	butter or light oil for frying

Simmer pears with sugar and water in a covered pan until fruit is tender. Process briefly till still chunky and leave to cool.

Mix all dry ingredients in a bowl. Combine milk, butter and beaten egg. Make a well in the dry ingredients, whisk in the milk, butter and egg mixture, and stir in the fruit purée.

Heat a non-stick frying pan, brush with oil or melted butter and pour in about 2 tablespoons of batter for each pancake. Cook over moderate heat until small bubbles appear, then turn and cook the other side.

The pancakes should feel firm in the centre and have thin and crispy edges. Serve at once and sprinkle with cinnamon sugar.
Makes approximately 8, *serves* 4

14 FEBRUARY

Valentine's Day was celebrated by sixty pairs of lovers at Stephanie's. It was pretty quiet in the dining rooms. All hand-holding and murmuring. We gave tiny posies of Cecile Brunner rosebuds and iced heart-shaped cakes to each table.

The heat is extraordinary. Since mid-January we have had day after day of more than 30°C. On several days the temperature has climbed to 37°, 39° and even 41°C. It does not bear describing conditions in the Restaurant kitchens. And we are not getting our traditional cool change in the late afternoons, but instead enduring nights when the temperature does not drop below 20°C. I have taken to having cold showers at about 3.00 in the morning. I stagger to the bathroom with my eyes still closed, turn the tap on hard, blot myself vaguely dry and go straight back to bed quite damp and fall into a few hours of sleep. Rosie, my woolly poodle, has abandoned her bed and sleeps stretched out on the wooden floor. In the Restaurant kitchens we are making an effort to stay calm and be kind to each other. My hot car feels as if it might suddenly go whoosh and vaporise.

1 5 FEBRUARY

*B*read-tasting at Phillippa's today. Phillippa Grogan has a great food shop in nearby Armadale. Influenced by the wonderful Clarke's food store in Kensington Church Street, London, where she worked for several years, Phillippa's sells superb breads and preserves, offers morning and afternoon teas and light lunches, and stocks a select range of fine local and imported goods. Phillippa's will make most of the bread served at the Cafe. Some of the breads are her own developments. We particularly liked a fig and anise loaf, and a hazelnut and vinefruit loaf. And my favourites for all-purpose munching were the *pane francese* (apparently an Italian recipe thought to approximate French bread, although it does not and is eminently more satisfying), the *ciabatta* slipper loaf with its beguiling chewy crust and big holes, and a marvellous honeywheat loaf that contains soaked grains and seeds. Its texture is chewy and grainy without, as Phillippa says, 'tasting like birdseed'.

We went home with bags of bread and that evening tried many more. The flour-dusted *pane toscana* with green olives was delicious. This part of the project is enormous fun.

I have also been busy tasting tea. I drink many cups of tea a day, but as I like it really weak and black and as no one else in the family drinks tea, I have frequently resorted to a tea bag or a personal infuser. Now I am surrounded by plastic envelopes and tins from several tea blenders and I am having to think a good deal more deeply about the flavours and characteristics of different teas. I have just enjoyed Prestige Darjeeling, a one hundred per cent Darjeeling tea from the Himalayan foothills. It is so good and the tea is beautiful. What I have been missing! A medium-length leaf, greyish-black with flecks of silver and deep brown, with a delightful aroma that stimulates even when sniffed from the tin. Later today I shall try an Assam when I feel my energy waning, and perhaps in the very late afternoon a sophisticated Lapsang Souchong, the classic 'smoky' tea of China, this example picked from a province formerly known as Fukien but now called Fujian. The designer of the Cafe describes the colour of the stain she wants for our shelving as 'tea'.

17 FEBRUARY

*D*ay Two of testing in the home kitchen: pasta, poultry and meat dishes today. One of the best dishes was the sweet and sour lamb, the recipe for which is in *The Cook's Companion* and includes raisins, although I am now wondering whether it might be better with prunes. We are using a relish made from sweet peppers, tomatoes and raisins to accompany grilled pork sausages. I don't want the public to think I am obsessed with raisins. The sweet pepper and raisin relish is an Escoffier recipe gleaned from Elizabeth David's *Spices, Salt and Aromatics in the English Kitchen*. This is a wonderful book but seems to be appreciated less than her volumes devoted to the Mediterranean region.

We also made a rich oxtail sauce to spoon over bulging pasta parcels filled with a garlicky potato mash. As we sweat and mop our brows it is difficult to remember that it may well be very cold when we open the doors.

Another simple pasta dish will combine fettucine with sorrel leaves and rocket and be sauced with sliced mushrooms melted in fabulous farmhouse butter. At least two of our enterprising cheesemakers are willing to have a go at making farmhouse butter. 'Farmhouse' means butter made from cream produced by the farmer's own cows. Believing in the concept of benchmarks, we will also sell French butter. The finest French butter is a revelation but it tells a story of a country where cows do not have access to green grass all year round, hence its creamy colour. As always good produce reflects its environment.

Maggie Beer and I are hoping that her trials of a revised method of cold-smoking kangaroo will be completed in time for us to offer one of her favourite dishes on our first menu – duck egg pasta with smoked kangaroo. We will add our own touch with some spiced leaf chicory tossed through the pasta.

I adore a roast chicken. It is a very difficult dish to get right in a restaurant situation. To be perfect it should be roasted, carved and eaten – no waiting around. But the best compromise, which I hope turns compromise into a virtue, is to roast a chicken, let it rest in its roasting juices, then lift the meat from the bones and ease it into largish pieces and nestle it on salad leaves. Use the buttery winey juices as both sauce and dressing for the salad. Then it must be eaten quickly before the leaves feel greasy and wilt.

We had reasonable success with this in the afternoon's testing, and then tonight (35°C again!) I cooked another chicken, this time for old friends Jim and Melita.

My first husband, Monty, and his Greek restaurant partners worked side by side at the restaurant Jamaica House for more than fourteen years in complete harmony. Jim and Melita were shocked and saddened when our marriage ended and with it my involvement in Jamaica House. However, they had no choice but to continue in their business venture with Monty. It was a rewarding time for them all. It seems that the secret of their partnership was that no one felt the need to jostle for centre stage, or feel threatened by the others. They also truly understood the qualities each person brought to the partnership and in all those years I never heard any one of the three say a nasty word about another.

As we talked tonight, Melita remembered one of the first times she met me, in happy days, when we all gathered at our home to eat dishes I had been testing for a new menu to be offered at Jamaica House. Just as we were doing this evening. The first occasion would have been twenty-eight years ago and it is a sobering thought to realise that one doesn't change much over such a long time. There is still a Jamaica House in Melbourne, now in its fourth location in Lygon Street, Carlton. Melita is renowned for the way her beautiful eyes will well and spill with tears as she remembers something very dear to her. But she also laughs through her tears and so did we all, then and tonight. Life is so rich. And so I cooked the chicken and splashed it with Maggie's verjuice and surrounded it with little potatoes and fat cloves of garlic, fresh bay leaves and finally some pickled cherries.

I covered a big creamy platter with soft green leaves and quickly arranged the meat and all the bits. And they loved it. We ate in the garden, which was lit by flickering citronella lamps, and we mused on how rare it is to feel so relaxed and so at peace with food that is aromatic, easy to enjoy and not demanding.

CHICKEN FOR MELITA

1 × 2 kg free-range chicken
sea salt
freshly ground pepper
1 lemon
2 tablespoons olive oil
2 tablespoons unsalted butter
12 small potatoes
12 fat cloves garlic, unpeeled

4 fresh bay leaves
4 whole cloves
½ cup verjuice
4 handfuls of soft salad leaves, washed
   and dried
pickled cherries or crabapples or
   spiced peaches (if available)

Season chicken inside and out with the salt and pepper. Slice lemon into 4 fat slices. Squeeze 2 slices all over skin of chicken. Place the other slices in the cavity. Rub bird with olive oil. Slip butter into the cavity. Place bird with the potatoes and garlic cloves into an oiled baking dish with the bay leaves and cloves and roast on its side at 200°C for 30 minutes. Turn the bird onto its other side, and roast a further 30 minutes.

Remove baking pan from the oven and pour the verjuice over the chicken. Shake pan to blend the verjuice with the other roasting juices. Roast a further 15 minutes. Test the thigh of the chicken to ensure that the juices run clear. Leave the chicken in the baking tray with all the juices for 10 minutes.

Arrange salad leaves on a warmed platter. Remove the chicken legs and divide into thigh and drumstick pieces. Remove wings. Remove breast fillets and cut into long pieces, keeping the skin intact. Arrange all the meat, potatoes and garlic over the salad leaves and spoon juices over. Scatter with the pickled fruit if using. Grind over extra pepper and maybe extra sea salt.

Serves 4–6

Will had made me a gift of a Corsican ewe's milk cheese, a Brin d'Amour, round and flattish, covered with a bluish mould and rolled thickly in rosemary and savory, as well as a splendid French camembert. Both cheeses had softened superbly and the camembert bulged with a creamy sheen.

I was reminded of a book I read many years ago by Sheila Kitzinger, an enthusiastic exponent of the pleasures of natural childbirth. An image that has always stayed with me was her suggestion that the labouring woman should yield to her contractions like a surrendering camembert, or words to that effect.

Memories of past times, old friends, perfect food, good wine and looking forward to a bright future. What more can one ask for?

19 FEBRUARY

The builders have started at the Cafe! Nothing much to see yet but the tension increases one notch. There is so much to do and it spans many disciplines. We are all out of our depth now and then and that is when panic can get a grip. Both Angie and I continue to have the nightmares regularly, usually at the same hour. Three a.m. is our bad time.

The graphic designer, Guy, has presented us with a second set of roughs for a business logo to consider. I have had a consultation with Brian Wane, the sommelier at Stephanie's, to set guidelines for the new wine list. We did not receive any objections to our licence application but we do have a new set of forms to be filled in. We must also organise insurance.

Will is going to sail on HM *Bark Endeavour* from Madeira to London in early March and has painted a graphic picture of what might happen to him as he clings to the mainsail of the three-mast sailing vessel built as a replica of the ship in which Captain Cook made his historic voyage to the eastern coast of Australia in 1788.

Will Studd has his romantic side. He first inspected HM *Bark Endeavour* when it was docked at Station Pier in Melbourne in 1995 before its inaugural voyage around Australia and retracing of Cook's route to England. Will was captivated, and signed on as crew initially for the Melbourne–Sydney leg. Apparently it was every boy's dream come true. A tall sailing ship, a swaying mast, the creak of the rigging, testing one's body against the elements, working as a team . . . He found it very addictive, and later sailed the Cairns–Cooktown leg. When he was offered a place on the boat for its final sail from Madeira to London he could not refuse, even though the timing was not great vis-à-vis his new business. His stories after the event were very stirring. The boat detoured to the island of Alderney so Will could surprise his father, who actually came on board. It sailed around the south coast of England past Brighton and Margate and places that were very important in Will's childhood, and then entered the Thames. London Bridge was opened up for HM *Bark Endeavour* and the climax was when Her Majesty The Queen came on board!

For an Englishman, happily transplanted to Australia, it is not difficult to sense all that this could mean. And he says he gets very seasick, too!

I have set up a budget projection, and worked through and costed our estimated staffing. Prices keep coming in for services and equipment. Mostly they are on budget. We must negotiate with all of the producers and suppliers of the high-quality produce we wish to stock. Even writing all this down brings on a dry mouth. And when all of the above is done there is another list that is just as long.

The heat does not help. I walked under a brilliant crepe myrtle tree today which seems to have shed most of its party frock in protest at the lack of moisture. The pavement was a mass of pink frills. It is distressing to look at the plants in both public and private gardens. Even some of the drought-resistant Australian native plants in the local park have given up.

21 FEBRUARY

*R*estaurant Week will be with us again in three weeks. Advance planning is essential. The annual Melbourne Food and Wine Festival touches most Melbourne foodies in some way. There are special dinners and lunches, visiting chefs, lectures, demonstrations, photographic exhibitions, chefs' tables and events too numerous to mention.

Restaurateurs are asked to offer bargain-priced lunches at $19.97 for a week, and the demand is extraordinary. In one and a half hours, from the moment the announcement appeared in this morning's newspaper, Stephanie's Restaurant became fully booked for that entire week. In the meantime, we needed an extra telephonist to inform the hundreds who called that sadly there is no more room, and we decided to extend the event for the next two weeks of the festival. Full again in another two hours, for two weeks this time. We will revert to our usual menu at its conclusion.

I wonder where these lunchers are at other times? Do they only eat out one week of the year? Is the appeal of a bargain so strong? Do they not wonder what the full menu of these establishments might be like? The only way to cope with the huge numbers is to streamline the offerings, warn the suppliers, hire extra plates (everyone arrives within fifteen minutes), hire extra staff and anticipate the deluge.

I have made bookings to attend a couple of special events during the festival, and also to join in walking tours to explore Melbourne's Middle Eastern shopping street and one of our most populous Asian markets.

Together with three other colleagues I have been asked to submit recipes to Qantas, who will select a menu that will run on First and Business Class domestic flights during the festival. This afternoon I visited the Airline Catering Facility at Tullamarine Airport, which was an extraordinary experience. Like many other frequent flyers I have mused on the lacklustre food that is served and often thought I could do better. Here was an opportunity to have a go. It is not an easy task and at the end of our session with the flight chefs I suspect we all were filled with awe at the huge task they oversee each day.

Preparation benches covered with thousands of plastic food trays stretched to infinity. Dozens of operators concentrated to ensure that each one being filled was identical.

Our recipes had been cooked and rather anxiously we inspected the results. The most obvious fact was that nothing looks great jammed into a plastic rectangle or square. And, as was explained to us, limits are imposed on the style and range of appropriate dishes due to the processes to which each meal is subjected. No fresh herbs or delicate crispy garnishes can expect to survive the blast-chilling and reheating these dishes go through. Sauces may not be too light or flowing in case of turbulence; bones must be extracted from poultry and fish. Bits cannot stick up out of the trays as they will prevent efficient loading in the trolleys. Rare meat, and especially rare fish, are considered health hazards and are automatically excluded. Apparently the travelling public has overwhelmingly expressed a preference for a hot main dish.

My potted prawns were considered a possibility, as was a red pepper mousse. I had wanted to serve the mousse with olive bread, but the flight kitchen's alternative suggestion was a slice of bread spread with cream cheese, which I could not agree to. One of the nastiest things about airline food is the cold, sometimes damp bread. I made a counter-suggestion of a rusk-type crouton, which they thought would be possible. Then my oxtail dish was struck out on several grounds – too difficult to eat in the cabin, and too knobby, which meant it might not load well. We discussed my chicken dish and they thought it might look a bit ordinary. I had to tell myself not to react too strongly. If they used a quality chicken and were generous with freshly chopped tarragon in the cooking it should taste delicious, I said, probably a touch too quickly. The passionfruit bavarois recipe had been adjusted so that the texture was no longer melting, and the plum cake had been totally misunderstood. But they said cheerfully that they would redo it. Around the room similar discussions were taking place with the other three chefs. It will be interesting to see which dishes are finally chosen.

The hot food issue interests me. The best dishes I remember eating on aircraft have tended to be cold. Once on a British Airways short flight between London and Paris I enjoyed a thick slice of a country terrine with olives, cornichons and a separately offered crusty and non-chilled roll; Alitalia offered an antipasto platter that was well-flavoured; and I have enjoyed excellent open sandwiches on local flights. If the public understands that their food is to be cooked, chilled and reheated why wouldn't they prefer great sandwiches, or sliced ham salads or similar items?

23 FEBRUARY

Sunday, and Harvest Picnic Day. Ten years ago, as a member of Victoria's Bicentenary Committee, I developed the idea for an open day where families who are interested in food could come along to meet and talk with the specialist producers and suppliers of the growing range of high-quality ingredients and products that have enlivened our markets and shopping streets. The organising committee set strict guidelines for participation and thus began an event which has become astonishingly popular. It is now held at Hanging Rock, among magnificent old gums, and this year the organisers again estimated attendance at 30,000.

Interestingly in the 1997 Discussion Paper on Victoria's tourism industry, produced by the Department of Tourism, the event does not rate a mention in the Victorian calendar, a most serious omission.

Like everyone else we packed a rug and a picnic basket and set off early, arranging to meet friends outside the potato stall. My first taste of the day was just-cooked new season's Nicola potatoes, rolled in butter and parsley. Followed swiftly by freshly opened oysters, then soon after by a bruschetta of thickly sliced tomato and buffalo mozzarella, and a little later by a Scottish black pudding grilled and offered on a slice of potato scone. Once again the temperature was more than 30°C, so an icy granita of fresh orange juice was delicious and much appreciated, and then I felt ready for a glass of wine.

White balloons floated in the air, children squealed and played chasey. The crowds were thick around each stall. Stall-holders I spoke to were exhausted but exhilarated by the genuine interest and enthusiasm for their products they encountered all day long. The Harvest Picnic is a people's day and the organisers are to be congratulated on their efforts to keep the concept within the original guidelines. But why was Crown Casino permitted to promote its forthcoming venture, many of us wondered.

24 FEBRUARY

This morning I had an interview link-up with Nahum Waxman, owner of Kitchen Arts and Letters, a specialist bookstore in New York, and Sue Fairlie-Cuninghame, the executive editor for food and wine for *Vogue Entertaining*. We were discussing an essay by Waxman in which he protested at the growing number of Americans who do not understand how to cook. One of the starting points for my writing *The Cook's Companion* had been my concern at the lack of cooking ability of not just the present generation of young people, but of their mothers and fathers also, therefore I was presenting a parallel Australian point of view. I think Waxman and I shared a similar hope that young people can be persuaded to try to prepare their own meals, but we acknowledged that they need information of a more basic, accessible kind than that provided by a gorgeous and glossy cookbook.

The success of *The Cook's Companion* speaks for itself. I am stopped in the street almost every day by someone saying how they love the book, how it remains open in the kitchen, how their husband or partner has also found it fascinating even though he has never opened a book about food before, and the letters that come are saying the same thing. Thank you is the overwhelming message, thank you for showing us how and helping us achieve success. I am thrilled with all this and with the growing realisation that this book I have produced may well make a difference.

And then, to continue a day of media attention, I was interviewed by Ann-Maree Moodie for the book she is writing, *Local Heroes*, which is intended to be a celebration of success and leadership in Australia, to be published later in the year. Ann-Maree told me that many of the interviewees for her book found it hard to credit that they had succeeded. I share this feeling, although it seems to contradict the preceding paragraph where I have openly acknowledged my joy at the publishing success of *The Cook's Companion*.

It would be foolish to deny many of the manifestations of success – requests for interviews, requests for my opinion on an amazingly wide range of topics, requests for donations, for advice, requests to sit on committees; being recognised in the street, in the supermarket, in taxis; earning a comfortable income and so on. Those who are work-driven know there are always new levels they can aspire to, new things to learn, and never enough hours in the day. But at the same time one can experience flashes of contentment, and a certain confidence in expressing opinions, and positive pleasure in one's achievements. And I do know that one cannot have everything.

In the evening we invited all of those who have so far joined the team of Richmond Hill Cafe & Larder to come and meet all the business partners and each other and to hear about the likely start-up date. We also tasted some wines submitted by two vignerons, both of whom are interested in having their wines represented as our house wines. I would like to encourage the European habit of meeting a friend or colleague after work for a leisurely half an hour and I intend to offer simple savouries to balance the wine and set the mood for a great evening. Maybe people will even pick up a piece of cheese or a loaf of bread to take on home.

RICHMOND HILL CHEDDAR BISCUITS

170 g unsalted butter	*salt*
250 g plain unbleached flour	*cayenne pepper*
150 g mature cheddar, grated	

Blend butter and flour in a food processor until the mixture resembles breadcrumbs.

Add the cheese and seasoning and process until the dough forms a ball. Wrap the dough and chill for one hour.

Roll the pastry out to a thickness of 5 mm, cut into shapes, and bake at 200°C for 15 minutes.

Makes approximately 30.

27 FEBRUARY

We now have a framed kitchen and the shell of the coolroom has been installed! Lisa took some pictures of the empty space that will soon be so busy, with me leaning on a ladder and wires dangling from a skylight in the roof. The upstairs tenants are building surveyors, not architects as we had previously thought. They say they are delighted that we are to be the new tenants and they are already anticipating quality coffee breaks.

Angie and I had a huge day today, sorting through and refining our ideas for the opening stock. In between all of this we interviewed and confirmed the appointment of a third-year apprentice chef, and discussed a mural for the wall with a young painter, Sarah Faulkner. We are both pretty excited about this and Sarah has promised to get back to us soon with a small sketch of what she believes will work well on the large wall. She showed us examples of her work and we feel confident we will be thrilled with her ideas.

The heatwave is over for the time being. What a relief to sleep under a light cover again. We can now anticipate Melbourne's magical March weather, clear sunny days and cool evenings. The plants in my garden have visibly relaxed. The colours are brighter, the roses have flowered again, the agapanthus need to be cut right back and the first pink buds are fat on the windflowers.

March

2 MARCH

Our final testing session for the Cafe today: fish, shellfish and desserts. It was our best session so far. With at least one last-minute surprise.

Early in the summer I pickled some yellow peaches by poaching them in a spiced vinegar syrup and then covering the fruit pieces with the reboiled and somewhat reduced syrup. The peaches tasted wonderful, as did the syrup, which was a deep rose-pink from the skins. However, after a few weeks I found that the flesh was breaking down in the jars and although they still tasted good they no longer looked perfect. All was not lost, though. I puréed the contents of one jar (including one cardamom pod from the syrup) and developed a subtle and delicious sauce for a platter of air-dried salmon which we shall serve with a salad of green papaya, pounded in the Timorese manner, with fresh tomato, raw peanuts, lime juice, chilli and a judicious slurp of fish sauce.

Now we are left wondering whether I have enough of my 'mistake' for the entire menu. There are still good peaches in the marketplace but it seems back-to-front to intentionally make a mistake. I would prefer instead to invent something else once the peach purée is no more. The combination of the sweet (peach purée) with the sour (lime) and the salty (fish sauce) and the hot (chilli) represents the classic tastes of Thailand and readers could easily substitute another fruit purée for my peach pickle. The green papaya salad is common to other Asian countries, notably Thailand, but it was at the Timorese stall at Darwin's Mindil Beach market that I first saw it made and tasted it.

The air-dried salmon has been developed by my friend John Wilson of Mohr Foods in Sydney. The fish is cured in a mix of spices and flavourings and is then partially dried. The final product is soft and moist and quite lovely. John is about to set out on a six-week investigation of fish markets and smokehouses in Japan and Europe and hopes to come home with his head buzzing full of new ideas. Always this push for the new. We commiserate with each other but agree that the stimulation of stepping outside one's own daily grind to take a wider look is not only essential but also life-renewing.

Sydney oyster farmers are reeling from the results of a widespread outbreak of hepatitis A that has supposedly derived from Wallis Lake oysters. Two hundred cases have been reported and within days oysters from anywhere are being rejected by the entire community. This sort of tragedy can devastate small producers in a few weeks. Most Sydney rock oyster leases are in inlets or rivers. Sadly the general public and local authorities have not been scrupulous in how they treat their rivers, with the result that most are heavily polluted. As oysters are filter feeders it is easy to grasp the problem. Since 1990 fisheries authorities have required that all oysters gathered from the leases be depurated for twenty-four hours in fresh water. Somehow this system has either been insufficient to kill the pathogens in the oysters or people affected have eaten oysters that for one reason or another have not been treated. For many holiday-makers, knocking oysters from the rocks, rinsing them in sea water and downing them on the spot has been thought a romantic and delicious thing to do, with all its connotations of freshness and harmony with unspoilt nature. The fact is that because of the far-flung effects of our thoroughly modern pollutants it is unrealistic to think that these quiet stretches of inlet or bay are pristine.

The freshly opened oysters we will offer at the Cafe will be from Tasmania, and served with watercress sandwiches. No need to test them, but we did test bowls of mussels steamed with coriander and, a bit later, fish dipped into a spicy chick pea batter and fried.

Fish and chips is a standard in many cafes and I want to offer it – but with a difference. In the old town of Nice in the south of France, especially in its covered market, one can buy a piece of *socca*, a flat, rather greasy and floppy wedge of hot griddlecake cooked on an oiled metre-wide circular iron hotplate. *Socca* is made from chick pea flour, water and salt. It is not refined food and approximates to the appeal of hot chips on a cold day or to my childhood memory of the jam-filled sugary doughnuts bought from a caravan parked in the Queen Victoria Market. Like these, *socca* can be indigestible and heavy but it is a dish that brings a rush of memory.

A slightly more refined version is *panisses*. The same batter is cooked like polenta and poured onto an oiled dish or tray to cool. It is then cut into pieces and fried. I wonder whether Alice Waters named her seminal

Californian restaurant, Chez Panisse, after this most basic food? She has
certainly written of her affinity with the ingredients and the direct cooking
that one can experience in the south of France.

Earlier today I read an article called 'Eating in the Street' in *SLOW*, the
magazine of the Slow Food Movement, in which Maurizio Maggiani,
an Italian food writer, recalled the charms of *farinata* he enjoyed as a boy in
La Spezia in northern Italy. Once again it was a pancake of chick pea flour
mixed with water, this time baked. Variations included topping it with fresh
rosemary leaves, thinly cut fresh onions or fresh whitebait, and Maggiani
also wrote of the delights of fried *farinata*.

> The dough of water and flour must float and fry in the oil; the zinc-plated
> copper pan must be burning hot and olive oil is the only oil that remains
> healthy at such a temperature. Cooked this way, the farinata comes out firm
> and soft, and when Orso cuts you a large piece and lays it on the paper, you
> have in your hands a perfumed wafer just waiting to be inserted into the
> correct opening, where it melts on the palate without any crumbling or
> indigestible raw pieces or the stench of burnt oily deposits.

The Slow Food Movement, with its logo of a little snail, has become well-
known throughout Italy and is spreading. (One hesitates to say anything is
happening 'fast' when speaking of the Slow Food Movement!) There are
branches in France, Spain, Germany, Japan and Australia. Founded in the
late 1980s in Italy by Carlo Pertini, the movement was initiated as a counter
to the ever-growing homogenisation and standardisation of food through
multinational fast food chains, industrialised agriculture and the cult of food
as fashion. The manifesto of Slow Food recognises that food is as much an
expression of culture as language is and that its traditions must be respected
and protected. Slow Food has 'conviviums' in several Australian states.

Anyway, we will serve our fish in a spicy chick pea batter, and I hope it
will be flathead tails, that sweet speciality from Port Phillip Bay, with
panisses, onion rings soaked in buttermilk to crisp them before frying, and
a bowl of yoghurt, made green with chopped coriander leaves.

When I was a child growing up on the Mornington Peninsula flathead
were in plentiful supply. My father and brothers had a small boat and went

out at least once a week in the spring and summer, leaving very early before the sun climbed too high. They would return before lunch with a bulging wet hessian sack – mostly flathead, a few nasty couta with vicious teeth, garfish, the odd gurnard with its poisonous spine, and very occasionally a snapper. But it was the flathead that we all remember. And the many ways Mum handled it. As we scraped the scales onto newspaper spread under the pump tap a long way from the house, she used to say 'If this were Europe there would be a festival – they would organise it for October and November when the tea-tree bushes are all in flower. People would come from far and wide to eat this sweet lovely fish and sniff the honey scent of the flowers'.

I think in her mind's eye she saw kiosks on the beach with charcoal burners or simple grills, as she had experienced on holidays in Malaysia and Greece. Stall-holders would be rushing plates of golden fillets to waiting, hungry and appreciative diners. Now in the 1990s the supply of local fish has dwindled and we are told that still the largest percentage of fish eaten in Australia is imported, and is then sold pre-crumbed and frozen.

There is a worrying push to outlaw professional fishermen from our local bays and inland waterways in the belief that this will improve fish supplies. Responsible professional fishermen accept that they must agree to regulation, with implications of quotas and closed seasons, but they angrily reject the claim that the recreational angler is necessarily more environmentally aware. For the consumer the important fact is that fish caught in Port Phillip Bay, at Lakes Entrance and around our coastline is the freshest fish Victorians can eat. Frequently these varieties are on sale less than twenty-four hours after being in the water. Other more expensive and more 'fashionable' varieties may be four days out of the water and have had quite a rough time getting to market. Rarely is anything simple in the food supply business!

PANISSES

1 litre warm water	*100 ml olive oil*
300 g chick pea flour	*black pepper*
salt	

Pour water into a bowl. Slowly add the flour, whisking well. Add salt.
Rest batter for 4 hours to allow flour to swell and absorb the liquid.
Skim any froth from the surface and add the olive oil. Stir in well.
Grease an ovenproof dish and pour in the batter to no more than
1 centimetre in thickness. Bake in a hot oven at 250°C for
approximately 15 minutes, or until it has a golden crust. Grind over
black pepper before serving. Alternatively, allow the mixture to cool,
cut into pieces and fry in plenty of hot, clean olive oil.
Serves 4–6

I have already mentioned my efforts to authenticate 'Matisse's shrimp', and
the 'shrimp' – or prawns, as we know them – were delicious, served with the
waxy potatoes. Will's wife, Bonny, had the idea of cooking and presenting
the dish in flowerpot saucers. We needed something that could hold the
very hot rock salt for a long time without cracking. I will experiment with
this when I can get to a garden shop. Everyone commented in astonishment
at the shine and colour of the mayonnaise we plan to serve with the dish.
The only secret is the quality of the eggs, and to make the mayonnaise with
a wooden spoon not a whisk. Less air is beaten in this way and the finished
product has a gloss that is never achieved with the whisked product.

The prawns were quickly followed by a salmon dish and a platter of
grilled red mullet. Many of us prefer to eat our fish fairly simply, allowing
its freshness and flavour to be the dominant impression. I have restricted
myself to a refreshing salad of orange and radish to accompany the salmon,
which will have a mix of olives, parsley and preserved lemon spooned over
it. The grilled fillets of red mullet will be served with a pot of one of my
favourite condiments, anchovy butter.

Desserts are to be very simple, with a luscious chocolate roulade for the
chocolate cake fans, a pot of bitter chocolate cream topped with cognac

mascarpone for the hopeless chocoholic, and then a few more that are less daunting. An orange-infused crème caramel, forever a favourite, a splendid open apple tart glazed with clotted cream, and an ice-cream terrine striped with amber quince sorbet and cream-coloured botrytis ice-cream.

We are also hoping to convince our diners to eat more fine cheese, so the cheese offerings will suggest an accompanying bread, and the selection will rotate most days and certainly with the seasons.

Nicky Reimer, our chef, and Justin Dowd, second chef, were justifiably pleased with their efforts and I think the planning can now move on to assembling ingredients, and establishing preparation lists. A good feeling.

CHOCOLATE MUD CUSTARD WITH MASCARPONE 'CREMA'

250 g bittersweet couverture chocolate,	*1 whole egg*
chopped	*3 egg yolks*
100 g unsalted butter	*mascarpone*
80 g castor sugar	*cognac* or *other liqueur*

Melt chocolate together with butter over a bain-marie until softened. Remove from heat and stir gently with a wooden spoon until well-combined and glossy. Cool a little.

Whisk sugar, egg and yolks until well-combined (but not fluffy). Pour chocolate mix into egg mix and whisk gently to thoroughly combine but not cause bubbles. Pour into small coffee cups or moulds.

Cook in a water bath at 180°C for 10 minutes. Remove and cool to room temperature. When cold (but not chilled), top the dessert with mascarpone whisked till smooth with cognac to taste.

This is best made several hours before it is needed and stored in a cool place as it will become too hard if refrigerated.

Serves 8

4 MARCH

*P*utting on my other hat, today is menu-change day at Stephanie's. It is
always difficult but hopefully less so today, as almost all the dishes were
thoroughly tested last month. The new team in the kitchen understands that
from now on my intention is to inspire, to suggest, to test and taste, but not
to be in there mixing and chopping with the team. Having said that, I will
do just that today, but I will move from one cook to another and not allow
myself to be solely responsible for a dish or a process as I once did. My
former role was to be everything to everybody for the first week of the
menu. Result was I felt crushed and crumpled, my prodigious energy
depleted, sore to the soles of my feet, and unable to respond enthusiastically
to the hard work of others.

Work on your business not in the business, some advisers say. I hear this
but I am not entirely convinced. The best businesses, the trailblazers, while
almost certainly not the most profitable ones, are those where someone
cares passionately about the product and knows enough to fix it if
something goes wrong.

Yesterday the architect rang to tell me that the cheese room was to be
installed today and where did we want the phone? Help – we had only
vaguely considered phone placement and now it had to be decided in an
hour. Angie found Telstra to be most helpful and apparently they are on the
job. Fortunately Angie is now able to put in time as the backroom person
while Will and I speed along trying to keep all the balls in the air. Lisa will
leave her job as a publicist in a month but at the moment she, too, is doing a
bit of this and a bit of that.

5 MARCH

*N*ew menu satisfactorily delivered at Stephanie's, although one of our
newest dishes, the ginger-rubbed roasted duck, was such a runaway success
that five of us spent much of the evening boning and slicing umpteen ducks.
A private function ignored almost all the other options on the menu. This is
not good menu planning, so I will have to look at changing the wording of

the other dishes – it is possible to change the demand for a dish by changing its description on the menu. And as I have also said before at other times and in other places, the word 'crisp' is the ultimate turn-on. I sometimes wonder if a dish of 'crispy cardboard' would be a great success!

The young ginger shoots are no more but we have been able to buy new season's ginger with pale-pink fingers and nearly transparent skin. While this ginger is almost fibreless and is excellent with the duck it is not satisfactory when sliced and fried as a wispy garnish for roasted scallops. Its extreme moisture content means that each shred instantly shrivels in the hot oil, leaving us with deliciously flavoured oil, but no crispy wisps!

I am also very pleased with the new lamb dish. Inspired by the South Australian development of an ancient grain from the Middle East, Greenwheat Freekeh, which I commented on in January, the dish has evolved from slices of a roasted leg to become a rack of lamb rubbed with a paste of saffron and sumac. I changed the accompaniment to freshly steamed zucchini, roasted tomatoes and grilled eggplant, a bright and fresh note in the centre of what is an aromatic but bronze-looking plate.

Appropriately the evenings are now cool so that my decision to include a caramel rice pudding and a rhubarb and raspberry crumble fits in nicely with the weather. They were both very successful.

A rushed visit to the Richmond site was pretty exciting. The cheese room shell is in place, tiles are on the kitchen walls and the kitchen canopy was being fitted. The builder assured me that all is on track for a finish in three weeks' time.

6 MARCH

Our graphic designer, Guy, who was responsible for the design of an earlier book of mine, *Stephanie's Seasons*, presented us with our corporate 'look' this afternoon. We were all thrilled with the warmth of our clotted cream and butter-striped menus and produce tags and wine labels. A few special problems are still to be solved. To print or not on the tamper-proof ribbons that will finish off each jar? In-house laser printing or professional printing? Angie and I are doing a bit of shivering in our shoes at the prospect of new skills to be learnt. Among them is obviously going to be the formatting of menus, wine lists and shelf labels, as well as special announcements and newsletters. Will professes to be unfazed by all this, but we shall see.

A lightning dash to Nexus, the interior designer's studio, this morning to decide on bar stools. They are sleek chrome with polished wood seats. Is the stain for the shelving too dark? Another sample has been ordered. Are the walls too white? Everyone must be asked to pass by and take a look. Each visit confirms my pleasure in the space – it is so sunny and inviting. We have been measured for an awning – quote still pending.

Meanwhile out in the wider world a Grand Prix is being held this weekend. The community is divided between those who strongly oppose it, those who are thrilled at the idea, and those who do not care one way or the other. Most of Melbourne will be affected by the race in some way, even if only by having to cope with crowded streets and rerouting of traffic. Local traders are unsure how they are expected to continue to trade as all cars are to be banned from Albert Park, the suburb where the race is held, from Saturday morning. My hairdresser is very close to the track and intends to open as usual but confesses to having no idea how his staff or his eighty customers will make it to the salon.

7 MARCH

When I was a teenager my mother used to go on and on about the need to develop 'hobbies'. At the time I found this odd – I was already an avid reader, as was my sister, and my brothers seemed to have all sorts of outdoor interests. Mum was overwhelmed with her own 'hobbies'. Books towered beside her bed. If one opened a little-used cupboard, bundles of raffia would be certain to fall out, or skeins of silk thread or tapestry linen; sticks of cane were found soaking in the bathtub; bonsai trees were pruned with nail scissors (I have never understood the appeal of this); blocks of rag paper for watercolour painting stood behind chairs in her study; other cupboards were full of finished works or shoeboxes crammed with seed packets; the kitchen was a workshop in action, with notes and lists pasted to the refrigerator, stuck under bowls and so on as Mum worked on several things at a time.

My father's recreations were classical music and photography. He found Mum's habit of flitting from interest to interest irritating and he would sometimes criticise her. She would be crestfallen, as her self-esteem was very shaky. But they were a great team and when they travelled, Mum painted quick, lively watercolour sketches and kept a travel diary that mixed historical facts with meals eaten and personal, rather quirky, anecdotes. Dad took movies, and back home he would entertain the family and neighbours. In his late seventies he also mastered the technology to convert all his Super-8 film to video, resulting in a wonderful archive of lives lived to the full.

Now, at eighty-eight, Dad is writing down his memories of the latter part of his life and he spends a lot of time reviewing these videos. Yesterday he asked me for an atlas so he could better follow his and Mum's travels. Today it was their trip through the Brenner Pass and into northern Italy. I think he is communing with Mum as much as anything else, and I find him wistful and melancholic yet at the same time stimulated after a morning's viewing. Dad is still using the electric typewriter, but I would be happy to get him a word processor. His fingers are stiffening, and he is ashamed of the mistakes he makes, yet he has no interest in mastering any more technology, he says.

Old age is not great. There is no one to share the memories with, and daily there seems to be a loss of faculty that inevitably means one little bit less independence. Dad's shakiness has long meant he needs a walking frame, and now the frame is one with a seat so he can rest after ten minutes. Stiff and swollen fingers make it harder to put on socks and shoes, or drink soup without spilling it; deafness makes it harder to have a conversation or to follow a debate; running children or balls or frisky dogs are terrifying when one's legs are wonky. Steps are impossible. A movie in an upstairs cinema has to be foregone. Saddest of all is that the world has shrunk to become not much bigger than his room. My father's lively mind is happiest in the past rather than confronting the pretty horrible state of world affairs. For one formerly passionate about world politics and to whom we all turned for the big picture to help us better understand every territorial conflict, he now admits to skimming the newspaper and finding most of it irrelevant. And yet he still reads several large-print books a week, he entertains his fellow residents with a carefully selected and compiled weekly programme of classical music, he looks forward impatiently to our visits and phone calls and to televised concerts or ballets, and he is mentally alert.

In contrast many of the residents sit and sleep in chairs all day long, and seem never to speak to anyone. So yes, Mum, 'hobbies' are all-important. He is just so lonely.

8 MARCH

*T*oday is International Women's Day. One has become used to the pronouncements that there is no room for complacency. The struggle continues for basic rights, for workplace equality, for child care, for meaningful participation in decision-making at all levels. All of these are legitimate concerns of Western women, who have already achieved a certain standard of living and legal protection, and who have a free choice whether to be active in these struggles or not. Not all groups in our society are so well looked after. Aboriginal women actively participate, seeking to focus attention on the chronically disadvantaged status of almost all their people. International Women's Day also seeks to draw the developed world's notice to the lack of human rights and basic inequalities endured by women in less fortunate parts of the globe.

The wider world offers daily evidence of the horrors experienced by men, women and children in underdeveloped countries and a televised documentary last night, showing the children dying in camps in Somalia and Rwanda, was chilling and terrible. That such horror can be visited on one group in the community by another group, or that a nation has to endure mass starvation year after year, is inconceivable to us in comfortable middle-class Australia.

It also gives rise to a sort of 'horror-tolerance plateau' that is very disturbing. In programme after programme we see these dying bodies, listless in the emaciated arms of their mothers; we see children and whole families trailing down dusty roads balancing rag bundles on their heads; we listen to international care officers predicting greater and greater disasters, and what can we do to change anything? Apparently nothing. We can and do write fat cheques and post them.

But nothing changes.

Struggles justified in terms of the perceived superiority of one race, one gender, one religion or one ideology are the ultimate obscenity. And here, by a circuitous route, I find the greatest relevance for the women's movement. When decision-making is achieved after thought for the greatest good and with due consideration for the global picture, when compromise is seen as a virtue not a capitulation, we may achieve fairer distribution of the world's goods. I have found women to be more prepared to debate and discuss and proceed to a decision than men, who prefer to dig in verbally to establish and defend their position. More and more women are no longer fooled by these tactics and seek alternative structures in which to achieve more equitable outcomes.

9 MARCH

A free day. Holly has the car all day so as I am without the means to go anywhere, I intend to cost the new menu for Richmond Hill Cafe & Larder. This is quite difficult, especially for one who for twenty years has offered a fixed price menu in which averaging was the dominant principle. An expensive dish had to be balanced in appeal with something of more moderate food cost. Without any undue modesty I think I have done this very well. Whereas now I have to calculate quite differently.

I have always disapproved of establishments that charge for bread. We will not do this but as we intend to offer a basket of interesting bread and pots of superior cultured butter on the table, the cost has to be added in somewhere. I also have to factor in community expectation of a cafe rather than a formal restaurant, and balance this with my conviction that the food will be excellent, the portions appropriate and the total experience a pleasure.

In a few days Angie and I will have coffee with our fruit and vegetable supplier. Angie has been a customer of his for ten years but he and I have exchanged only a few words. With a change of suburb comes the opportunity to rethink one's suppliers. Joe Toscana has the reputation of being an honest trader, an enthusiast about quality, and someone who enjoys supplying those who will notice the difference. Sounds like my man!

I hope to offer a green salad that will cause a customer first to stare or sigh with admiration before eating it and then to find that the leaves are tender, well-washed and dried, that the balance of extra-virgin olive oil and droplets of quality red-wine vinegar and the grain or two of best sea salt and the grind of pepper are beautifully balanced, and that it has been thoroughly turned in its dressing so that no liquid remains in the bowl and each leaf has a slight sheen. Maybe a freshly baked garlic crouton or three might be tucked at the sides for some crunch. Such a simple dish but so rare to get it right.

As I worked my way through the menu, I noted the dishes where tender loving care and exceptional produce can transform the ordinary into the special and I added on a dollar. Tender loving care costs in time and wastage as well as adding costs in the form of selective purchasing. Those in the industry all know about pre-dressed salads, and greens that are three days old, and poor oil, and rancid mixes with too much poor-quality vinegar.

I have already spent a few hours in discussion with the butcher. Jonathan Gianfreda is well-known to Melbourne restaurateurs and his retail shop in Smith Street, Collingwood, is very well-patronised. He is an enthusiast, an enterprising trader and someone who enjoys being associated with serious players. He is already planning the ageing of our steaks, and we have discussed the percentage of fat I would like in our hamburgers. His sausages are great and we will simply list them as Jonathan's sausages and allow the varieties to change every few days or with each order. Deliveries twice a day – no problem, he says. And his expertise extends to smallgoods as well. Jonathan is interested in trying my Spanish recipe for blood sausage with fennel and chestnuts and, as it is almost chestnut time and chestnut grower Elizabeth Seaton is promising me a fine crop from her property in Victoria's north-east, we will try in a few weeks.

Michael Canals will continue to supply the fish. I have been a customer of the Canals family for twenty years, and initially dealt with Michael's father and mother. Jack and Josie Canals were already the second generation of a proud Spanish–Australian family dealing in fish. Michael now has his own business as a wholesale supplier and can always be relied upon to provide the best fish available on the day. One can never ask for more than this. Other restaurateurs prefer to have their supplies flown in from around the country. I have done a bit of this in my time and have had some traumatic afternoons trying to trace live crabs, or boxes of scallops that have somehow been offloaded between Brisbane and Melbourne, or between the Eyre Peninsula and Adelaide and Melbourne. Now I prefer to let Michael worry and he is quick to tell me if something cannot be guaranteed.

This direct liaison with suppliers is one of the most enjoyable parts of my work. I have met some amazing characters. Notable among them is Jim Mendolia of Fremantle, who has single-handedly created an industry first with Fremantle anchovies and then with Fremantle pilchards or sardines. Both fish were ignored by Anglo-Saxon Australians and regarded as suitable only for fish bait. Jim's canned sardines are delicious, his cured sardines – which he markets as Auschovies – are also very good. He has agreed to experiment with a couple of products for me to sell in the shop and is confident they will work. At the moment he is very chuffed that Will is to present a box of Mendolia sardines to Her Majesty Queen Elizabeth, who is to board HM *Bark Endeavour* after its sail up the Thames to dock in London. HM *Bark Endeavour* was built in Fremantle, hence the gift as a further offering from the city.

Once the Cafe is up and running smoothly I am looking forward to moving around the country a bit and encouraging a few more enterprising individuals to think of new projects or different ways of quality value-adding.

1 0 M A R C H

A public holiday and a family outing with Dad to our beautiful Botanic Gardens for lunch. I was horrified to hear that he had fallen in the street yesterday and worst of all was that he was not able to get up. He lay until a passer-by helped him to his feet – and he is not a lightweight! No actual damage done except a severe blow to his confidence. I initiated discussion about motorised wheelchairs, which was summarily dismissed.

A strike of all public transport workers changed everything over the weekend. Grand Prix race-goers were ferried to the track in private buses, many who had not yet decided whether to go or not stayed away, few left home to shop unless they had no choice, and instead of traffic chaos we had a largely deserted central business district. I fear that we will now experience some pretty powerful paybacks, or 'union bashing', as it is more popularly known, from our State government, which does not like to be crossed and which seems reluctant to negotiate with anyone holding a different opinion from its own.

In preparation for my Italian sojourn with Maggie Beer in September and October of this year I have been reading and enjoying *Under the Tuscan Sun* by Frances Mayes. Mayes is apparently better known as a poet (not by me) and her writing is delightful. Somewhere early in the book she describes the Tuscan hillsides in high summer as being like lion's fur, evoking at once the dark blond but rough and tufty look of the harvested slopes. In the preface she tells of an Italian neighbour burying a tendril of an old vine so that it will shoot out new growth. She interprets this as a romantic but compelling metaphor for the way life must change if we are to push forward in our thinking.

Back in Australia our travel agents inform us that our three residential cooking schools are all but full.

13 MARCH

*Y*esterday a man came and suggested that I invest in the cultivation of truffles in Victoria. These rare fungi that appear seemingly from nowhere have a penetrating perfume and are highly prized in the kitchen. They command astonishing prices of up to $2,000 to the kilo. The best black winter truffles come from the Périgord region in France; the best white truffles occur in late autumn in Piedmont. Apparently there have been encouraging harvests in New Zealand. My friends in Tasmania have had a similar project underway for four years now and are hoping for results next year. I think I shall wait and see what happens. There is little question that everything connected with truffles is mysterious and capable of conspiratorial interpretation. I shall wait until my friend and colleague George Biron returns from a visit to New Zealand for a longer and more dispassionate account of results. George is actually going to view for himself New Zealand's claims to have found *Boletus edulis*, the magnificent cèpe or porcini mushrooms. Despite marketing claims to the contrary, no *Boletus edulis* has ever been identified in Australia. Its cousins, among them *Suillus luteus* and *Suillus granulatus*, are prolific in our pine plantations. However, their texture and flavour cannot compare with *Boletus edulis*. Its distinctive swollen stem is a major identifying difference but, as with all similar fungi, microscopic investigation is needed for accurate identification.

Autumn is well-established and it is wonderful. I wake to crisp air and enjoy the caress of my feather doona. My very special crabapple, 'John Downie', is displaying an excellent crop of crabs, each the size of a large walnut, as scarlet as a robin on one side and golden on the other. Even its slender trunk is two-toned, golden one side and green the other. Today I noticed the first red streaks in the vine leaves.

14 MARCH

*I*n preparation for stocking the shelves at Richmond Hill Cafe & Larder I have been talking with Mary Walker of Tasmania's Hill Farm Herbs and Tracklements. It is a delight to be able to share a concept that is instantly understood. We are to offer a range of seasonal preserves in limited quantities and hope that the customers will be thrilled to see the quince jelly arrive while they may be sad to see the end of the redcurrant jelly. Mary is very pleased to have the opportunity to work with more fleeting products than her usual range permits. The quality of her work is outstanding. She is creative, intelligent and practical, a winning combination. Many creative people are not at all practical but both Mary and I rush to answer faxes meticulously, make lists and number points, and winkle out unclear detail in a way that is delightfully similar. I wonder how much this has to do with the fact that both of us spent years as reference librarians?

Our initial range will reflect late summer. We will have a peach chutney and an unusual peach marmalade, blackcurrant jelly and spiced cherries, an apricot and apricot kernel jam, to mention a few, together with mustards, and my own contributions of grilled eggplant bathed in balsamic vinegar and extra-virgin olive oil.

A gathering of foodies tonight as Julie, her husband, Damien Pignolet (part-owner and executive chef of Sydney's Bistro Moncur and Bistro Deux at the Sackville Hotel), Maggie and I dined at Stephanie's with Chris Manfield of Paramount restaurant in Sydney. Damien and Chris are presenting sessions tomorrow at the Melbourne Food and Wine Festival Masterclass. Maggie and I are participants only this year so we were very relaxed and there was much hilarity.

15 MARCH

The Masterclass is the annual showpiece of the Melbourne Food and Wine Festival. It is a fantastic event, easily one of the highlights of the Australian food calendar. A mix of local, interstate and international presenters offer fascinating sessions and in between are longish morning and afternoon tea breaks to encourage networking and conversation, as well as a communal lunch, so that the weekend is an in-depth plunge into the world of food and wine. Regrettably I had a throbbing headache resulting from our party the night before.

But temporary discomfort was not enough to spoil the experience.

I watched and listened to visiting Chicago restaurateur Charlie Trotter expound his philosophy of a life devoted to the pursuit of excellence. We had lunched together at Stephanie's yesterday and in conversation it did appear that Charlie was obsessed with food and its preparation. His books display plate after plate of intricately worked dishes, mostly showing brilliant colour with some unusual flavours and juxtapositions and an inventive use of oils, essences and purées. In his class he showed himself to be a consummate professional and an outstanding presenter – articulate, able, interesting and efficient.

Elizabeth Chong is an inspirational Melbourne food identity. Elizabeth started classes in Chinese cookery in 1961 (I have already mentioned that my mother was one of her early students) and she has become the voice of Chinese cookery for most non-Asian Australians. She is proud to be the granddaughter of a market gardener and the granddaughter of one of the thousands of Chinese who came to the Victorian goldfields in 1850. As a small child Elizabeth lived in West Melbourne, where the Queen Victoria Market was her backyard.

From Elizabeth's class I learnt (at last) how to deal with bitter melon, that improbable-looking brilliant green vegetable with all the warts and varicose veins. She combined it with black beans and beef in a stir-fried dish. Like all Asians Elizabeth understands the central importance of vegetables and believes in the specific benefits that each one contributes to bodily harmony and health. Food is medicine as well as nutrition and pleasure, and the choice one makes of what to cook may be influenced by how one is feeling as much as what is in season. Black beans give the stomach a positive feeling of happiness. The enjoyment of *fu gwar* or bitter melon is seen as a sign of maturity. There is a Chinese saying that one only eats bitter melon for half of one's life! Bitterness is one of the five fundamental flavours but one that small children do not respond to.

Elizabeth was most emphatic that we understand that stir-fried, green-stemmed vegetables must be cooked. They should retain a crisp texture but should not be left hot but raw. And that Peking cabbage, whether stir-fried or braised, should be cooked until it is soft and mellow.

'We Chinese do not like raw vegetables', she said. And then another piece of Elizabeth wisdom. Australia has now experienced more than twenty years of Asian migration. The ingredients grown by these new arrivals are inevitably being adopted and adapted, and this is to be encouraged. But we must take notice of the potential and qualities of the various ingredients. Cooking methods must be appropriate and authentic – Western cooks have much to learn from Asian cooks.

Hooray! Perhaps someone will listen. I do not appreciate uncooked snowpea shoots in salads. They are an exquisite vegetable with steamed prawns or as a dish on their own, but served raw they are indigestible and one is liable to choke. And I have had many unsuccessful stir-fried mixtures that are partly scorched, too oily, and undercooked.

ELIZABETH CHONG'S STIR-FRIED BEEF AND BITTER
MELON IN BLACK BEAN SAUCE

1 tablespoon fermented black beans
½ teaspoon sugar
pinch salt
2 cloves garlic, peeled and bruised
light soy sauce
2 bitter melons, washed, halved
*   and seeded*

2 tablespoons peanut oil
300 g rump or fillet steak, sliced and
*   marinated in a light splash of soy*
*   sauce, rice wine and a light dusting*
*   of potato or corn flour*

Rinse the black beans under cold water and drain. Mix in a small bowl
with sugar, salt, garlic and a splash of light soy sauce.

Cut each melon in half, lengthways. Scoop out the seeds and
surrounding pulp. Cut the melon across into 1 cm slices.

Bring some water (enough to cover the melons) to a rolling boil,
and blanch the bitter melons for 1–2 minutes, until they are slightly
softened and become a brighter green. Rinse immediately and briefly
under cold running water, drain and put aside.

Heat the wok until very hot, add the peanut oil, and coat the
surface of the wok. Add the beef slices, stir-frying over a high heat
until the colour changes, then add the black bean mixture, stirring
constantly until fragrant. Add the bitter melon, combining carefully
and quickly for the flavours to marry.

Add a little water or stock in a thin drizzle, stir-frying to combine
all the seasoning evenly. Serve immediately. The Chinese would
probably offer a clear soup with this dish as a flavour contrast.
Serves 4 with rice

Marieke Brugman and Sarah Stegley of Howqua Dale Gourmet Retreat
contributed a thoughtful session entitled 'Pioneers, Partnerships,
Pilgrimages', in which they evaluated the shared experience of twenty years'
professional involvement in this chameleon-like world known as Australian
cuisine. Impossible to paraphrase the paper. Sufficient to note that more and
more intelligent practitioners are speaking out against the media's need to

categorise cooks and Australian cuisine, and its tendency to support elusive and ill-founded notions of regionalism in a continent where almost everything is available almost all the time, rather than contribute to the less modish debate which recognises that the existence of a rich and varied cuisine is inextricably linked to real-world issues of land care, monopoly retailing, and education.

Late last spring, as part of the events surrounding the launch of *The Cook's Companion*, I spent a weekend at Sunnybrae, the idyllic country restaurant owned by George Biron and his partner Diane Garrett. Tucked away at the foot of the Otway Ranges, Sunnybrae has the appearance of an expansive country homestead. Its windows look onto an extraordinary organic garden, much of it given over to the growing of vegetables in serious quantities. The lunch I planned on that occasion started with a vegetable antipasto including artichokes. There were sixty guests and I remember being astonished that George was able to pick all the artichokes from his own garden. And that was before the Great Garden Expansion. George is inspired by his garden and by all manner of edible growing things.

The well-researched paper George presented at the Masterclass today was on mushrooms. I appreciated his excellent bibliography. The centrepieces on each table were moss-covered 'gardens' planted with clumps of varied fungi for us to sniff, handle and learn about. The room was lit only by soft glowing lights (mushroom-shaped, of course), tucked in each fairy ring of mushrooms, and we seemed to be in an enchanted forest. There was much discussion about the likelihood of Antipodean porcini and truffle cultivation succeeding. I have already noted the facts about *Boletus edulis*, and New Zealand appears to be ahead of us on both counts. To accompany his tasting platters of varied mushrooms George had made a special bread brushed with a highly aromatic truffle oil as it came from the oven. Each plate offered a different sauce to illustrate the versatility of mushrooms – a dark soy dressing, a delicate saffron cream, a rich red pepper relish, and a smoky bacon sauce.

To conclude the session George passed around his 'poison box' containing innocent-looking mushrooms that were in fact the poisonous yellow-staining mushroom, *Agaricus xanthodermus*. I found this very disquieting as they seemed the same as the mushrooms I collected as a child. It is true these did not smell very pleasant but I don't recall sniffing each mushroom when I was ten. I do not like the idea of being warned away from one of the very few naturally occurring foods we still have. Picking mushrooms has always been associated in my mind with country walking and nature's bounty. Will I ever do it again now?

16 MARCH

*D*ay Two and with headache absolutely entrenched I started the morning with a session on sherry. What a way to go. Wine writer Tim White strutted and declaimed and leapt from idea to idea, swirled his *copita* and encouraged us all to assume this same exuberance. It must have been the sherry. And it was fabulous. Sparkling, delicate fino and manzanilla, surely the perfect aperitif. On to the nutty amontillado, and finally to the rich and syrupy oloroso. In between we nibbled on prawns and anchovies and ham and black pudding and parmesan and fruit cake. A fabulous session and the smell in the room was exhilarating!

Damien Pignolet is a constant in my life. We have been friends for twenty years and have experienced a great deal together. Damien is a master of technique and could probably give a memorable class on how to boil water. This time his class was on charcuterie and the detail was extraordinary.

Damien remembered that the best terrine he had ever made in his life was a venison mixture and it was baked in 1981. If pressed I am sure he would have been able to remember the date. It is this attention to fine detail that makes his classes exceptional.

We saw him emulsify a sausage mixture by hand, insist on precise poaching instructions for boudins blanc that had me rushing back to Stephanie's Restaurant after the class to check the temperature of our poaching liquid, and explain the fine points of working with caul fat and spice mixtures, and of properly sealing terrines and rillettes to ensure their keeping qualities. The tasting he offered us was most generous and the texture in the rillettes and the boudins again was exceptional. Having lived in Tours, the rillettes capital of France, I think the Tourangeaux might have found Damien's version a bit refined, without the little shreds of browned *rillons* that were always present, but then probably Damien might find their version too rustic.

And there were so many more highlights. I can still taste the mango sorbet offered at the conclusion of Chris Manfield's stunning dessert class and the wasabi-flavoured flying fish roe from Babak Hadi's caviar session. Maggie attended the class presented by Henri Krug where the lucky attendees had a guided tasting of the great wines of Krug, including the exceedingly rare Clos du Mesnil wines of 1981 and 1985 and the Krug Collection wines of 1973 and 1976. What a weekend. It is not possible to attend every session, so inevitably one has regrets. But then there is always next year.

1 9 MARCH

*T*he pressure is on. The works are proceeding at a rapid pace at the Cafe and the opening date is now possible to determine. The kitchen equipment arrives in two days' time. We meet to review paint colours and canvas samples for the awning. We are still waiting for a telephone number in order to print stationery. Angie and I have decided on our opening stock. Orders are being placed. Our liquor licence application has been conditionally approved. This means that all is OK as long as the fire and health authorities approve. Everything has been done in accordance with their regulations, so we should not have a problem. The wine list is still a bit vague in patches. One cannot order wine as a wholesaler without a licence number from the Liquor Commission, so that approval is very important.

Time is what we need. Time to chase up miscellaneous items. Time to think. Time to understand the implications of the cash registers. Time to review the pile of CVs received. Lisa is onto that now. Rosters will have to be redone in the light of our latest decision to open six days a week. We feel that this decision was necessary although we are also aware that Will is somewhere swaying on a mast in freezing seas in the English Channel and knows nothing of our thinking. We tried without success to contact him on board. Surely he will approve?

I have written to Dom Christopher at the Benedictine Community at historic New Norcia in Western Australia to see if they are able to supply enough of their excellent olive oil for us to use in our canned sardines. I would love to have a truly Western Australian product. And we have ordered sleek pepper grinders made of Tasmanian blackwood from Tasmanian woodcrafters. I must ring Damien for advice about choosing a laminator for our menus. Not enough minutes in the day.

But still we have time for fun.

Tonight Lisa, Angie, her husband Duffy, Dur-é and I attended a clambake at The Pavilion restaurant, part-owned by Dur-é. The event had been designed by Gail and Kevin Donovan, the operational managers of The Pavilion (formerly Jean-Jacques-by-the-Sea), and was a happy mix of Australian barbecue and New England clambake, reflecting the backgrounds of this energetic and delightful couple. Such special events are another part of this truly extraordinary Melbourne Food and Wine Festival.

When we arrived the pits had already been dug on the beach and filled with wood and stones. The strong wind whipped the fires to a fierce roar. The shellfish were swaddled in wet seaweed and rested on wire frames, waiting for the moment to be judged just right for their ultimate sacrifice. We were entertained by a delightful brass band called Itchy Feet whose band master twitched and jerked through a marvellous Chaplinesque routine as they syncopated along the boardwalk. The food was sensational – a succulent and sweet crayfish with melted butter, juicy crabs, milky sweetcorn, and, of course, the clams.

The sun sank, the moon rose, the waves glistened, the silver sand darkened, and still we cracked claws and sucked the juices and sipped wine (when we had a free hand). What a joy it was. Conversation was almost superfluous.

20 MARCH

Restaurant Week is upon us at Stephanie's and is running as smooth as silk. They pour in and they file out! One hundred and fifty people a day for lunch. A choice of three entrees and three main courses, home-made bread, one glass of Victorian wine, tea and coffee and that will be $19.97, thank you very much. The kitchen is amazed at how straightforward it is. There has been a great deal of backroom planning for it to unroll like this, and of course considerable additional wages. Too soon to see if it covers our costs. The downside is that because the demand is so huge we have had to offer dishes that are very simple to prepare and serve. And of course the choice is restricted. It saddens me that so many of the customers cheerfully announce that they also came last year. Twenty dollars a year is their outlay for lunching at Stephanie's. They are not experiencing the Restaurant as it is during our usual trading. And they are saving perhaps $10. Dinners are very quiet. There are so many activities vying for the attention of food lovers this month.

I think I am witnessing something absolutely exciting and moving. Lisa is shedding her cocoon and emerging as a strong and beautiful butterfly. When I met Lisa's father thirty-one years ago in London he was an exceedingly charming but unresolved human being. He had no difficulty finding employment but it was all temporary, and all pretty marginal. Once we opened Jamaica House in 1966, the year of Lisa's birth, Monty found his metier. A superb host, personally organised and a hard worker, demanding but fair with his employees, he found that the restaurant gave him a stage and he loved playing on it. I see signs that our daughter is going to reincarnate his success. Although she confesses to panic at the prospect of so many new systems to absorb (and we all do), she also has a new sparkle in her eye, and a thoughtful way of assessing information and acting upon it that fills me with confidence and delight. She is going to follow in her father's footsteps, with more than a little help from her mother. I am sad all over again that Monty is not around to be thrilled by his little girl's triumph.

22 MARCH

I have just enjoyed a two-hour walking tour down Sydney Road, Brunswick, with Greg Malouf, the chef at O'Connell's Hotel in South Melbourne. Greg's family is from Lebanon and together with his Syrian sister-in-law, Amal, he is enjoying introducing food lovers to yet more exotic and unfamiliar flavours. Greg combines appreciation, knowledge of and respect for the traditional ways and dishes of the Middle East with his own thoroughly modern approach to menu design. He incorporates a traditional flavour or technique and creates something that is new and yet culturally appropriate. This is what makes Greg's food so satisfying. It is familiar and yet different and very exciting.

We started with coffee and pastries at Balhas, the surprise for me being the semolina cake baked with a layer of clotted cream and soaked in orange-blossom water, then excellent but more familiar baklava, and *barma*, a roll of *kataifi* pastry filled with pistachios and walnuts and soaked in syrup. *Kataifi* is fine pastry that is cut into shreds and is usually rolled tightly around a filling of minced nuts, baked and then soaked in syrup. Greg described other uses for *kataifi*, including wrapping poached brains and walnuts like sausage rolls. I have used this same *kataifi* pastry teased into a nest and baked to hold an 'egg' of nougat ice-cream with an orange and mango sorbet 'yolk'.

At the Turkish butcher we tasted paper-thin slices of *bastourma*, silverside rolled in a fine paste of fenugreek, chilli and sugar and air-dried. It was delicious. Greg explained a traditional way of enjoying this. The slices are lightly fried, an egg is cracked over them and the pan is brought straight to the table for the diner to scoop the contents with flat bread. Greg uses it in a salad with goat's cheese, rocket and a well-seasoned red-wine vinaigrette and he sprinkles the salad with sumac. Sumac is an oft-mentioned spice. It is ground from a purplish-brown seed, lemony in flavour, and Greg uses it in many dishes. Also popular with Greg is *za'atar*, a mix of wild thyme, sumac and other spices that is sprinkled onto freshly baked flat bread, or on the unbaked dough. Greg says he regards *za'atar* as his Vegemite!

The fruit and vegetable shops in Sydney Road had cases of the first fresh pistachios in their pink and green suede coats, and also the first fresh green olives for pickling. The supermarkets had bundles of golden tobacco leaves for use in water pipes. I bought some twisted ropes of haloumi cheese in brine and tasted another appealing snack of baked haloumi on slightly sweet flat bread. The cheese bubbled and melted like mozzarella but with an additional tang. Greg says he normally washes and dries the haloumi before slicing, flouring and frying it to add to a spinach salad.

This busy suburban street is home to more and more Middle Eastern businesses and I was transfixed by the sight of a dark-skinned woman, completely veiled in a rich purple chador, standing in the middle of busy Sydney Road while the Saturday morning traffic whirled around her. What a cultural mix we have.

This excursion is my introduction to another strand in the fabric of Australian cuisine. And what do I intend to do with all this new information? It is a culinary reference – a resource – to be filed away, but it definitely starts my brain ticking. There are flavours and products I want to think about a bit more. I have already mentioned my first try at using sumac with lamb and freekeh. I am certain that *bastourma* will be on my next menu, somewhere. I am left wondering how I can experiment with pomegranate molasses, or dried limes or spiced Lebanese lamb sausages. But today's trip has another benefit, that of greater understanding. When I visit the Middle East I will have been given some culinary and cultural understanding. At the Masterclass, Tim White quoted Lawrence Durrell from an article Durrell wrote for the *New York Times* called 'Landscape and Character'.

> As you get to know Europe slowly, tasting the wines, cheeses and characters of the different countries, you begin to realise that the important determinant of any culture is after all the spirit of place. Just as one particular vineyard will always give you a special wine with discernible characteristics so a Spain, an Italy, a Greece will always give you the same type of culture – will express itself through the human being just as it does through its wild flowers.

The 'spirit of place' is what we respond to when we travel and the discovery that each place can be so different is what gives life its particular savour, and what affirms for me that there is no one place, or people, or flavour, that can ever assume superiority. Difference is to be forever celebrated.

2 9 MARCH

*T*he Cafe looks very exciting. Sculptor Frank Bauer has spent the last three days installing a web of black and silver wires that criss-cross the ceiling, on which tiny lights are suspended. They look absolutely wonderful. Our builder, Ken Van der Jagt, eyed this installation a little doubtfully and said it seemed like an adventure playground for spiders. I hope he is proved wrong. I also hope these little lights are very resilient – changing them will be a nuisance. The marble top to the bar was installed as I watched. Angie and I stared in amazement at all the shelving in the larder and hoped we have ordered enough stuff to fill it! And is there still enough space for the customers?

I rang Elizabeth Seaton, my chestnut grower, to secure supplies. She says the cockatoos are looking interested and that this is a sure sign that the harvest will be soon. Two fruity treats this week. A colleague gave me two purple peaches, those glorious last fruit that have a greyish skin and brilliant juicy crimson flesh, right to the stone. Imagine a Bellini made with this purée! And then Sarah, the painter of the mural, gave me a bag of prune-plums, small pointed fruit as large as a very big grape, firm and meaty and sweet. I would love to have more of these; they would be the ideal plums for pickling. Sarah, Angie and I have discussed the painting and now we have to trust the artist. The mural is to be a dreamy but strong depiction of a laden table and some people gathering and planting, with an Australian background that at once establishes our own 'spirit of place'.

I leave for Adelaide in a couple of hours to spend a weekend with Maggie to do further work on our menus for Tuscany. Julie has persuaded us that the logical outcome of our adventure is a book! By planning the menu outline in advance, which will then be edited and reproduced in booklet form for our students, we will have a good chunk of the book structure complete before we leave. Although we do know that the best-laid plans will almost certainly change.

What an extraordinary life! When I return the construction of the Richmond project will be complete and once more I will be overwhelmed with tasks. But for now, the month ends and I am about to immerse myself in Italy.

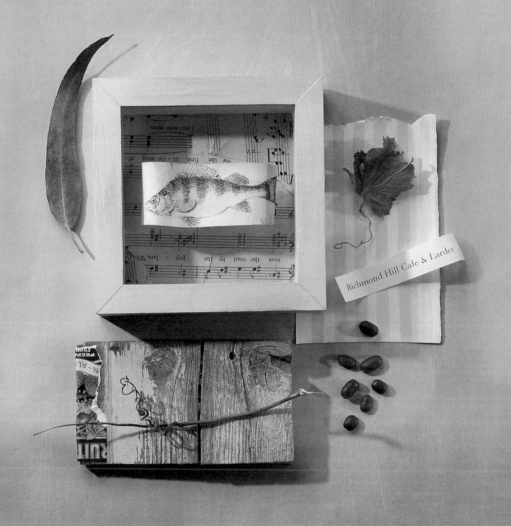

April

1   APRIL

*U*ntil very recently both my brothers, John and Christopher, lived in the
Northern Territory. John still does and is a senior public servant with the
Department of Education. My younger brother, Christopher, has left his life
in the Top End after twenty-five years working with Aborigines to establish
indigenous projects that offer tourists an accurate, absorbing and enjoyable
way of learning about the Territory and Aboriginal culture. Christopher,
his wife, Catherine, and children Caleb and Lilian, are now living in
Strathalbyn, on the Fleurieu Peninsula, where Christopher is the tourism
officer charged with promoting this part of South Australia.

Dad was eager to check out their new life so Chris and I decided that
en route to my few days with Maggie in the Barossa I could build in a short
detour to Strathalbyn. I expected there would be some difficulties getting
Dad there. And there were. Dignity is very precious. Even at the airport,
where he had to be transferred in a wheelchair, I watched his shoulders
slump and his mouth settle in a grim expression. As our luck would have it,
this Easter weekend was a popular day to be flying. On our flight were seven
others in wheelchairs – six were intellectually disabled elderly people, one
was a young and elegant Italian man, beautifully dressed, the lower part of
his body wasted and twisted. We boarded without fuss or delay but at the
other end it was another story. Adelaide airport has no air bridge and it was
a long and arduous process to move eight wheelchairs down the passageway
of a plane, and then to manoeuvre these same chairs and passengers onto a
hydraulic platform with luggage and minders. There was a lot of confusion
and distress. Two of the wheelchair passengers were blind and became
frightened and disorientated as they felt themselves swaying and bumping
while the platform was slowly lowered to the ground. Half an hour after
landing we reclaimed Dad's walking frame, met Christopher and Caleb,
and started the drive to Chris's home. All problems were forgotten as Dad
settled into the front seat of a comfortable car and off we went in
sparkling sunshine.

The Fleurieu Peninsula has been home to the indigenous Kauma and
Ramadjeri people since the beginning of Aboriginal history. Visitors today
can go to the Signal Point Interpretive Centre at Goolwa to learn more of

the area's early history and associated legends. Its European name derives from a French explorer. The whole Peninsula is known for its spectacular natural beauty and for its untouched nature reserves. The Coorong, one of the twenty conservation parks to be found there, is a popular destination for bird lovers and for all those whose spirit responds to solitude, and an ever-changing mix of wild and gentle landscape. Dad reminisced that he had first crossed the Coorong when he was sixteen years of age. I was reminded of a weekend I had camped there on a meandering drive along the Great Ocean Road from Lorne to Adelaide many years ago.

Today the Fleurieu is known as the 'produce basket' of Adelaide, said Christopher the tourist officer. It was noticeable in the variety and frequency of roadside notices advertising produce for sale. We bought just-picked sweetcorn (four for $1) and could have bought strawberries, raspberries, youngberries, silver beet, red potatoes, honey, farm eggs, and manure. We also passed a farm that produces turf and another growing horseradish. As with so many country roads in South Australia, wild olives abound here as do old unpruned apple, almond and quince trees. It is a gentle landscape of dry stone walls, simple timber cottages and more substantial stone homesteads. Winemaking plays an important role in the economy of the region, which is collectively described as the Southern Vales and includes the well-known sub-regions of McLaren Vale and Langhorne Creek.

The town of Strathalbyn was settled in 1839 by Scottish immigrants. Its High Street offers a tourist promenade of restored heritage buildings now operating as antique and second-hand shops or craft shops, and other specialised businesses aimed at the tourists. Strathalbyn is fortunate to have been able to preserve its historic buildings in a manner that ensures they are both a living museum of how things were and a major contributor to the town's economy. The number of very attractive bed-and-breakfast establishments certainly suggests that the town is a popular destination.

Christopher and family have bought a sprawling stone house with a wrap-around, wide, country verandah just made for deep cane chairs and lazy afternoons. Their block slopes gently to the Angus River, lined with mighty river gums. Kookaburras laughed as we inspected the boundaries.

We installed Dad in a chair on the verandah with a shady hat and the paper. A nearby golden ash shimmered in the autumn sunshine. The clouds drifted and the sun became too fierce for him. It took two of us to heave him from the chair. He hated to ask and therefore sounded irritable. Then it was a little breezy out of the sun and he needed an extra sweater.

Oh, my father. You strode like a Colossus through my childhood. Capable, strong and certain. A builder of things, a teaser of ideas. He loved to be loved, to have his work approved of, even admired. His beliefs were founded in idealism tempered by a distrust of the fanatic. He disliked confrontation and approved of moderation in most things. Many times I believed him to be sitting on the fence over an issue to discover later that his understanding was very deep and left him hesitant to declare that black was black or white was white. So much of the world is more accurately seen in shades of grey.

And now he is a man diminished. His dignity slips from him little by little. Unfamiliar showers can scald, toilet cubicles are not intended for bulky frames and the elderly need time and privacy and help with buttons. I rack my brains for recreational possibilities that are interesting, not too far, have smooth paths, easy access, car parking close at hand, and yet allow sight and smells of the natural world. Almost every experience seems too hard in one way or another. The alternatives are dreadful to contemplate.

He has so looked forward to this trip but a walking frame cannot safely negotiate a stony track beside the river. He must admire it from the manicured carpark. And everywhere there are steps. Even a change of level of two to three centimetres can bring on a disaster. He stumbles. I feel the tremble in his fingers. My heart breaks but I cannot help him with this.

2 APRIL

And on to the Barossa Valley to celebrate the Vintage Festival. The Lutheran community still exerts considerable influence in the valley. The Vintage Festival may not commence before the end of Lent. There will be vineyards to visit, festivals to attend, parades to see, flavours to enjoy and

Maggie has bought tickets to the Vintage Ball and has insisted that I bring my dancing shoes.

We called in to the Woodside Cheese Wrights on the way, where Paula Jenkin is crafting her beautiful cheeses in a disused butter factory, and we bought a selection of cheeses for Maggie. Last year I was one of the judges who awarded Paula's ashed goat's milk cheese, Edith, the prize for Best Australian Specialist Cheese. Paula and her partner Simon Burr are typical of the small band of specialist cheesemakers around Australia who have changed the nature of cheesemaking and have contributed to our improved standards. Like most small producers they have not found it easy. For many consumers the cheeses are confronting and powerful and quite unfamiliar. One of the aims of Richmond Hill Cafe & Larder is to provide a collective showcase for these brave individuals so that their product will be displayed proudly and properly, and they can feel reassured that it will be promoted to an appreciative audience. But, as I also know, it takes more than a few appreciative food lovers to pay the bills.

We lunched with Maggie and Colin Beer in their walled courtyard. Dad was in high spirits and thoroughly enjoyed both the conversation and the delicious Kangaroo Island chicken that Maggie had prepared. He and Christopher returned to Strathalbyn and Maggie and I settled in for a few days of Italy planning. We firmly resolved to work all day and play later. A few exceptions were allowed. Tomorrow I am to do a session at Yalumba winery at the Harvest Festival that is part of the Barossa Vintage Festival discussing the produce of the Barossa, and Maggie has to supervise at her new export kitchen. Tonight we are dining at the Wild Olive Restaurant. Once the Pheasant Farm Restaurant and the launching ground for Maggie and Colin's products, it is now operated by Sue-Ellen Hope, formerly of Stephanie's, and her partner Pierre Barellier, formerly of Jacques Reymond's restaurant in Melbourne. It was great to see Sue-Ellen again, always bubbling and positive and with prodigious energy. She confessed that she was missing Melbourne and was not sure about country life as a long-term option.

As we drove home we passed tractors piled high with grapes heading for the weighbridge. In the clear, cold night air each breath we drew brought the unmistakeable smell of crushed grapes and fermentation.

It is very stimulating being among winemakers. What I enjoy is their down-to-earth manner, the mix of farmer and craftsman. Their vocabulary offers a mix of sensual imagery as they speak of juice and bunches and fruit and skins, and just as enthusiastically they move on to discussions of dirt and rain.

3 APRIL

Today Maggie showed me the export kitchen that she and Colin have just had officially opened by the Premier of South Australia with appropriate pomp and ceremony. I was speechless. It is very high-tech and the equipment makes one gasp. Regulations controlling food production are exceedingly strict, even more so since the food-poisoning scandal in South Australia in 1995. On any day that the plant is producing for export a government inspector is present the entire time ensuring that all is as it should be. To have expanded to this after ten years as a cottage industry is a magnificent achievement. The product cooked yesterday, Maggie's exceptional Pheasant Farm pâté, is being packed and will be on its way to Japan in a few hours. This is commercial production achieved without any compromise in quality. The absence of preservatives has implications for shelf-life and makes the distribution that much more hair-raising, but that is how Maggie and Colin want it and their commitment to this standard is why the product is exceptional.

Maggie is developing some exciting new products. The public would be amazed to learn how long a new product takes, from the first glimmerings of an idea until the first feasibility testing takes place. I find it fascinating. From time to time over the years I have been asked to contribute an idea or a recipe for mass production. Always on closer investigation what is being proposed is a compromise, or a watering down, or a substitution to make it last longer, be more stable and so on. Always the modifications would result in a lesser product. I have always said no.

Today's Yalumba Harvest Festival (inspired by the success of the Victorian event, I wonder?) is held on the Signature Lawn beside the magnificent and classic buildings of Yalumba, built of local sandstone in

1849. Local artist Rod Schubert has built an assemblage of life-sized corn dollies in calico dresses on top of wheat stooks, surrounded by brimming baskets of fruit and paper poppies. There are more than thirty stalls offering a wide range of local delicacies. I had samples of many products sent to me to inspect several weeks ago but I looked forward to an early wander to make sure I had experienced absolutely everything. Although breakfast was only a couple of hours ago I could not resist a speck bun with a dill pickle, and as I walked I munched a caraway-seed pretzel from the Apex bakery. The crowds were gathering fast.

Woodside Cheese Wrights were represented and I bought one of Paula's rare Artym cheeses that she had been rubbing with olive oil for months. The Artym had matured to a creamy-coloured dense-textured cheese, ideal for grating over pasta. Unsurprisingly it was not cheap, as a hundred litres of goat's milk is required to produce just ten kilos of cheese. I also bought a Tomme, another chunky round cheese produced from rich Jersey milk.

Kangaroo Island is developing a reputation as a food lover's destination. The chickens are excellent (if hard to find) and here today was a stall selling magnificent marron. The marron on display in the tank was a beauty, and was six years old. The industry is in its infancy on Kangaroo Island but there are hopes to have sufficient quantities for a limited commercial operation by the end of the year. I still purchase live marron (with a registered licence to do so, I hasten to add) from Warren Moore of the Denmoore Marron Farm, south of Perth. Warren's operation is highly organised and he seems to have no problems supplying a hundred or so creatures a week.

This is one of the points being emphasised by such events as the Yalumba Harvest Festival. Many of the producers here are comfortable supplying a purely local market and are quite unable to cope with a state-wide or national demand. 'Small is beautiful' is a convincing philosophy from a local point of view. But rarely does it make economic sense to remain small. The winemakers of Australia have long understood this. Once again the achievements of Maggie and Colin Beer stand out. They started small, they serviced a growing state-wide business first, moved to national distribution and have now made the big decision to export, with no special expertise other than clear thinking, a belief in planning, hard work and total commitment to their product and quality.

And, as Maggie told me recently, it is necessary to come to terms with the special madness of small business. She says she read somewhere that it is like 'dancing with gorillas, dangerous, and they never get tired'.

I have to become accustomed to the wildlife in the Barossa. Everywhere is invaded by millipedes. These disgusting creatures are like crunchy tiny snakes, each maybe three centimetres in length. They seem to like pale surfaces and cling to the white stucco of the house. They bend and twist themselves into hooks and loops so that a line of millipedes can seem like a message in shorthand. They also like rain and after rain it is quite impossible to put one's foot down without hearing a crunch.

They are on chairs, in the bath, in your bed, and in your water glass. Staying calm is necessary! They do not bite, nor do they appear to do any harm at all. They do have an odour, though.

And then the possums got at my special Artym cheese!

4   APRIL

All morning we have worked on our menus for Italy. The Italian Slow Food Movement has compiled a directory of recommended businesses in many cities and small towns in Italy. We are delighted to find that the butcher recommended by one of Maggie's former employees is also recommended in this book. We have made contact with an Adelaide distributor for high-quality Italian wines and we are meeting him tomorrow. Tonight is the ball! Maggie is very excited. She loves to dance.

Today for lunch Maggie made a quick sauce agresto. She stuffed the food processor with basil, walnuts and almonds and added quite a lot of her verjuice as well as olive oil. This delicious sauce was enjoyed with generous dollops of fresh goat curd bought yesterday from Paula Jenkin and yesterday's bread rubbed with garlic and grilled. We will use this combination or something similar for one of our Italian lunches.

This dish in many ways sums up our aspirations for the Italian experience. To put together a simple fresh cheese with a sauce that uses the herbs in the garden and very good quality aromatics proves that memorable culinary moments can be as easy as this. Maggie lives her life with complete integrity. Her philosophy is 'only the best', but the best can be a freshly picked pear, or freshly laid eggs, or yabbies from the dam. I hope I live this way, too. We have no need of truffles (although we certainly don't pass up the opportunity to taste them when they are in season, which they will be at the very end of our Italian holiday), or other rare and exotic ingredients. Just what is in season and fresh and of good quality. It all seems so obvious to us and yet I am still shocked by seeing the convenience foods that are the preferred choice of many I would have thought were converts to the foodie cause.

Supper at the ball was not until 10.00 p.m. so Maggie had invited our table of revellers for a bowl of pasta. This proved to be another of her quick specialities: fettucine tossed with currants soaked in verjuice, with toasted sliced garlic, olive oil, loads of parsley and generously shaved parmesan.

It was so cold and the ball was to take place inside a giant marquee erected on the football field. Our breath preceded us in great puffs of steam. One had to dance or possibly freeze to death. Four hundred tickets had been sold and for most of the evening almost everyone was on the dance floor. It was great fun, if rather like standing in one's underwear outside in the garden on the coldest night of the year!

The local ladies excelled themselves with the cakes at suppertime. I had forgotten about country suppers. Brandy snaps, chocolate eclairs, cream horns, melting moments, lamingtons, chocolate rum balls, apple slices and much more. The only thing I missed were airy cream sponges. I am determined to put a cream-filled sponge on the menu at the Cafe in memory of all the suppers at school socials.

COUNTRY-STYLE SPONGE CAKE

3 eggs

1 tablespoon hot water

75 g castor sugar

2 drops pure vanilla

75 g plain flour, sifted

jam or lemon curd

200 ml cream, firmly whipped

icing sugar

Butter and flour a 20 cm sponge tin and rap against the sink to dislodge extra flour. Cut a circle of baking paper to fit the base of the tin. Preheat oven to 200°C.

Place a pan half-filled with hot water on the stove and bring to simmering point. Choose a basin that will fit snugly over the pan and tip in the eggs, hot water, castor sugar and vanilla. Whisk quickly for about 5 minutes until egg mixture is warm to the touch. Do not allow the water to boil or the basin to touch the water.

Transfer mixture to an electric beater and beat until the mixture has trebled in volume and is very thick and pale. Sift the flour over the mixing bowl and, using a flexible whisk, very gently but thoroughly fold in the flour.

Tip into the prepared tin and bake for 20 minutes. Cool on a wire tray and when quite cold split and spread with jam or lemon curd and whipped unsweetened cream, or any other combination you fancy. Dust top with icing sugar.

Serves 6–8

Variation   Sometimes I sprinkle an extra 2 tablespoons of castor sugar over the raw mixture just before putting it in the oven. The cake will then bake with a crusty top. Scented leaves such as lemon verbena, blackcurrant or rose-geranium can be placed on the raw mixture before the sugar. The scent will perfume the cake.

5   APRIL

I spoke with Lisa this morning. She was full of cheer and described a feeling of having decisively 'crossed over' from her former life to this new one. She said that she and Jane and Ken, the builder extraordinaire, and Nick Haddow, the cheese room manager, toasted each other with a caffe latte at the coffee shop next door. Their toast was to a great project about to be completed.

Today Maggie and I finished planning each day's menu. We have made lists of equipment we will need to provide, and supplies we will need to purchase. Both of us have a list of the recipes we must write in order to complete a booklet for each student. We have challenged each other when deciding on the dishes. What are we teaching with this meal? Why is this dish there? Each dish is to be matched with a wine. This is being organised by Negociants, an Australian firm that deals directly with the best Italian wine houses. The wines will be delivered to the door at Villa di Corsano. We have also confirmed that Peter Lortz, a former waiter at Stephanie's and a multiskilled young man, will accompany us as waiter, wine master, driver and linguist (Peter's mother is Italian, his father German). Now we have a staff of three: Peter Lortz, Peter Bevan and Tony Phillips.

At this stage we are still in need of a skilled person 'on the ground'. Maggie's network is incredible. She has just published *Maggie's Orchard*, her second book, and as part of the book promotion she will be working with a former staff member who is now a chef in Sydney. This same staff member has recently returned after a cooking stint in Siena! How extraordinary. Maggie is certain he will have an idea of how to enlist the help of a local restaurateur.

'The good things in life are free' should be tattooed on my head.

A few days of distance from problems, a few days of clean air, long vistas of grapes and olive trees and of drooping golden willows and massive pear trees have reminded me all over again to concentrate on natural beauty and the good in people and filter out the negative and the manipulative.

How can one sustain a sad thought when in Maggie's company? She radiates goodness, empathy and appetite for life. She often refers to her husband Colin as her rock. I see him also as a leprechaun, very droll and twinkly of eye, shrewd but fair in business. The combined Beer charm is very powerful. They are romantics in the best sense. They both allow themselves to dream of future projects – and then Colin does the numbers!

For dinner Maggie cooked one of her specialities: quickly seared fillets of kangaroo with anchovy butter. No one cooks kangaroo as well as Maggie. It was crusty on the outside, rare and juicy inside and full of flavour. I have included her recipe in *The Cook's Companion*.

6 APRIL

*S*unday, and today the Barossa Vintage Festival procession marches from Tanunda to Nuriootpa, a distance of five kilometres, and is applauded all along its route. We watched from Jan and Brian Linke's bakery, in the main street of Tanunda. Those with businesses on the street invited their friends and there seemed to be one long party as we waited for the parade to reach us. Others less fortunate sat in deck chairs at the roadside and shared a laugh with friends. Kids raced everywhere. The annual scarecrow competition is very popular. Wild and wonderful scarecrows are to be seen in fields and in very unlikely places. On this day many of the best scarecrows were tucked between buildings or dangled from shopfronts. There are few airs and graces in the Barossa. Robert Hill Smith, the owner and general manager of Yalumba, had a glass of his prestigious Yalumba 'D' in one hand and a pie in the other. The Nuriootpa town band oompah-pahed down the street in magnificent costumes heralding the arrival of the parade. The floats were many and varied, some very simple and others that had obviously taken months to design and put together. Each of the wineries was represented, and there were some weird and wonderful vehicles. The Lutheran church entry had a lifeboat rowed by disciples. The slogan on the float read 'I am the vine, you are the branches, Jesus is the No. 1 lifesaver'.

There were tankers, vintage cars, penny-farthing bicycles, beautifully brushed draught horses and steam cars, coopers coopering in syncopated time, giant wine bottles and more brass bands.

7 APRIL

*B*ack from the friendship and relaxation of the Barossa and ready to accommodate some changes in my life. The first delivery of bottled preserves from Mary in Tasmania arrived today. Peach marmalade and pickled cherries and apricot jam and apple jelly. Already we are talking about the winter collection, which will feature quinces, crabapples and green tomatoes, to name a few.

The printer is doing a valiant job but has warned us it will be touch and go to achieve all the many and varied labels and menus we need.

The licensing inspector is concerned that we erect some sort of physical barrier to prevent unaccompanied children entering our licensed premises. For a day this seemed insuperable. Finally he agreed that Will's antique cheese press would be sufficient, if placed at the side of the entrance to the Cafe. Problem resolved in the best possible way. The press looks fantastic, its giant screws resting on two full-size cheddars (which are in fact fakes).

So many people to contact. So many forms to fill out. So many things to be purchased. So many questions.

10 APRIL

*D*ad took another tumble in the street today and fortunately once again there was a passer-by to help him to his feet and collect his scattered glasses and cap. No damage to his bones but again damage to his confidence. I must try to walk with him at least once a week. He desperately wants to keep his mobility. I have also engaged a physiotherapist to assist and to walk with him. For some reason he doesn't seem keen on this.

His mind is very sharp and today on our walk he went over the detail of a part of his life he is recording. His earlier unpublished volumes of autobiography, entitled *The Timid Adventurer*, finished in about the mid-1950s. I am thrilled that he is persevering in creating a complete memoir that will be treasured forever. Apart from its personal value, he has been so involved with community and social issues that when I read a few pages I am instantly reminded of matters that have long since passed from my conscious memory but that were very important at the time.

Tonight Dur-é and I have invited convention organisers to a cocktail party at Stephanie's as a marketing exercise to demonstrate that our restaurant is much more versatile than many believe. We have set up one room with theatre-style seating and with a screen, as it is frequently used by pharmaceutical companies, and another room with its tables and chairs mostly removed to show how the space looks when used for a stand-up gathering, and in yet another room we have set out a long conference table.

One of the things we do best is catering for a variety of small functions and it has proved very difficult to spread the word that this is another service we can offer.

We both spoke to the thirty or so guests and once again marvelled that they all seemed unaware of Stephanie's as anything other than a wonderful place to come for a birthday or other celebration. We hope that good business will flow on from this exercise. I must say the Restaurant looked fantastic. The cocktail food was good, too: rice paper spring rolls, mushroom pies, anchovy pastries, delicate chicken breast sandwiches, and gutsy small pizzas topped with roasted and skinned red peppers.

14 APRIL

There is palpable excitement in the air today at Richmond. The final touches are being tackled. So tactile is the unpolished marble bar that we all caress it over and over again. Ken, our builder, has just mounted the panels of Sarah's mural. The original brief included 'something growing, someone working at food preparation, a laden table, and excitement, colour and energy'. We have all this as well as strong shapes and rich colours, a kelpie dog asleep in the milking shed, and the unmistakeable topknots of eucalypts, giving us that all-important immediate 'spirit of place'.

In the kitchen the first stock is bubbling on the kitchen stove. The coffee machine is being tested constantly. Wine glasses are hanging from the racks and exotic bottles and cases of wine are arriving by the minute.

The last of the delivery cardboard cartons are crushed and carted out of sight. Rubbish removal is looming as a huge problem. Our tiny carpark is reached via a narrow winding lane. I have already crunched the side of my car when leaving a few nights ago. No commercial rubbish contractor we have yet found can bring a truck up this lane, so cardboard and all rubbish will have to be physically dragged down the lane for collection from the next side street. I prophesy that this whole issue will need creative solutions – and soon – or we will have considerable complaints from our neighbours. How do restaurants in other inner-city suburbs cope with this, I wonder? Or indeed in Venice? We are going to ask our suppliers to transfer our deliveries into plastic tubs and to remove their cardboard and foam containers.

Simone Jenkins, late of Neal's Yard Dairy and Carluccio's in London, has done a fantastic job of supervising a team made up of the daughters of the partners. Fleur Studd and Amy Clemens and their friends have weighed and wrapped and labelled an assortment of goodies. Holly has unpacked, stamped and arranged our collection of food books for sale. By the end of the afternoon we had clean shelves neatly loaded with labelled stock all looking as if it had been there forever. I have caught Simone's cold and we do not move far from a box of paper tissues.

Some time during the afternoon I had a flashback to the opening of Jamaica House thirty-odd years ago. Baby Lisa was firmly rolled in a bunny rug and in her carry basket near to the kitchen in case she yelled for food. My dear friend Joyce came to deliver something – was it flowers? Was it radishes? I can no longer remember – but I do remember that she took one look at this scene from Hell, rang her usual employer to say she would not be in, rolled up her sleeves and Saved the Day! Those early days are largely blotted from my mind. I do remember that in about six weeks I lost a lot of weight and for one of only two periods in my life was able to wear Size 10 clothes!

The cheese room is looking more and more fantastic.

The craggy interior of a three-year-old Parmigiano-Reggiano looks dramatic on the slate bench, surrounded by aged gruyere from Heidi in Tasmania and cloth-wrapped cheddars from Pynengana, also in Tasmania. The smaller wheels and barrels and rounds of hard cheeses sit on olive-oil-seasoned slabs of wood in the main cheese room, humidified and temperature-controlled at 14°C; the soft cheeses are in an inner room kept at 7°C. The pungent and ripe smell that is so appealing to cheese lovers is contained behind closed doors.

Will was advised to season his wonderful old iron cheese press with deodorised fish oil. Angie's eldest son, Johnno, duly spent a couple of hours rubbing this stuff into every crevice. The result is a beautiful cheese press that smells like Hypol. When we were children it was customary to insist on us swallowing a spoonful of this disgusting fish oil every day as a supposed preventative against colds. We all held our noses and banished the press for a couple of days. Fortunately the smell evaporated quickly and it does glow most beautifully.

At 6.00 p.m. we decided that apart from tables and chairs, and the awning (promised for today but it didn't happen), we were done. We all crowded onto the footpath to admire this glowing, exciting space. It was quite a moment. And achieved in just two months of actual work, preceded by three months of dedicated planning.

15 APRIL

*T*he tables and chairs were to arrive today but a most extraordinary thing has happened.

Someone has stolen our chairs from the warehouse.

The interior designers attempted to convince us to accept another chair and in the panic that ensued they nearly succeeded. Sanity prevailed by the morning and we rejected the replacement and hired classic bentwood chairs until the replacement chairs can be obtained – a matter of two or three weeks, we are told.

17 APRIL

*W*e have invited our friends and relatives and all those who worked on the project to experience our 'soft' opening. All systems are to be tested, so the assembled gathering – too many, as always happens with such an event – were offered the full menu and the full wine list. Although no money changed hands, we also put the bills through the cash register to test that system also.

All the first nights I have experienced (first and second location of Jamaica House, first and second location of Stephanie's, and now Richmond Hill Cafe & Larder) have been agonising. And there has always been a drama – a blocked sewer, a smashed window, the chairs being stolen, a new ordering system installed on that very day, and so on and so on. Others tell me of their experiences and they say that everything was fine at their openings. Are they lying? Am I just super-sensitive? I cannot say. But all my first nights have been physically painful. Hard to breathe through the tightness in my chest, the quickly forgotten but horrible experience of not being able to move fast enough. One's brain races ahead of one's hands. And some of the new staff are slow to suck telepathic thoughts from me to their hands. We are all stuck in quicksand it seems to me.

On this night, after about one hour, the haze cleared and wonderful calm descended. Nicky and Justin smiled triumphantly and said 'Hey, we're getting the hang of this'. And then we started to roll as a team. The food looked OK and the friends and relatives seemed to be having a very happy time.

Of course there was plenty wrong with the evening. The floor staff couldn't find their sections, they confused one dish with another, some of the coffee was served cold, we ran out of bread, the tables wobbled on the old floorboards. And some of the guests thought they were at a real paid-up night and grumbled at delays. But we now have three blessed days to meet and discuss what went wrong before the real test – the public. Accolades, flowers and kisses from this audience but most of them are hopelessly one-eyed and we love them for it.

1 8   APRIL

*T*onight was a long-planned dinner at Stephanie's with Dur-é and Mietta O'Donnell and Tony Knox. For twenty-one years Mietta and Tony owned and operated Mietta's restaurant, in its last fifteen years (the restaurant closed in 1996) housed in an elegant Victorian building in the heart of the city. Mietta's was as well-known for its patronage of the arts as for its food. Performances of all sorts, from poetry readings to song recitals, were held in the downstairs lounge and when the pair decided they had had enough there was a sad sigh from the arts community. After a day in the anxiety of Richmond Hill Cafe & Larder it was reassuring and relaxing to meet with these old friends and enjoy the elegance, perfect food and soothing environment of my other restaurant!

There are such a lot of stories about Stephanie's Restaurant and so many can never be told. There was the diner who sobbed all over Dur-é in the toilets because 'all she wanted was an omelette'. There was the woman who removed most of her clothes. There was the man who rang many times to check details for his Proposal Dinner; the roses were delivered, but the couple never showed up. I reminded everyone of the evening when we entertained a super-critical fellow restaurateur many years ago. The waiter delivered her food with a fine flourish – a beautifully roasted pigeon. Somehow the plate touched the wine glass as it was put on the table and in a freak accident, the plate broke cleanly in two halves, depositing pigeon and perfectly reduced pigeon sauce all over the table in front of the astonished celebrity guest. There were many such stories. We laughed till we cried remembering other horror incidents.

At Stephanie's the crab salad has given way to a new entree of quickly seared tuna on a rich baba ghanoush with caponata and a trickle of extra-virgin oil. Caponata is that unctuous mix of eggplant, celery, olives, capers and tomato. I used the recipe given by Mary Taylor Simetti in her fascinating book *Pomp and Sustenance*, which includes a small amount of cocoa that, as she states, gives this lovely vegetable dish a baroque and Moorish touch. She suggests serving it either cold or at room temperature, sprinkled with toasted almonds.

My head cold made eating and breathing difficult to accomplish simultaneously and my sinuses have started to ache. I have arranged a few days away from Stephanie's to concentrate on The Opening.

19 APRIL

*O*ur new pastry cook at the Cafe rang to report a sick baby. She will not be at work for our first day. I guess this misfortune can be seen as a reminder that life is rarely smooth and that staff crises will be part of our lives forever. The search is on for a competent person to fill this temporary gap. A willing but inexperienced pair of hands will not be sufficient on Tuesday 22 April, our real opening day.

Thank goodness we arranged a couple of days between our soft opening 'rehearsal' and the real thing. My cold is making me light-headed and I cannot concentrate. Where is my renowned energy?

I am going to take to my bed.

2 2 A P R I L

D-Day. The pastry cook resigned yesterday. I will do the dessert work for the first week while we try to find a solution.

Our picture is in both the *Herald Sun* and *The Age* 'Epicure'.

We cannot now expect to creep into the marketplace. We are definitely open with a bang not a whimper!

2 3 A P R I L

*Y*esterday, on Day One, I rose in the dark and raided my garden for branches of dogwood with bright strawberry fruits, crimson grapevine leaves, thick stems from the persimmon tree dripping with heavy fruit not yet fully ripe, and dainty arching sprays of Easter daisy.

Barely had I finished arranging this autumnal collection when the very first customers walked through the door. We were full in half an hour. In the kitchen we scrambled to find our feet and at the same time we scrambled eggs, and fried eggs, and baked eggs, and dished up congee and burnt the toast and couldn't find the marmalade and fought for control. We even had our first complaint in that first hour. The congee was insufficiently seasoned. Although we were sad to be chastised so early the customer was quite right. By the next one we had adjusted the broth, added extra chilli to the dipping sauce, corrected the salt level and remembered to add the salted duck egg to the bowl.

CHICKEN CONGEE

1 × 1.6 kg chicken	*2 cups medium-grain rice*
1.5 litres good chicken stock	*1 fresh chilli, seeded and finely sliced*
2 tablespoons peanut oil	*3 spring onions, sliced*

Poach chicken in stock for 45 minutes. Cool in stock for 10 minutes then remove, discard skin and cut breast into fine strips. Return stock to boil.

Heat oil in wok, fry rice for approximately 2 minutes and transfer to saucepan. Add boiling stock till it reaches 5 cm above rice; cover and cook gently for approximately 30 minutes, or till rice is soft and soupy. Place shredded chicken and a few slices of chilli and spring onions in bowls, and ladle in soupy rice broth. Serve with Dipping Sauce.
Serves 6

DIPPING SAUCE

1 garlic clove	*3 tablespoons water*
1 red chilli, seeded	*3 tablespoons light soy sauce*
1 teaspoon sugar	*juice from 1 lime*
1 tablespoon rice-wine vinegar	

Grind garlic and chilli in mortar and pestle to form paste. Combine with other ingredients in bowl. Stir well to dissolve, and set aside.

25 APRIL

*D*ay Four and the first time I have had a minute to reflect on the rollercoaster we seem to have let loose. Thoughts, feelings and images tumble chaotically in my head . . .

As I have already mentioned, the pastry cook resigned on the day before we opened. The reality for The Gang of Four – Nicky, Justin, Rachel and Nicole – has been work from early morning until late without breaks or food or even toilet stops! A few loyal old-timers from Stephanie's have returned to work as casual cooks during our peak service time. We have coined a new concept – seamless service, where breakfast flows into lunch flows into afternoon tea flows into bar menu flows into dinner. We are so busy. The Cafe seats sixty-five plus eight at our slinky bar stools, and yesterday we served fifty for breakfast and one hundred for lunch and around seventy-five for dinner, with more customers drifting in and out for a glass of this or that at other times.

'More staff!' is the cry from the floor, from the kitchen and now from the cheese room. Lisa and Jane are at work by 7.30 a.m. and do not leave until after midnight.

In the office Angie is looking a lot less calm than usual. No time to bank the money, no time to pay the bills, no time to fathom the intricacies of the new accounting program, no time to complain that the hand-towel roller doesn't work properly – just deal with the phones that ring on all four lines constantly. We must buy a safe, as well.

We should feel excited but it is impossible to get past the stress and panic. Although there have been moments! The room is full of warm light and even when at capacity the noise level is buzzy but never painful. In the late afternoon, around 4.30, we have a slight slow-down and it was then that I had my first sense that if we can get on top of the systems we have a wonderful business here. It is also the time of day when rich autumn light floods the floor and our customers feel mellow as they sip on a glass of wine or a coffee and read the paper.

Today the food looked good.

We abandoned a separate afternoon tea menu and are instead offering the cheese and dessert options as listed on the main menu after 3.00 p.m. The bar menu with more extensive savoury items is available from around 4.30. And we ordered four more bar stools and some larger table tops.

Changing systems after thirty-six hours is pretty bold!

26 APRIL

*T*his month has become one long blur and here we are a few days from its end. One of the curious aspects of writing a diary is that even though one knows that later on the currently traumatic happenings will just take their place as part of the pattern of the year, while we are in it we are stumbling and crashing and stressing and have no ability to stand back and organise or send for reinforcements.

Every day brings some tiny improvement although customers are still clamouring at the door and there is no way we can hire and train staff fast or effectively enough. Both Lisa and Jane have shed a lot of weight. I never lose weight, no matter how hard I work or how stressed I am. (As soon as I say this I am reminded of Jamaica House and how I did so!)

Anna Dollard has come into our lives. Formerly an editor in a major publishing house, she has just returned from travelling and is interested in experiencing something different. We contacted her at just the right moment and she has responded instantly to our cry for help. Anna has taken over the telephones for now and is bringing her exceptional organising skills to bear on the reservations book and the table plan and in making things happen. Within three days we had staff lockers and an extra desk!

Bertie, a young English cook who was invaluable at Stephanie's before Christmas, has just returned from travels in north Queensland and we have been quick to grab his services to relieve the kitchen. Damita, the sister of a former head chef at Stephanie's, has been recruited to use both her skills as a bookkeeper and her interest in the hospitality industry. She has slipped cheerfully from polishing cutlery, to juicing oranges, to manning the cash register to counting the cash after service. Multiskilling is a marvellous thing. Margaret, a childhood friend of mine, who has recently retired from her job as a psychologist, turned up with fantastic striped egg cosies she has knitted. They look like hats for pixies, with tiny woollen tassels.

29 APRIL

*B*ack at Stephanie's life proceeds at a different pace. Business is slow. Affected, some assume, by the opening at Richmond. This may be true to some extent but many other establishments are also quiet due to the shadow cast by the imminent opening of the Crown Casino. This casino is to be the biggest, brightest, most diverse in the continent, even in the southern hemisphere, we are told. Built to attract the high-rollers from Asia, it has cost an obscene amount of money. There are to be more than a hundred eating establishments, employing thousands of staff at rates purportedly negotiated at more than the base rates for the rest of the industry. No wonder there is anxiety in the air.

Tonight we launched the 'new' old grain Greenwheat Freekeh at Stephanie's Restaurant. The kitchen prepared a delicious array of dishes designed to show its versatility. We made a soup with the whole grain and sprinkled it with the magic spice sumac, and the silken flour made beautiful blini that were topped with rolls of *bastourma* and rocket. The cracked grain pilaf that we serve with our lamb dish was equally good with a fried quail egg on top, and we made kibbeh by working minced lamb with the cracked grain to a smooth paste, tucking a knob of haloumi cheese inside and frying these little patties. And we made small *bisteeya*, the appealing sweet and savoury party dish from Morocco, which consists of pigeon, eggs, cinnamon and sugar. It is not at all traditional, but I like to serve pieces of pickled turnip with these little pies.

After the launch Holly and I sat down and enjoyed a quiet dinner but we did talk loudly, encouraging the room full of diners to relax and not to whisper. Why do they whisper here and then shriek to be heard in other places?

And so the month ends. The weather has been extraordinary. Daytime temperatures in the high twenties, the autumn colouring glowing most beautifully in the sunshine. There has been no rain at all and for a good part of rural eastern Australia it is a disaster. Drought will have its repercussions for us all later on. In the short term I note that the menu I have planned for the Wine and Food Guild early next month was conceived assuming that Melbourne would be cold and blustery at the beginning of May. Of course it still might be.

May

1 MAY

*T*oday I think I saw the tiniest chink of light at the end of this tunnel.

Jane came to work looking rested and with her enthusiasm restored after a proper night's sleep. We had worked on the front-of-house roster together and there was comfort to be had once she saw that I had now realised the full extent of the problem. To cover seventeen hours' service a day, six days a week, with an almost uninterrupted stream of customers from 9.00 a.m. until 11.00 p.m. needs an army of energetic, able and willing waiters and bar staff. We simply have not recruited sufficient people. I spent four hours in the basement with a giant piece of paper, pencils, highlighters, erasers and a calculator. At the end of this time it was clear that we are ninety hours short of waiting staff and fifty hours short of bar staff. An advertisement was placed in the paper and I hope to review and recruit from a rush of applicants on Saturday afternoon.

In the kitchen Nicky took her first day off! Justin had one yesterday.

Progress is measured by the fact that in Week One everyone worked like animals to cover the total hours, but in the second week everyone had a day off. Next week we will have secured extra cooks and the hours will plummet. The service is smoothing out although there is still work needed on fine-tuning of dishes and on speed, especially at breakfast. I had wanted to offer a few surprises on the breakfast menu – congee was one of them. However, the public want eggs! Or pancakes. Or fruit. Or toast. Two serves of congee (and one of those not up to standard) sold in ten days is not sufficient. Lisa and I have been having a bowlful each morning but congee is going to disappear. The kitchen is basically OK other than having a desperate need for a second coolroom and more dry-goods storage space downstairs. Plans have been drawn up, the architect has walked through the space and we have been promised at least the other coolroom in two weeks' time.

The shop and cheese room are running smoothly but need an extra member of staff. Sophie Heath will join Nick, Simone and Angie next week and together with the part-time staff they will continue to service an ever-growing stream of customers with tastings, advice and sales. The shop looks better and better as we introduce some select fresh items – a bucket of beautiful artichokes in tight, bright-green bud, for example, and a basket of organically grown avocadoes from the unlikely area of Red Hill on the Mornington Peninsula. Freshly harvested hazelnuts and walnuts will be next.

We have had our first letter of complaint, so things must be almost normal! Mediocre coffee, slowness of service, and alleged rudeness. Plus I have had two rival coffee firms challenging my love of country for not choosing to purchase product from them. *Plus ça change*, and all that. More importantly for the morale of drooping staff, who are suffering aching feet and overloaded brains but still smiling, are the more generous remarks of the majority who love the Cafe, love the cheese room, love being able to buy good bread, and have overwhelmingly welcomed us to their neighbourhood.

Lisa now has my cold and we both went home early.

My favourite dish of roast chicken has not been successful. Its timing is not suitable for the speed of service required, so away it goes. I have been testing a new chicken dish – a variation of the French bistro classic, chicken slowly cooked with wine vinegar and fresh tomatoes. The sauce is absolutely delicious. It is softened at the end of the cooking time with a knob of butter, freshened with parsley and served with boiled potatoes. Tonight I ate it in front of the television. Tomorrow night will be its debut for the customers.

CHICKEN WITH RED-WINE VINEGAR AND SHALLOTS

2 tablespoons extra-virgin olive oil
40 g unsalted butter
2 × 1.8 kg chickens, jointed
    (2 drumsticks, 2 thighs, 2 wing
    joints, 4 breast pieces on bone)
16 cloves garlic, peeled and blanched
    3 times in water
1 cup red-wine vinegar

16 shallots, peeled, blanched in water
    or chicken stock until just tender
1½ cups tomato purée or sauce
1½ cups chicken stock
extra 40 g unsalted butter
salt and pepper to taste
2 tablespoons roughly chopped
    flat-leaf parsley

Heat oil and butter in a heavy-based enamelled cast-iron dish and brown seasoned chicken pieces very thoroughly over moderate heat.

Remove and set aside. Do not crowd pan and do not hurry this stage. Lightly colour the garlic. Remove. Wipe out the pan with a paper towel.

Return all the chicken to the pan with the thighs and drumsticks on the bottom. Increase heat and pour over the vinegar. It should hiss and bubble fiercely. Shake pan to ensure that all chicken pieces absorb some of the juices. Watch closely as the vinegar will reduce quickly. When almost all the vinegar has disappeared, lower heat, add garlic, shallots, tomato and stock and bubble together, shaking the pan for a minute or two. Cover and cook gently either in the oven at 180°C or on top of the stove for approximately 30–40 minutes. If the latter, use a simmer mat to prevent sticking.

When chicken is tender and you are ready to serve, shake in the extra butter, taste for salt and pepper and sprinkle with parsley. Serve with boiled new potatoes.

(In the Cafe, for extra finesse, we remove the chicken pieces to a hot dish and strain the buttered sauce over the chicken to hold back any stray bits of tomato skin. It's up to you.)

Serves 8

2   MAY

I have been picking up the windfalls from my cherry guava tree, or strawberry guava (Cattley guava, *Psidium littorale* var. *longipes*). It crops very heavily. Each little fruit is the size of a cherry with a purple leathery skin. One bites into wonderfully aromatic deep-pink juicy fruit that is very acidic and richly perfumed. It intrigues me that the lower fruit ripens first – why does this happen, or is it that the ripest fruit from the top of the tree falls before I notice it and when I have my attention focused I see the carpet of ripe fruit on the ground, some nearly ripe fruit on the lower branches and completely green fruit at the top? The ripe ones make delicious ice-cream and Phillippa tells me they also make lovely jam. I stewed some to have on my breakfast muesli. The flavor was very good, but I wished I had passed the fruit through a sieve as the tiny seeds are as hard as pellets of leadshot. I just keep a bowl of them in the kitchen and eat a few whenever I pass by. In Louis Glowinski's reference work *The Complete Book of Fruit Growing in Australia* I read that each one hundred grams of the fruit contains 300 milligrams of vitamin C, compared with approximately fifty milligrams for the same amount of citrus! Down the road my neighbour has its cousin, a feijoa. It is not as advanced as the guava but as I pass by it has the same perfumed sweetness.

The persimmon tree is sensational. Its long, leathery leaves are streaked scarlet and gold, like rich Chinese silk. The fruit (rather small this year) is shiny and deep gold. This morning I watched as a glossy blackbird dipped his yellow beak into one fruit. I have already removed a few of the tree's overladen branches to use in the Cafe as decoration; I am sure it was grateful as its central trunk immediately straightened up. My own back could do with some straightening. I am unsure what action I have been doing that has resulted in considerable lower back pain. I have not been to the gym for two weeks due to my early morning starts at the Cafe. I am off today to see if some stretching exercises will help.

And they did.

3 MAY

*W*onderful sense of madness today at the Cafe. At one point I simply had to overcome my fear and take over the reception position at the door as Lisa was needed to manage a section. Some of the floor staff seemed to wilt before the onslaught. We have sixty-five chairs and yet we served 155 for breakfast and 175 for lunch. Seamless service again – breakfast melts into lunch with still not a seat spare. It was very exciting! Lisa looked enchanting with her short soft curls and a striped green and brown skinny top. 'Just like a peppermint cream', I told her as we made brief contact. Never in my wildest imaginings had I thought I would be working alongside Lisa. She is so good at it. I am very proud of her.

As one group would leave there were many waiting. The trick was to wipe down the table fast enough so that the next in line felt that the table had waited just for them to arrive. Sometimes we didn't make it and there were a few who left, disgruntled. I felt quite light-headed with the responsibility of overlooking the sea of eaters and assessing who was likely to leave first and how one could join a few tables to accommodate a larger group!

I returned to Stephanie's later in the day to check the venison for the Wine and Food Guild Dinner on Tuesday. The myrtle tree in the Restaurant garden has plump blue-black berries and we will tie sprigs of the resinous fruit and aromatic leaves to each venison loin before roasting it. The sauce will be finished with a splash of crème de cassis and I am hoping for a rich ruby-bronze sauce in which the carved slices will rest, the colour and fruitiness of the flavours echoed by braised red cabbage with apples, and the acidity mellowed by a rich and creamy gratin of potatoes.

Back to the Cafe and twelve interviews for new floor staff. We do not have a private office so I set out two chairs in the middle of the basement, balanced a piece of wood on top of two garden chairs from my own garden and, feeling as if I was playing charades, invited each applicant into my 'office'.

I met some interesting young people and have fitted many of them with trial shifts next week. Nicky has recruited sensibly in the kitchen. The cheese room learnt its lesson this morning – the big guns all have to be there on a Saturday morning. Bridge Road on a Saturday is a very exciting place, five minutes away from the football stadium, so hundreds of passers-by are decked out in colourful beanies and scarves, all the fashion boutiques are buzzing, and there are people everywhere. We are definitely the flavour of the week. How long will it last, I wonder?

Nick in the cheese room suggested an outdoor hot-dog stand. We all think it is a great idea. Good smoked frankfurters, crusty half-baguettes, quality mustard, caramelised onions – I think it would be a huge success. We have applied for an outdoor seating permit and now need to consider whether this snack stand would also be permitted.

I felt euphoric as I drove home, and even more so after relaxing with two glasses of wine (Knappstein's hand-picked riesling, and Gary Crittenden's nebbiolo). With a victory over the British Tories to be celebrated and another great week successfully lived to the full I might just move on to Darjeeling tea.

9 MAY

A quick round-up of events. Glorious sunshine yesterday so I walked from the Cafe to my medical appointment in nearby East Melbourne. It was a delightful twenty-minute walk through Melbourne's Fitzroy Gardens in their full autumn glory. The lawns sparkled under their dusting of freshly fallen golden elm leaves. Sadly my doctor discovered something worrying in my left breast. I have to have further tests next week. A moment of dread and then I pushed away the possible implications of this, other than to remind myself that it is in the same site where I had a benign lump removed a few years ago.

We are told that one in twelve Australian women will develop breast cancer at some time, which is a frightening statistic. And more than that. It is the third most common cancer diagnosed in Victoria and the third highest cancer killer. When is it considered an epidemic, I wonder? We are told that early detection means more cures; we are also told that mammograms are an imperfect diagnostic tool. Like many others I have an annual check-up, do a bit of tentative self-examination when I remember, and hope that it won't happen to me.

The Wine and Food Guild Dinner was a great success. Melbourne obligingly moved from Indian summer to freezing autumn on the day so that my planned menu of warming chestnut soup, venison with myrtle leaves, and prune and armagnac tart seemed just right. We hadn't made the prune tart for years and I had forgotten how delicate and crisp the orange-flower flavoured crust was. As the VSOP armagnac was added to the ice-cream parfait just before churning there was no chance that any of its alcohol would be driven off, as would have happened with a cooked custard base ice-cream, so it was a very, very heady dessert.

PRUNE TART WITH ORANGE-FLOWER PASTRY AND ARMAGNAC ICE-CREAM PARFAIT

300 g prunes (stones removed)

ORANGE-FLOWER PASTRY

250 g plain flour	*1 teaspoon orange-flower water*
salt	*150 g unsalted butter, chopped into*
1 egg	*small pieces*
1 teaspoon cognac or *armagnac*	*castor sugar*

Soak prunes for one hour in strong Earl Grey (or other) tea. Drain very well in a strainer first of all and then on a clean cloth.

Sift flour and salt onto the work surface, make a well in the centre. Break in the egg, add the flavourings and the butter. Using a pastry cutter, work the liquids into the flour. Push the dough away from you using the heel of your hand to smear it across the bench. Gather pastry into a ball. Dust it with flour. Give it a minute's working, divide in half and then flatten each portion into a disc. Wrap in plastic. Chill for one hour. This pastry is very delicate and it may be easier to roll it between two sheets of plastic, or on two pliable silicone pastry sheets (obtainable at good cookware shops and indispensable for pastry work). Drape one half into a 22 cm flan tin.

Cover with stoned prunes. Roll out the remainder of the dough and cover the prunes with this. Seal the edges very well and scatter the tart with castor sugar. Bake at 180°C for about 45 minutes until pastry is a deep gold.

Cut into wedges and serve with armagnac parfait, other ice-cream or thick cream.

Serves 6–8

ARMAGNAC ICE-CREAM PARFAIT

The parfait is a convenient technique to know, resulting in a smooth ice-cream without the need for an ice-cream churn. I have used this base to create many delicious desserts. One that I have used over and over includes crushed amaretti biscuits soaked in espresso and chopped chocolate-coated coffee beans.

1 cup castor sugar   *2 cups (500 ml) cream*
¾ cup water   *2 tablespoons armagnac* or *other liqueur*
8 egg yolks

Boil sugar and water, stirring until sugar is dissolved, until the syrup registers 112°C on a sugar thermometer. Meanwhile beat yolks in an electric mixer until pale and light. Pour hot syrup over the eggs, beating constantly. Continue beating until mixture is cool.

Combine cream and armagnac and whisk until cream is very firmly whipped. Fold into egg mixture, pour into appropriate mould and freeze.

This same cold weather has brought problems to the Cafe. The heater is not working and the vital part is coming from Japan – by sea! Why it was not flown here I cannot say. In the meantime we have hired temporary heaters that look like giant mushrooms. They look eccentric rather than elegant but they are very efficient. A more important alteration will be the installation of a glassed-in wind lobby.

I have often likened Melbourne to Paris. Both are energetic, bustling cities that host myriad diverse cultural activities and that seem to love cafe life. In Paris one spends part of every day in a cafe and this is becoming the norm for Melburnians also. When I thought about it yesterday, as the wind whistled and the air had an icy chill, I had a memory flash of the glassed-in lobbies and the rush of warm air as one opens the door of a Parisian cafe on a winter's morning. Well, we will have our own warm lobby soon!

So much media interest. The spectacular cheese room is very, very photogenic. All morning we have been the centre of attention. Nice but a bit inconvenient for the customers. One journalist even made it obvious that the customers were in her way! I am glad it is the cheese room not the Cafe that is the focus as we still need a bit of time to sharpen up our act.

Three new front-of-house staff employed today. Rosters moved to realistic hours and we have big hopes for next week. Oops, Nicky has just rung to say she is in bed with a tummy upset. Life rarely runs smoothly in this industry.

1 0   M A Y

*T*he future of Stephanie's Restaurant is under review. Our staff have been marvellous. Resigned to the fact that the outcomes are unknown, they have loyally supported Dur-é and me but there is still long-term uncertainty. They see us both involved in other businesses and other areas of endeavour, be it committees or teaching, networking or writing, and they wonder.

Dur-é and I have had to come to terms with the fact that no one wants to take over Stephanie's Restaurant and the long-term view is even more unsettling for us. There are matters that can never be talked about in a diary such as this, no matter how tempting it is to explore all the angles. One reason being that there is always more than one version of complex issues. But our partnership is in jeopardy. Discussions are taking place which add considerably to the level of tension in my head, to the already swirling mix of ideas, plans, emotions, calculations, frustrations and excitement. I am in a state of extreme mental ferment. And I am still choked with a head cold.

Ultrasound and mammogram yesterday and breast surgeon today. She says there is only a low level of concern and to return in three months for a further check-up, just before I leave for Italy.

So there is no certain way out. I have to hang around for the time being.

Mother's Day tomorrow. We are fully booked at Stephanie's and closed at the Cafe.

1 2   M A Y

*A*t Stephanie's Mother's Day was, as predicted, a full-on day with over ninety guests.

All went well until the last half-hour when Jeff was burnt on the arm by a gush of steam from the steamer. We also have another injured team member with young Steve, our newest recruit, off work with badly burnt feet. 'Fire and knives', Dur-é often reminds those who think they might like to spend a day observing in the kitchen. And it is true that although there are often enticing aromas wafting around, the professional kitchen can be a dangerous place for the unaccustomed player. Greasy floors, tight corners, pots simmering with boiling stocks or water, vats of frying oil, leaping flames from the grill, hurrying cooks or waiters, knives on slippery boards. The first-aid box is always well-stocked, and a bucket of sand is always in reach, as is a fire blanket and an extinguisher. Cooks in my kitchens are meant to wear protective shoes that can be quickly kicked off if they are in contact with boiling liquid, and the sleeves of their jackets are fully rolled down to protect skin from unnecessary burns.

At the Cafe partners' meeting this morning we mulled over what the implications of our wind lobby will be in the summer. Will it trap heat? Will the waiters be able to service the hoped-for outside tables? The landlord's son came to look and was unhappy with the plans. And then the architect was unhappy with the concerns voiced by Will. So a stalemate has been reached. Maybe nothing will happen now?

We have Nicky the chef at the Cafe, we have Nicole the third-year apprentice, we have Nick the dishwasher, we had Nicky the builder's Rhodesian ridgeback, we have Nick in charge of the cheese room, and we have Nick the accountant. We even had Nick the licensing solicitor! Wow.

Nicole tested a new dessert today based on lavender honey. We shall top this frozen dessert with new season's walnuts and grapes drizzled with more warmed honey. I like it so much that I think it will be part of the Tuscan adventure.

The team that crafted *The Cook's Companion* – me, Julie, editor Caroline and Penguin designer Sandy – all met late in the afternoon to discuss the design of my latest project. As mooted in February, this is to be a reprint of my mother's recipe book, with annotations, culinary comments, and reminiscences from me, my father, my two brothers and sister. The cover design is brilliant. The central motif is to be a Sunbeam mixmaster – surely one of the most important milestones in kitchen liberation, certainly to the women of my mother's generation.

Caroline has read the text of this 'new' work thoroughly and, having lived through the editing of *The Cook's Companion*, she knows me very well.

I was so pleased that she instantly recognised the similarity in voice between my writing and that of my mother. I pointed out in my notes to Caroline that both my mother and I were/are very shy, and needed some way of connecting with people. For both of us it seemed/seems to be food. Mum tried other things, as sometimes neighbours made her feel guilty that she was not more involved in community affairs. She tried many things and hated most of them. She felt ineffectual at the Mother's Club, was uninterested in tennis or golf, loathed being a Guide leader, was never happy with her dressmaking efforts, but she did enjoy painting classes, embroidery classes and swapping fuschia cuttings with like-minded enthusiasts.

Shyness can easily be misinterpreted as being uppity or as off-handedness. While one is curling up inwardly at suddenly being or imagining that one is the focus of attention, defensive mannerisms can just happen. Or so it seems. I don't understand it really. Why am I so obsessed with how others will find me, and why am I certain that usually their conclusions will be negative? The remembered agony at age ten of crossing the narrow strip of beach, which seemed a mile wide, certain that every eye was scornfully assessing my milk-white skin, before sinking thankfully into the water with my shrieking (brown-skinned) classmates. Why did I cross the road in Paris rather than greet an approaching fellow Melburnian, panicked at the thought of the conversation I would have to have? Why do I avoid social gatherings that I know will be full of strangers, even though it is likely that some may even want to speak with me?

From time to time I have been inveigled onto boards and committees. I accept out of a feeling of guilt that I am not doing enough and then suffer the reality that I do not perform well in such forums. I do not grasp the implications of thorny issues quickly, I fail to detect hidden agendas, and I do not enjoy direct confrontation. It has been a slow lesson to learn that there are those who thrive on such activities and like nothing better than to initiate lists and delegate tasks, and that one need not feel guilty about letting them get on with it.

Back to Mum's book. It is informative and charming, but to Mum its major importance was the tangible evidence that her efforts were valued by others. Another similarity. Not for the first time I shake my head at human nature. One can receive approbation on a daily basis and know the satisfaction of a task well done but so often, for so many women, they need someone outside their close circle to tell them they have done well. This need for recognition is also a strong motivator and can push the procrastinator to complete projects.

I hope my sister and brothers will enjoy their reacquaintance with Mum's words as much as I have done.

18 MAY

We had our first Richmond Hill Cafe & Larder staff meeting today since opening. More than twenty-five people were present. (And we thought we might have a staff of ten!) Not only were we able to go over certain service issues, and restate policies regarding uniforms and meal breaks and other humdrum matters, but it was important to sit together and be relaxed for the first time. Some staff members were introduced at last to their colleagues, hitherto just faces in the blur. We followed formal proceedings with a tutored wine tasting – concentrating on recognising styles of wine rather than specific vineyards – and after that a serious cheese tasting, again with each product introduced as an example of a style of cheese. We all discussed the style of wine we would like to drink with a certain style of cheese. No one agreed, so it was great fun.

19 MAY

The wind lobby is back on the agenda. A revised plan offers wind protection but will not impede waiters as they move in and out to service the soon-to-be arriving outdoor tables. Further drawings and quotes are now coming in. The second coolroom is promised for this Friday.

Gentle pressure from Simone in the larder for more goods to sell. She wants baked items, especially sweet biscuits, and ready-to-go veal and chicken stock and even potted custards. We would love to do all this but so far cannot see that window of opportunity either in terms of time or available space in the kitchen. The customers would also like something sweet with their coffee. I am pondering all of this. This afternoon, practising for Italy, we made a batch of roasted almond and espresso biscotti. And Rachel made irresistible brownies.

DOUBLE CHOCOLATE BROWNIES

¾ cup melted butter
¾ cup Dutch cocoa
1½ cups castor sugar
few drops pure vanilla extract
3 eggs

100 g plain flour
¼ teaspoon baking powder
1 cup bittersweet couverture chocolate,
　　roughly chopped, or chocolate chips
pinch salt

Heat oven to 160°C. Line a flat swiss roll tin (approximately 16 cm × 22 cm) with baking paper. Combine butter and cocoa in a large bowl. Mix well. Add sugar, vanilla and lightly whisked eggs. Mix in other ingredients. Pour into prepared tin and bake approximately 20–25 minutes until firm but still moist.

Allow to cool completely before cutting into squares. Dust with icing sugar or cocoa if you wish.

Makes 20 squares

Simone has arranged small displays of organically grown potatoes and apples. She asked the kitchen to boil some Pink Fir Apple potatoes this morning and doused them with Ravida olive oil from Sicily, salt and pepper and offered them on the counter. I found all sorts of reasons to return for another sample. Today our greengrocer sent a box of gorgeous bumpy green and gold tomatoes hanging in bunches from the vine. I reminded Simone of the movie *Fried Green Tomatoes at the Whistlestop Cafe* and suggested they be displayed with a bag of Queensland polenta so that customers could make their own fritters. The recipe is in *The Cook's Companion*. The store copy was stolen today.

The Cafe had a wonderful review in the local paper and I was so pleased that the reviewer commented on the friendly staff, on the lack of pretension in the entire establishment, and on its light and bright feel. All aspects that have been uppermost in our minds from Day One.

My father had a cataract operation yesterday and was amazed at how simple it was. He was feeling fine when I visited in the evening and is now eagerly anticipating the improved vision he has been promised.

Dad is such a good thinker that it is a great help to me to air my business woes with him. There are not many people with whom I can do this. My children tend to feel weighed down by my problems. It is inappropriate dinner party conversation, and few of my closest friends have any experience of large borrowings, partnerships, or business risk-taking. Although Maggie does and she is visiting in a few days for further Italy discussion. I'm sure I'll talk about some of my personal and business concerns with her, as she will with me. 'Tell me yours, and I'll tell you mine' sort of thing. Dad also sometimes feels weighed down by my problems. I try to reassure him that it is very helpful to me to articulate the issues, and often his insights are very wise. Such conversations usually slip into memories and reminiscences.

Dad is still writing down his memoirs of his life with Mum, and he is steadily moving through the rich years that lie in his extraordinary library of home videos. I can't bear to think about it for more than a few seconds at a time but some day when he is no longer with us the family will have a wonderfully complete picture of our parents' lives, perhaps even in a printed form that I may have reshaped from all this growing material – Mum's notebooks, her printed articles in early *Gourmet* magazines and letters to us from abroad, Dad's movies and commentaries and his own extensive writings.

20 MAY

Lisa's birthday. We will celebrate tonight at the Flower Drum restaurant.

21 MAY

$\mathcal{A}$nd we had a wonderful meal, the highlights a plate of small scarlet prawns, steamed in the shell, to be peeled and dipped in a bowl of soy, and, after the Peking duck, a bowl of exquisite vegetables topped with crunchy chestnut-sweet lotus flowers which Gilbert Lau brings in from Hong Kong. Each creamy, pearly petal tasted absolutely delicious. Gilbert and I commented to each other on the effects of the first week of the Casino being open. In the newspaper it is claimed that one million people visited the Casino in its first eight days.

23 MAY

$\mathcal{M}$aggie arrived today, that bright ray of sunshine. It was my day at the Cafe and she amused herself browsing in the larder and admiring the cheese room, and then she signed all the copies we had bought of *Maggie's Orchard*, her latest book. We had a simple meal at the Cafe and set our agenda for two days hence, when we intend to fire off our next round of faxes and letters to all those involved in the Italy venture. Maggie is such a marvellous friend. She is a good listener and then offers examples of lateral thinking so that one sees possibilities that didn't seem to be there beforehand. And her enthusiasm for food and fellowship is the best antidote to the blues that I know.

And I have had the blues lately. I had hoped to steer a careful course towards a bright future without encountering resentment. It doesn't seem to be possible. Can one equate a business disappointment with a broken marriage or the death of someone loved? I don't think so. I have been mulling over the traumas I have experienced so far in order to restore my sense of proportion.

I fell in love for the first time when I was a precocious fourteen. My love moved away to a different school. We corresponded daily and met about once a fortnight. For two years we planned a life that would allow us to be together forever. Eventually the effort of maintaining a relationship over a distance proved too much and it fell apart. I remember my grief and how

I wept into my teacup and my pillow, and how I knew that no one else could possibly know or understand the pain I felt. When I woke in the mornings it would take just ten seconds before I remembered and then I withered inside all over again. My breakfast stuck like a stone and could not be swallowed. My eyes brimmed and spilled. How did I get over this? I imagine the pain became less raw, and then became a numb spot, and then something caught my interest and I found that I had gone an hour, half a day, eventually even a day without thinking of him. And eventually I met another. Forty years later my first love and I are still good friends.

The day my first husband and I finally separated, after a couple of false starts and delirious reunions, has to register as one of the biggest traumas of my life. Again the sobbing, both of us this time, and the pain. Oh, the pain that did not go away. And the need to keep on working, and the terrible nights, and having to deal with the terrors and nightly wanderings of our two-year-old who was equally traumatised and bewildered about where her Daddy was. And the collapse at work, the shame of being sent home because I couldn't cope with the classroom, and the rumours and the gossip and all those who wanted to tell me where he had been seen and with whom. There is little to compare with this sort of despair. I have tried to be supportive now and then for someone dear to me who is going through the same thing, but of course one can do nothing but listen, and make tea, and maybe take the kids for an outing. Even now, more than twenty-five years later, there is still an unpleasant jangling in my head when I think of it. I went to see this man as he lay dying and I kissed him tenderly. We held hands once more but it was too late to say anything to each other.

And there was a further trauma when another man in my life became more and more obsessed with a particular anxiety. He took refuge from the world by simply not communicating with anyone. This was not only shocking but terrifying. No one could penetrate his wall of silence or help him with his pain. The biggest healer was time.

Then my mother died. Nothing prepares one for this. She had been visiting my brothers in Darwin. She called me from my sister Diana's house, near Melbourne airport, and said how odd it was that she felt so breathless, almost as if she had asthma. Dad collected their car from Diana's and started the drive to their home, an hour away. They called in at the Restaurant for a moment and I went to the carpark to say hello. Mum looked pale but was quite cheerful. She had a cutting of a bougainvillea that Christopher had stripped of all soil to comply with regulations. She hoped it would strike – it was such a lovely flower. Two hours later she was dead.

It was probably a blood clot, but no one ever told us exactly. Mum had long ago decided to leave her body to the university, so we sat around and waited until the undertakers came. My mother lay like an icy pillar on the floor of her bedroom. My father was alternately incoherent in his grief and then polite and capable with documents and so on for the grim visitors. Diana clutched me all night and shook. I dissolved every few minutes, and still do from time to time, although twelve years have passed.

Such traumas are so powerful because they represent a loss of love, or so it seems to me. I must not allow commercial matters and upsets, no matter how grave or unjust they seem, to assume an importance in any way comparable to these primal experiences.

2 6 M A Y

*T*oday is the first day of the Convention on Aboriginal Reconciliation. In the same week the report on the Stolen Children will be published, detailing the stories of Aboriginal children who were stolen from their parents under a policy promoted by welfare agencies, government and the church during the 1940s, 1950s and 1960s. Official policy was that any white home would have to be superior to a black home. I have not read the report but those who have or those who officiated at the hearings have been devastated by account after account of broken lives, fruitless searching, pain and grief. Compensation, and above all an apology, is being demanded by Aboriginal leaders. This has already been forthcoming from church leaders and from some State premiers. And yet the headlines in this morning's newspaper quoted the Minister for Aboriginal and Torres Strait Islander Affairs as saying 'I don't think you've got to put all the weight on one word – apology'. And the prime minister has ruled out compensation.

The Chairman of the Reconciliation Council, Mr Pat Dodson, said yesterday, 'This is a great moment, this is a great chance, this is an opportunity where we can go forward, simply by a word that acknowledges that this happened, that these are the facts, that this happened in Australia'.

Aboriginal Australians have suffered almost every possible injustice at the hands of white Australians both past and present. It is humbling to realise how non-violently and philosophically they have endured the destruction of their culture (not to mention their health). I find it extremely depressing that our policy-makers fail to appreciate what Aboriginal Australians can contribute to important understanding of this curious continent, especially its care.

I also believe that Australians will never achieve a mature sense of self and of place until we are reconciled to the idea that our identity lies in acknowledging our diversity. And with this understanding must come an appreciation of the richness and relevance of Aboriginal culture.

If we permit or encourage inequitable community standards we are inevitably inviting a society founded on discord and violence and an abuse of scarce resources. In a world where daily we have evidence that putting profit before other considerations makes no economic or moral sense, we must come to terms with our past in order to prepare for a better future for all Australians.

The prime minister is also due to introduce his ten-point plan of Wik amendments to the *Native Title Act* this week. The High Court upheld an appeal by the Wik people of Cape York and determined that native title could co-exist with pastoral leases. The pastoralists were unimpressed with this decision. It is hard for ordinary Australians to grasp why the notion of co-existence is so frightening to giant pastoral companies. I find it equally difficult to understand why farmers on freehold land that is unaffected by the decision should also feel disturbed by it. And what does all this anxiety tell us about their belief in negotiation? Many commentators are suggesting that the implications for future race relations in this country will be forever shaped by the manner in which the decision is upheld or amended. In such a tense climate the catalyst for some malcontents is the Independent member for Oxley, Pauline Hanson. For more liberal and moderate Australians there is much to be appalled and horrified by.

I do not want to live in a society divided by hate. If ever a symbol of reconciliation was needed it is now.

3 0 MAY

*T*he new basement coolroom at the Cafe is a reality. But the wind lobby is not going to happen. Sliding doors cannot slide uphill and the entrance is on a distinct slope. The wind engineer who came to study the problem felt that the constant opening and closing of both inner and outer doors would do little to control the draught. The next idea being investigated is a curtain of air said to block eighty to ninety per cent of draught. The partners are prepared to go and stare at one already installed at a nearby convenience store before making this decision. We are very confused.

At Stephanie's the numbers are still dreadful. I suggested that the pastry cook make the Christmas puddings now. Last year we had a successful mid-year Christmas and we plan to do so again. We all stirred the mixture, which entailed kneeling on the floor and pushing a heavy paddle through a huge tub of forty kilos of pudding mix. Thank goodness the electric mincer coped with the eight kilos of suet needed. The kitchen smelt marvellously of spice and fruit and brandy as the basins jiggled for six hours.

I shall serve the new pheasant dish to be premiered on Tuesday for the winter menu at the mid-year Christmas dinner. The first pheasants arrived today and are hanging in the coolroom at Stephanie's. They are delivered to us undrawn – that is, with guts in and head and feet intact. We find that after four or five days' hanging these birds roast to a melting succulence unlike any other pheasant I have tasted in this country.

Another new season's delivery has been the first of the Yarra Valley hazelnuts, hand-delivered by grower Jim Beattie. Jim encourages hazelnut lovers to roast the nuts in the shell and then crack them and enjoy the extra flavour. I am going to combine grilled scallops with sautéd Jerusalem artichokes, roasted hazelnuts and salad leaves as a juicy and lively entree.

I know that the dishes we are working on are as delicious as anything on offer anywhere in this city. And our high-backed, cushioned chairs are extremely comfortable. (A ludicrous review of a colleague's restaurant in the paper this week 'failed' the establishment because the reviewer didn't like the chairs!) There is no question that we are suffering from the opening of the Casino complex, along with every other non-Casino Melbourne restaurant, but also from the incorrect assumption that we sold Stephanie's at the end of last year. Our publicity was too effective!

Dur-é believes that the Cafe has had a lot to do with the drop in business. It is true that lunch figures are forty per cent lower than they were for the same period last year, but before conclusions are drawn it is important to register that the preceding year's lunches were also forty per cent lower than the year before that! It is easy to make statistics tell all sorts of stories. The reality is that the demand for lunches at Stephanie's Restaurant has been on a downhill slide since July 1995. Location, location, location, and the proliferation of city cafes and the serious 1990s, in which lunch has to be 'done' in under an hour, all have contributed to this changed pattern. If we are smart we will readjust and respond to this change in circumstance. I have ideas buzzing in my head.

Tonight Angie, Duffy and I ate in Stephanie's Restaurant and we all commented on how delightful it was. There cannot be more of a contrast between this smooth, calm, carpeted, confident establishment and our brash, bright, new venture that is still a bit rough at the edges. We finished our evening with a taste of a remarkable wine, Glaetzer's ratafia, which I purchased when in the Barossa last month. A ratafia usually means a wine or liqueur flavoured with fruit. This perfumed wine smelt and tasted like quinces and yet the back label only mentions 1996 Bush Vine Semillon and remarks on the wine's aromas of peaches and pears.

3 1 M A Y

Smoke-free day all over Australia today. I have had a short radio 'bite' to reinforce that at Stephanie's we responded to public demand several years ago and made our dining rooms smoke-free. The reaction was overwhelmingly positive from the very first day.

It is the last day of autumn and I have much to feel melancholy about.

But there is watery sunshine, the Washington thorn is a glorious dapple of gold and brown, and the *Hydrangea paniculata* 'Grandiflora' by the pool is quite lovely with its crimson and bronze leaves fanning in the slight breeze. My heart is heavy. I sense that the world turns slowly and that I have to experience some more shadow before springtime.

June

1 JUNE

I joined Will at lunch with a member of the Marketing Division of the Australian Dairy Corporation. Our intention is to raise the consciousness of those who make the regulations that great cheese is made from unpasteurised milk. Very good cheese can be made from pasteurised milk if production is in the hands of a passionate cheesemaker, and often very ordinary cheese can be made in other circumstances. We do not want Australia's best cheesemakers to be forever prohibited from doing their very best and to be barred from reinforcing their difference compared with the mass-market producers.

We claim that the issue is one of enforcing scrupulous hygiene and best practice rather than turning one's back on the knowledge and 'proof of the pudding' that exists in Britain and in France, where the most outstanding raw milk cheeses are being made and have been made for a long time. This officer recently returned from a visit to the United Kingdom and was impressed not only by the displays and flavours of the raw milk cheeses in Neal's Yard Dairy, the specialist cheese shop for pilgrims from all over the world, but also by the extent and popularity of the raw milk cheese counter at Harrods, a store that can never be thought of as an 'alternative' address.

If the winemakers of this country had continued to produce bulk mediocre wine our wine industry would be laughable. Instead it has a worldwide reputation. Our winemakers understood that they needed technological expertise, but more than that, the best of them have embraced the concept of *'terroir'*, allowing their winemaking to express the character of their own micro-climate and even the personality of the winemaker. They have also been interested in studying benchmark production in other parts of the world. The big advantage for the wine industry is that from its very early days it has been an attractive investment for moderate and big business and as such has enjoyed great press and prestige. This has not happened for the cheesemakers. Our friend from the Dairy Corporation insisted that our only chance was first to clone ourselves – in other words, to be in as many places as possible all over the country – grab media headlines wherever we could and be prepared to praise what is being produced under existing regulations. This can be a big ask when we believe that not everything that is called cheese is worthy of support. We end up being controversial and confronting when our aim is to raise standards.

We were not optimistic about imminent change in regulation.

2 JUNE

*H*olly and I went to see Kenneth Branagh's four-hour film of William Shakespeare's *Hamlet*. 'To thine own self be true' and 'Neither a borrower nor a lender be' had special significance for me as I listened to the Prince of Denmark pondering his options, 'To be or not to be'. I am currently considering my own options and my heart seems to be filled with stones. My attention drifted momentarily as the various paths open to me tangled in my mind. And then I was caught up again in this story of intrigue and lust and a son's love for his father. Often filmed versions of Shakespeare's plays are so lavish and beautiful that the power of the words is partly lost. Not so with this film. The poetry rang out and alternately thrilled, chilled and entranced. The action took place in magnificent palaces set in sweeping countryside under grey and threatening skies. Snow crunched underfoot, and fell softly in the graveyard scene, and the breath from the guards in their greatcoats came in icy puffs.

In Melbourne it is the second day of winter and we have had two days of steely blue skies and mornings and nights of 4°C. I have taken to wearing wool and cotton socks rather than nylon footwear. Astonishing, the comfort of a pair of socks!

My father had another fall and yesterday his doctor agreed to him having a full neurological check-up in case he has had a minor stroke. He is in great pain, with bruised ribs, but in reasonably good spirits. For the family there is an element of dread in this investigation. If the recommendation is for a wheelchair his whole life will have to change. I do not think the old folks' home can cope with this, certainly not without additional nursing assistance. The building falls short of what is ideal for a community of frail people. The corridors are too narrow, there are too many steps, the entrance ramp is too steep, there is only one lift and almost all the bedrooms are on the first floor. But the semblance of normal domestic life is maintained. It is far removed from the institutionalised character of the nursing homes I have seen. Each resident has his or her own bedroom and bathroom. The lounges are bright and cheerful, as are the staff. They do their best for anyone needing turning or lifting or assistance with showers and toilets, but they cannot possibly cope with more than a small percentage of the residents needing this level of care.

3 JUNE

*N*ew menu today at Stephanie's Restaurant.

And much later it has been successfully delivered. A delicate leek custard with a tumble of seasonal vegetables was absolutely sublime. Sadly, vegetable dishes are not as popular as they deserve to be. Too many diners equate the Big Night Out with luxury ingredients and have no concept of balance. One of the things I enjoy most about Italian food is the manner in which vegetables are cooked and presented with proper ceremony, but with never a thought that they are only appealing to non-meat eaters. There is no lack of sensuality – rather the reverse: vegetables are celebrated for their colours and their juices. Diners in Italy frequently order a plate of artichokes, or a platter of zucchini fritters, or grilled eggplant, or a vegetable antipasto to begin a meal. In Australia there is still a suspicion that such offerings indicate that the restaurateur needs to reduce the food costs.

Several of the newer staff members at Stephanie's were unaware that we have a special licence from the Fisheries and Wildlife Department permitting us to import live marron from Western Australia. The concern is that these wonderful creatures will escape if their entry is uncontrolled and take over the habitat of our own yabbies. A marvellous picture is evoked in the mind's eye of marron marching across the landscape, eager to drop into the first dam they find. All a bit unlikely, I think, given that in Western Australia the marron co-exists with the State's own yabbies, known there as gilgies. The marron are magnificent. Chef Michael made a rich stock from crushed crustacean shells and finished the sauce with a small quantity of shellfish butter. He also made a delicate and sweet seafood sausage to accompany the simply grilled but fearsome-looking marron.

We are told that crustacea have very simple nervous systems – I am not so sure about mine. I cannot become accustomed to the French habit of quickly cutting a live creature in half. They die instantly, one is told, but it doesn't do my heart any good at all, and my newest apprentice, Steven, looked absolutely aghast at the suggestion. I have decided we will dip the chilled, sleepy marron into boiling water for half a minute. They die without any sign of a struggle so I am convinced they are still too chilled to know what is happening. We will then transfer them to iced water, drain them and store until they are ordered.

I ate in the dining room tonight and tested the pheasant with a succulent pig's trotter stuffed with sweetbreads and wild mushrooms. The stuffing is based on the Pierre Kaufman version from the restaurant La Tante Claire in London, and we put a fat slice alongside the roasted pheasant breast. The stickiness of the trotter skin contributes richness to the pheasant sauce. With it a delicate moulded bread and bay leaf pudding, a refinement of the bread sauce we served with a stuffed chicken last summer.

And to finish I had a mandarin custard, with spiced orange slices scattered with dates and mint, and a sesame-seed biscuit, suggested by Chef Jeff. We are using the first of the new season's navel oranges. Next week we are to do a special menu for a television company and I can think of no better meal than these dishes. I shall start the meal with a demitasse cup of chestnut soup, followed by the pheasant and the mandarin custard. Perhaps I will include a small portion of one of our best cheeses.

7 JUNE

Julie and Damien ate at the Cafe with me tonight. I was so proud of the entire project. The dinner was excellent, the service splendid and Damien was absolutely thrilled with the space and everything we have done. I know it is pretty fantastic but it is very reassuring when a close friend endorses one's own biased opinion. We shared some freshly opened oysters, served with their top shell resting like a lid so that the customers can tell they have been opened minutes before. Damien and Julie enjoyed a spinach salad topped with a poached egg and I ordered a boiled artichoke with melted butter sauce. The comfort in the Cafe has improved, too, with the delivery of the correct chairs.

Sadly Peter Bevan will not be able to accompany us to Italy as the theatrical costume company he runs with Tony Phillips will be very busy at just the wrong time. He is very disappointed and we are all hoping he will come later in October, for a holiday, at least. Tony is still to be part of the team. Peter's replacement is to be Elena Bonnici. Elena has been a delightful personality in my life for the last few years. She has flitted in and out of Stephanie's kitchens; left once to make hats; on another occasion she left to start her own cafe, but has given that up and now is working casually at Richmond Hill Cafe & Larder. She wants to travel so is going to be able to fit in a few weeks' assistance in Italy before setting out for other adventures. Elena has assisted Maggie before at a cooking weekend, so she knows what to expect from both of us. Should we be pleased or horrified at being known as the two Earth Mothers – and not only by Elena?

And another happy detail is that my friends Jean and John are returning from Frankfurt at the beginning of August and will have nowhere to rest their heads until their tenants can move from Jean and John's own house. They are thrilled to be able to house-sit and dog-sit for me, and so am I. Jean is even more of a poodle lover than I, and Rosie will be in for two months of spoiling. It is the perfect solution all round. Jean can have my car, her youngest daughter can move into Holly's room, and no household routines need change!

Holly has been accepted for the overseas exchange student programme from the University of Melbourne and has received a scholarship towards the expenses. But until yesterday she had not been formally accepted by Jean Moulin University at Lyon. She is now very relieved and spent the day poring over the enrolment booklet and doing a very long sum to ascertain her likely costs for this eight-month sojourn. Holly has worked very hard this year at three different jobs, but she will still need some financial assistance. It is ironic that we will all be in Europe again, although this time probably not together. Lisa is coming to join us in Tuscany for the last two weeks of October when Holly will have just started her lecture programme. Maybe I'll slip over to Lyon for the weekend.

I am blessed with my daughters. The last time we were in Europe together the man who had been our guide drove us to our hotel in Rome, and after we said our goodbyes he came back to say to me how inspirational he had found it to observe how we appreciated each other. And we do.

Holly is the one who has conquered technology and to whom we both turn for help and guidance with all manner of electronic devices. The Internet holds no fears for her and her matter-of-fact approach to solving electronic blips is my confirmation that hers is a quite different generation. She rarely panics and does not exaggerate her emotional responses as both Lisa and I tend to. And I really enjoy having her around. Eight months without Holly will be life without some of its best bits.

Holly is very curious. An evening's conversation with her can sometimes feel like a cross-examination. 'And then what happened?' she will ask as I rack my brains to try to remember what actually did happen. 'And what did you say next', she continues, 'and what was the reply?' 'Give me a break, Holly', I have been known to say, but then she protests that I don't tell her things and this questioning is the only way she finds out. So I have to reflect and remember that she is not the only one who has accused me of not wanting to share my thoughts. But often my thoughts are half-formed. And they may have implications for other people or other projects that I don't feel ready to expose.

Am I secretive? Am I wanting to exclude her from my life? It doesn't seem so from my perspective. I feel that my head teems with millions of tiny ants, scurrying and worrying and scrabbling and sorting themselves into ever-changing patterns and combinations. And the ants move so very fast, much faster than speech. I have to seek for words.

None of this helps, of course. So I try to slow down, to think and speak carefully and deliberately, without omitting details, and to answer the next lot of questions. Then eventually we have dealt with this topic and I feel pleased that we have communicated, but tired, too. And the ants recommence their mad frenzy in my head. They never ever stop.

9 JUNE

*T*oday is a public holiday for the Queen's Birthday. This seems pretty anachronistic to me and the growing republican movement holds alternative celebrations on this day. Nonetheless the Cafe is busy as Melbourne enjoys its long weekend. I had some baked eggs for breakfast served in Spanish terracotta dishes and thoroughly enjoyed them. The combination of balsamic vinegar, butter and cream bubbles into a sharp little sauce that is quite delicious. I think fingers of toast should be served as well, for dipping and wiping out the dishes. When Julie and I were in Spain two years ago we lusted after these terracotta dishes. They cost only a few cents each and came in every shape and size. Most were unglazed on the outside and Spanish cooks use them directly over a flame. So beautiful and warm they looked, but so fragile. I brought a few home tucked among sweaters and some arrived intact, but some did not. I am hoping to find some more in one of our Spanish or Portuguese shops. The eggs look so much more delightful served in these rustic dishes than in the more usual white glazed ovenware.

BAKED EGGS IN A TERRACOTTA POT

1 terracotta or other ovenproof dish,	*1 tablespoon finely sliced spring onion*
15 cm diameter and 2 cm deep	*1 teaspoon balsamic vinegar*
2 egg-shaped (Roma) tomatoes	*1 teaspoon double cream*
2 tablespoons unsalted butter	*2 large free-range eggs*

Cut tomatoes in half lengthways and place under a grill, skins to heat source, until skin blackens and blisters. Allow to cool and peel skin off.

Preheat oven to 200°C. Brown butter in pan.

Place the pieces of tomato, brown butter, spring onion and balsamic vinegar in the terracotta dish. Put the dish in oven for approximately 5 minutes, so all ingredients are hot. Take out of the oven, add the cream, stir gently, and crack the eggs into the dish.

Return dish to the oven for 8–10 minutes until yolks are just firm

and the whites are still quite soft. The butter, vinegar and cream should .
have made a nice sauce that bubbles all around the eggs.

Serves 1

Today I decided to include an old-fashioned egg and bacon pie as an extra
option to the post-breakfast menu. This proliferation of menus has to be
watched. We now have an extensive breakfast menu that operates from
8.00 a.m. until 11.00 a.m., a post-breakfast menu from 11.00 until
12.00 noon, then a lunch menu, followed by an afternoon tea menu from
3.00 to 5.00, a bar menu until 6.30 and then dinner! Several customers have
complained that they want to eat a large breakfast at 11.15 or even later.
The kitchen cannot cope with this and also clean down the cooking area
and set up again for lunch. Hence the post-breakfast menu and the egg and
bacon pie.

What a long explanation for a tiny detail. It is this sort of working things
out that takes so long in a new venture. The solution, once achieved, is
simple – but getting there does not seem to be. And no sooner had we
introduced this modification than Lisa and I discussed the wisdom of a
brunch menu for Saturday (and maybe Sundays soon!) that could run
without interruption from early morning until late afternoon.

Will has imported the delicious French grey salt that is sold as Sel de
Guerande. Some may say that salt is salt but they cannot have tasted this.
It lifts any court-bouillon to new heights and adds a briny tang to everything
it flavours. Phillippa is going to use it in her breads. A few grains scattered
over poached salmon would be magical, or over a salad of boiled new
potatoes and very slim young green beans.

My friend John Wilson, who perfected the air-dried salmon that sells so
well, returned to Australia recently and we had a long conversation about
salmon. He loved the wild salmon he tasted in Scotland and he has new
ideas about different woods to use and is very excited about different
techniques. He discussed with me his plans to cure some salmon using this
grey salt, fennel and celeriac. I love the sound of this. John went on to
wonder how it would be with a salad of baby leeks. I can't wait to sample
the trial fillet!

1 2 J U N E

*A*ndy is leaving Stephanie's. He has been a good manager with a delightful sunny personality. I am very sad about this. Things are so flat at Stephanie's it was probably inevitable that some senior staff would start to look around. But it will be difficult to replace him and maybe we should not do so.

Today I did a photo shoot for *Vogue* magazine, to be included in a supplement of well-known Melbourne chefs and their dishes. The art director wanted a portrait of each chef doing something odd. My 'odd' pose was to sit on the balustrade on the first floor of the Restaurant, approximately nine metres above the ground. He would have preferred that I stood on it but I baulked at this. The hundred-year-old balustrade is well-worn and curved and although I have been feeling pretty depressed by the apparent impossibility of resolving conflicting interests, I decided it was not the day to end it all.

And then over to the Cafe to congratulate the staff on another glowing review. Once again the floor staff were singled out and praised for their friendliness and efficiency and the manner in which they handle the crowds at the door at peak times.

I went to a dinner to celebrate the 250th birthday of Maille mustard. I don't often go to these functions but felt I was in danger of becoming a hermit. Every guest received a tiny faience mustard pot. They were very beautiful. The representative of the company explained how originally the noble families of France had their own decorated mustard pots, which they took to be filled from a central pump. The company has opened a new museum in Paris to display these lovely pots. Different regions of France use different colours and different designs. A student of faience would be able to identify pottery from Quimper in Brittany, for example, and distinguish it from pottery from other major centres.

The dinner was very enjoyable as was the conversation with dinner companions Allan Campion and Michele Curtis, who are enthusiastic foodies. With my new-found interest in grey salt I was interested to hear that they had recently participated at a salt tasting. They both were enthusiastic about these unrefined salts and we agreed that the supermarket cooking salt is all attack on the tastebuds, with no mineral flavours or briny subtlety. I had a sneak preview of their lively little book *Chilli Jam*.

1 3 J U N E

I cannot escape a shiver of apprehension today. Friday the 13th, and it may well prove to be a watershed in my professional life. Possibly by tonight some major decisions will have been made and new directions set.

An excellent article in *The Age* today. Mike Richards passionately put the case for the necessity of this government apologising to Aboriginal Australians. He wrote:

> I have difficulty crediting the arguments of those who say: 'Why should I feel guilty for things I have not done?' Such people have missed the point. It is not a matter of guilt or blame but of responsibility and regret. It is a matter of acknowledging the truth of our past, accepting responsibility for it, and making reparations – beginning with an apology . . .

Richards went on to say that what is needed is leadership.

To be a citizen of Australia with a social conscience in the late 1990s is to spend a good deal of the time intensely frustrated and also depressed. There seems to be no forum in which to register one's disgust at the policies that prevail. Policies which from the vantage point of the outside world would suggest that Australians condone bigotry, are unwilling to take steps to acknowledge the effects of dispossession of Aboriginal Australians or to deal with greenhouse gas emissions, worship gambling, embrace totalitarian regimes, and on a more local level are indifferent to the crushing of the health and education systems while approving of government spending on lavish and spectacular entertainment.

16 JUNE

I have completed work on the facsimile edition of my mother's book. Originally titled *Through My Kitchen Door* and published in 1960, it is to be re-published as *Recipes My Mother Gave Me*. Caroline and I spent a few hours tidying up the manuscript on Saturday afternoon. It has been an enjoyable project revisiting so many old favourites. When we got to the chapter titled 'The Cookie Jar', my memory proved to be blank. And Mum had always been vague about oven temperatures and cooking times. Her oven was a wood-burning Aga, which had a little window on the door with a needle that wavered through a half-circle from somewhere at the bottom to about halfway to all the way down the other side. This was supposed to indicate the temperature and unsurprisingly was not very accurate. I decided to cook quite a few of these recipes, and what a pleasure that turned out to be!

I discovered a special glow of achievement in biscuit-baking! It was so easy and so satisfying. In no time I was removing trays of delicious-smelling biscuits from the oven. The kitchen smelt of spice and caramel and toasted coconut. My dog was going crazy – she sniffed and wagged her tail but I am afraid she didn't even get a taste. I lined the biscuits up on cooling racks and moved on to the next recipe.

These old-fashioned favourites had few fancy ingredients – cornflakes, coconut, almonds, mixed peel and, of course, sugar, butter, eggs and flour. As I creamed butter and sugar and stirred and spooned blobs onto trays I mused on the effort it took to keep those biscuit tins filled, with four kids' lunch boxes to prepare, not to mention after-school snacks and having something on hand when a friend dropped in for a cup of tea. Maybe one of the reasons I don't bake many biscuits is that my children don't drink tea. (Or coffee, for that matter.)

The biscuits tasted fantastic! In fact, they were a revelation. The current vogue is for Italian biscotti, dryish biscuits intended to be dunked in coffee or sweet wine. The deserved popularity of these has helped us forget many Anglo-Saxon confections. Although having said that, every food outlet now seems to sell a version of almond bread and yo-yos, or melting moments – I have even seen packets of them at my local florist. My favourites among Mum's selection were almond meringue fingers, and cornflake meringues.

Cornflake meringues had a subtle sophistication due to the inclusion of some mixed peel.

17 JUNE

Safely past the 13th and no huge decisions were made. The important moments in one's life probably can't be neatly programmed – they will happen when all the pieces come together.

> There is a tide in the affairs of men
> Which, taken at the flood, leads on to fortune;
> Omitted, all the voyage of their life
> Is bound in shallows and in miseries.
> On such a full sea we are now afloat,
> And we must take the current when it serves,
> Or lose our ventures.
> JULIUS CAESAR, ACT IV, SCENE ii

It is not always easy to recognise the flood tide, but the current must be taken.

20 JUNE

Holly has planned the American section of her travels and has impressed me greatly by obtaining all the information she needed regarding the Amtrak Rail system via the Internet. Days and times and destinations were all clearly set out and had she had her own credit card, she could have actually booked the ticket. Travel agents are no doubt aware that all of these services are so available. Unless they can offer an edge in terms of service or efficiency they may well become obsolete. Holly tells me I could even buy a car via the Internet!

Dad has had a second cataract operation, which has been as spectacular as the first. He is not wearing glasses for the first time in seventy years! And he is seeing new colours in the world! What an extraordinary operation. I am wondering (only tentatively at the moment) if I should have the new laser operation on my eyes to restore perfect vision. Probably not. I believe it is not as miraculous for long sight as for short sight. And then the other day I read of a new development to help the deaf. My most pressing problem is loss of hearing, and conventional hearing aids are only a poor solution. I know it is extremely irritating for those with perfect hearing when they meet someone like me who is stubborn and wilful and will not persevere with hearing aids. After all, this is exactly what I feel about my father, whose hearing is appalling. But, and it is a big but, the hearing aids are uncomfortable, difficult to adjust, they magnify every tiny sound so that the shrill barking of my dog has me leaping in the air and the noise of the exhaust fan in the kitchen seems like a jet landing. And their fake pink colour coated with ear wax is frankly repellent. The article I cut from the newspaper spoke of an implantable hearing aid that uses a sensor attached to the patient's eardrum and which registers sounds as vibrations that are then communicated to the brain through a system of nervous impulses. I might volunteer as a trial subject!

26 JUNE

$\mathcal{A}$ big gap.

I am dealing with potentially catastrophic events, which can never be detailed. Suggesting I am dealing with them is in fact misleading. Each new move is fielded, considered and replied to, and the possible ramifications are turned and scrutinised from every angle. The flavour is in my mouth all day, it is the stuff of my dreams at night, it limits my conversation and has sucked my energy in a whoosh.

And yet in the workaday world I function quite well. Or I think I do.

Last night at Stephanie's we had a most successful Christmas in June dinner. I was delighted by the response. We were very quickly booked out and I cannot say whether it was because the idea of steaming pudding on a cold evening was overwhelmingly appealing, or whether the public smelt a bargain. It *was* a bargain, and we all enjoyed the bustle and rush of a full restaurant of 135 diners.

I also liked being one of the kitchen team again after an absence of several weeks and the kitchen staff beamed and loved to have me there. A little bit of the ice around my heart melted as a result.

The menu started with smoked salmon on hot buttered blinis and then proceeded to the new dish of scallops and hazelnuts which I've been looking forward to trying. Scallops are in their prime at the moment, big and fat with bright corals.

TASMANIAN SCALLOPS ON THE HALF-SHELL WITH HAZELNUTS AND JERUSALEM ARTICHOKES

36 scallops on the half-shell
12 Jerusalem artichokes, peeled and
   resting in a bowl of acidulated water
2 tablespoons extra-virgin olive oil
6 tablespoons hazelnuts, toasted
   in the oven and the outer skin rubbed
   off in a dry cloth, roughly chopped
6 handfuls rocket leaves, checked for
   bruised or yellowing leaves
2 teaspoons hazelnut oil

sea salt
1 teaspoon sherry vinegar
black pepper
1 medium carrot, sliced finely in
   julienne shreds (easiest when using
   a Japanese vegetable-slicing gadget),
   deep-fried until crisp and drained on
   kitchen paper
vegetable oil for deep-frying

Remove scallops from the shell, cut away the dark intestinal thread on the side of each scallop and wipe each one with a damp cloth. Sprinkle with a few drops of olive oil and set aside in a bowl. Rinse the shells and dry in a warm oven.

Thickly slice the Jerusalem artichokes and cook in lightly salted water for 5 minutes. Drain and dry well on kitchen paper. Cut into 1 cm cubes.

Sauté the cubes of Jerusalem artichoke in half the olive oil, shaking and tossing until golden brown. Tip into a large, warm bowl with the toasted hazelnuts, rocket leaves, the hazelnut oil, sea salt and the remaining olive oil. Mix together.

Heat a non-stick pan and sear the scallops quickly (one minute on each side). Deglaze with a splash of sherry vinegar and quickly tumble the contents of the pan into the warm bowl with the other ingredients. (It may be necessary to sear the scallops in two batches. They must sear, not stew.)

A moment to rest and for the juices to mingle and then spoon the scallops into the waiting warmed scallop shells. Season with a turn from the pepper grinder and add a topknot of finely cut, fried sweet carrot to finish this bright and cheerful dish.

Serves 6

The main course was a partly boned, stuffed roasted chicken with which we served a simple braise of peas and globe artichokes and a delicate bread and bay leaf pudding, inspired by a recipe from English master chef Raymond Blanc, which I had also enjoyed with roasted pheasant.

One might question the wisdom of offering freshly shelled peas with the main course to 135 people, but I had expected to serve maybe sixty. I took a six kilo box home and shelled them while watching television.

One of the surprises of the last few years has been the appearance of globe artichokes in the winter. They are magnificent! Big, tender and sweet. Until now artichokes have always been an anticipated springtime treat and I have always championed seasonality. But I wholeheartedly applaud this new crop. It fits with the criteria of using what is freshly available and of the best quality. An important distinction and one which includes the artichokes but excludes winter-grown strawberries, for instance.

The artichokes were trimmed and braised in a mix of light chicken stock and extra-virgin olive oil. Once they were tender we left them in the now-reduced juices, and at service time they were quickly reheated and shaken in the pan with the perfectly cooked brilliant green peas.

Many, many years ago I spent a weekend with a very 'county' family in Somerset, in the west of England, in cheddar and cider country. It was my introduction to many things – thatched roofs; aristocratic accents confusingly coming from women decked out in shapeless tweeds, headscarves and boots; high tea and supper; freezing rooms where the dogs sat in the only warm spots; and bread sauce with roast chicken. I have never forgotten the bread sauce. It has been a favourite of mine ever since. Raymond Blanc's recipe gives bread sauce a classy makeover without losing any of its simple charm. This recipe for bread and bay leaf pudding is inspired by Raymond Blanc's recipe for bread mousse in *Recipes from Le Manoir aux Quat' Saisons*.

BREAD AND BAY LEAF PUDDING

600 ml milk
1 small onion, finely chopped
2 cloves
1 fresh bay leaf
120 g white bread, crusts removed,
    chopped into cubes
a pinch of ground nutmeg

a pinch of salt
scant amount of white pepper
1 egg
4 egg whites
butter for greasing moulds
8 rounds of baking paper, cut to fit
    the base of each mould

Bring milk, onion, cloves and bay leaf to scalding point. Add the bread and nutmeg, salt and a scrap of white pepper. Allow to cool, remove cloves and bay leaf and purée briefly in a food processor with the egg.

Whisk egg whites until soft peaks form then fold into the mixture gently. Taste for seasoning.

Butter 8 dariole moulds, slip in the paper rounds, ladle in the mixture.

Bake in a bain-marie at 180°C for approximately 15 minutes, until firm to the touch.

The bread puddings will stay warm in the bain-marie for up to three-quarters of an hour, loosely covered with foil if there are obvious draughts in your kitchen.

Serves 8

A few weeks ago when we were so quiet I had asked our pastry cook to make some Christmas puddings, and last night we were able to fill our huge stockpot with bobbing vacuum-sealed puddings and serve these fully matured puds with no effort at all.

Not for the first time after one of these no-choice designer menu dinners I muse on the advantage of doing it more often. We worked together like a well-oiled machine. No loss of quality, sufficient time to get every detail right, good humour reigned throughout both kitchens and the customers seemed to enjoy not having to choose. There will always be a few who regard a set menu as a challenge and have to do a bit of negotiation. We had one table requesting chilli sauce for their chicken, and they split open the delicate boudin blanc that accompanied it and added slabs of butter to it!

I think I feel a regular Tasting Menu coming on!

28 JUNE

John Wilson came to the Cafe to give me a tasting of his new salmon products as promised: cured and marinated with fresh horseradish, and cured, marinated and air-dried with horseradish. Horseradish and cured fish is an excellent combination. Twenty years ago I used to serve a fillet of hot-smoked rainbow trout with a ground walnut and fresh horseradish cream sauce inspired by a line from Elizabeth David. John's hope was that the clean hotness and flavour of the horseradish would create an exciting meld of flavour in the fish. And it does. The product is marvellous the first day but the aroma and flavour are elusive and diminish quite rapidly. It seemed to be captured better in the side that had been air-dried as well as marinated. Imagine if we had access to fresh wasabi! Its pungency must be at least six times that of our horseradish. I have heard that someone in New Zealand has successfully grown wasabi but it hasn't crossed the Tasman yet.

Thinking about this does give me an idea, though. What if I used the air-dried salmon and boosted the flavours by a side salad based on wasabi and seaweed? And used celeriac and leeks. My wasabi and seaweed samples are locked in the Cafe. My fingers are now itching to try but it will have to wait until tomorrow.

John has also made a pure pork and pistachio sausage that we will serve with a lentil salad. Altogether a good morning. It was refreshing to be with someone who shares my interests and passions and with whom I can have a reflective discussion about flavours, and about what is good, better or best without there being any paranoia or heavy sales pitch.

At other meetings during the day we discussed the near-riot conditions that still occur every Saturday. Lisa has as many as thirty people all waiting for tables at any hour of the day. The problem is most acute when it nears the time for a menu changeover from breakfast to lunch, or from lunch to the bar menu. We have decided to go ahead and introduce a brunch menu for Saturday trading. It won't shorten the queues but at least the full brunch menu will be available when customers finally sit down.

Our newly installed air curtain over the door has largely solved the draught problems. The application for outside seating is still with the local council and we now need to decide how to manage this additional area. The owners of a nearby cafe frightened us with stories of wild vandalism from a few disgruntled football fans. Their cafe chairs are thrown in side streets and the tables overturned on every football Saturday. If this is to be the case there can be no question of leaving anything set on the tables. I would prefer that our outside customers are as comfortable and well-equipped as the indoors folk but I do not want to risk our pepper grinders and plates vanishing, not to mention the tables and chairs! I suppose we will have to try it and see.

Nine weeks on and it is worth recording what a smooth team we now have.

Lisa has done a wonderful job and has achieved what she wanted – competent, efficient waiting staff who are friendly and who radiate enjoyment in a job well done and have no attitude problems. The kitchen is a joy to visit; Nicky has done the same there. She is ably assisted by Justin and no employer could ask for a more dedicated and interested pair. And Angie continues to add new strings to her bow and keeps a watchful eye on expenditure at the same time as noticing everything and everyone. Shop sales are steady and Simone is pleased. The latest consignment from Mary Walker includes fabulous pickled quinces and a green tomato relish. The cheese room continues to draw gasps of astonishment and Nick has it well in hand. We are also selling a lot of books! Anna is the quiet achiever – she has the books, the desktop publishing and a dozen other projects all moving along efficiently. Kelvin Monsbourgh has had input into our second wine list, which has been very well received.

So this is how it feels to have a popular success. I hasten to add that a successful bottom line does not come quite so quickly. As a consultant my role is to watch and to correct any mishaps or imbalances. And, of course, to have lots of good ideas. But for good ideas to flourish, I need the lump of wood that is squashing me down to go away. Maybe it will in a few days.

Both Stephanie's and the Cafe need new menus before I leave for Italy. And I must complete my contribution to the menu booklet that will form the kernel of the subsequent Italian book. I don't dare let my mind drift towards Italy yet.

The proof of the photo for *Vogue* magazine is abominable. I look like an old man with a beard. It is a mark of my general gloom that I do not insist on a reshoot!

I accompanied Dad to the balance doctor today. We must investigate thoroughly the possible causes of his falls. He had a very thorough examination and the doctor ordered a CAT scan in case Dad's loss of balance has been caused by a minor stroke, and a blood test to rule out thyroid irregularities. We will return in three weeks for the results. Dad's dear friend Dora died today, aged ninety-six. He is sad but philosophical.

30 JUNE

*T*he end of Empire in the Far East. Hong Kong reverts to China this evening. While today is the official handover, those whose lives are directly affected have made their plans and preparations years ago. Many long-time expats have had to reassess their future and decide whether to go or stay. Many Chinese have secured residency permits or citizenship in Australia, Canada or Britain. But there is a strong feeling that the majority of Chinese, both here and there, see the handover in a positive light. The new shift in focus acknowledges China as the motherland, with a hope that the motherland properly appreciates what she is taking over. There is much flag-waving and beating of breasts, gathering of world leaders, fine speeches, and pomp and ceremony.

The world looks on and fervently hopes that there can never be a repeat of the horrors of the massacre in Tiananmen Square in 1989. Like many others I find it hard to forget the bumpy progress of the tanks on that night, each bump signifying another murder and a crime against humanity.

Back at home I am thinking of earthquakes. Maybe my thoughts were stimulated by scenes on television of belching flames and smoke issuing from a volcano on the Caribbean island of Montserrat. It is a compelling image. Under the earth's crust there are heavings and rumblings with now and then a split or a crack, and some hot air and gas escapes more or less harmlessly, maybe singeing the ground a little and doing minor damage. But these small eruptions are warnings. The Big One is still there. Isn't this what they say about San Francisco? And so it can be with a life. Today will probably decide.

And on a more prosaic level, today is also the end of the financial year.

July

1 JULY

*T*oday I purchased the business equity held by Dur-é Dara, until yesterday my partner in Stephanie's Restaurant, and I am now the sole owner of this extraordinary institution. I now need to restore confidence among the staff, who have known that something was afoot but neither Dur-é nor I was able to relieve their anxiety, as our negotiations were long and painful.

3 JULY

*W*hat a rollercoaster of a year this is turning out to be. I confess to feeling very scared of the future. I have no option but to keep moving forward and meet whatever comes.

As with most small to medium businesses, the bank is an ever-present part of my life and although we are on fairly good terms at the moment, the balancing act is a delicate one. Looking back on policies prevalent in the expansive 1980s from the vantage point of the more serious 1990s, I can be proud that we did not become a casualty. Borrow more, borrow more, they invited us! Business credibility lies with paying one's staff appropriately, including all overtime, paying one's suppliers, maintaining a clean and safe workplace, and meeting the requirements of one's bankers – all matters of little concern to food critics or even the public.

So in the short term it will be business as usual but I must don my thinking cap and also consider the longer term. When a major life change looms my initial instinct is to say 'I can't do this, I can't do this'. And yet I also can't give up. My sense of responsibility sometimes seems overdeveloped. (Does it come from being the eldest child, I wonder?) My concern for how actions will affect others has frequently been unnecessary. I have found that the 'others' do not need my nurturing or my concern – they have found their own wings and are more than ready to fly away. And they will do so whenever it suits them, without the slightest backward glance.

My mother once told me that when I was about four years old (this was in 1944, when there was widespread fear that the Japanese were about to invade Australia), she was so determined that I would be independent that she constructed a little pack that I was to wear on my back should I be abandoned or be left an orphan. Goodness knows what I was to carry in it. Her horror was of her children not being able to fend for themselves should a disaster overtake her. We must be reared to manage our lives, never to be beholden to others for life's essentials. Sometimes it seemed that Mum didn't really think we were doing well enough. She withheld praise, apparently believing that praise would give us ideas, or lead us to think we had already reached our goal. Sadly I think what it did instead was to give each of us the sense that we were not achieving at a sufficient level. In our own ways the four of us still battle with limited self-esteem.

I have been encouraged by the writing of Stephanie Dowrick. I was given her latest book, *Forgiveness and Other Acts of Love*, by a dear friend who recognised that I needed extra strength at this time. Dowrick's first chapter is on Courage. Here is a sampling of her thinking:

> Fear is part of the human condition. But courage offers something that can balance fear, draw the sting from it, put it in its place, open us to life, and set us free . . .
>
> This notion – that courage is, or arises from, a mental attitude – brings courage into reach. We can't choose our feelings. They are like the elements: wind, rain, fog, cloud, snow, heat. They come and go. But attitudes are something else entirely. We can choose them, even when they seem a little reluctant to choose us . . .
>
> The events that are causing you grief don't change when you begin to face them, but the present moment does change, and so does your guiding sense of how you can relate to life . . . Perhaps the best that can be said is that you face life itself more truthfully and knowingly . . .
>
> Courage is as freely available to all of us and to any one of us as the sounds of waves crashing, of wind in high trees, of birds singing, of human laughter . . . Those sounds, too, are always there, but sometimes we don't hear them . . . Courage can be like that. We need to turn our attention towards it, pay it more attention than we do our fears, even when those fears are clamorous, clingy, familiar and demanding.

Reading these words has been a great solace to me. And by concentrating on their meaning I feel myself opening to this new experience and embracing it.

I was also helped by doing the flowers at the Cafe. Selecting branches of olive-green magnolia leaves with their bronze lining, and mixing them with dramatic red-hot pokers and caramel-coloured chrysanthemums and coral-pink liliums, was another version of hearing waves crashing. Their exquisite shapes and colours deserve attention and induce a feeling of optimism. The simple but incredible fact of their existence is humbling. So much is freely offered to anyone with eyes to see.

4 JULY

American Independence Day is not a bad day to be going it alone, as one friend commented. I had a terrific meeting with my senior staff at Stephanie's today. New positions and responsibilities were addressed but more importantly I felt a rush of energy again and knew that the staff were thirsty for it. They have all been caught up in the fallout and have known that the walls were shaking. I apologised for the too-long period of non-resolution, assured them the walls would not come tumbling down, and then we all got on with the business of planning the future.

Sophie was bubbling over with ideas for marketing and Valerie has seized the opportunity to be restaurant front-of-house manager. Brian has reacted positively to developing a series of winemaker dinners. My contribution was to suggest that maybe we should have the producer of a major ingredient along to the dinner on the same night as the maker of a wine that complements the dish.

My first-ever series of cooking workshops will start in two weeks.

I have selected themes that relate to sections in *The Cook's Companion* and have drawn menus from each chosen section. And I shall start a series of market-inspired lunches and Tasting Menu dinners to be advertised as Foodie Fridays. I want this new energy and direction to jump off the page to the general public and for them to say, 'Wow, things are really happening at Stephanie's – better get along there and take a look!'.

And I have drawn up a punishing schedule for myself before I leave for Italy.

The day finished with me in the kitchen. We had a busy evening, with three separate functions. It was a joy to watch this well-oiled team produce outstanding food, plate after plate of it. Precisely cooked, cared for, and perfectly placed on plates. Holly came to drive me home just as the main courses were finishing. She was reluctant to leave the kitchen and said how much she enjoyed watching. For cooks and kitchen groupies it is addictive, this fast rhythm, the controlled commands and shouts, the good humour, the slipping and sliding, the adrenalin rush. One plate a minute is our best average!

What a team.

5 JULY

The Cafe had its busiest day ever this Saturday. Just before the dinner service really got underway Nicky rang to say they had already done 400 covers that day! The only thing in short supply was bread. Another great team.

I picked a small posy from my garden with its promise of spring. Snowdrops, the first daphne, narcissus, thryptomene, and two *Iris stellata*.

During the late afternoon I had an interview 'live' for the BBC from the ABC studios. My partner in the interview was the Hon. Louise Asher, Minister for Tourism and Small Business. We thought we were to chat about food and wine in Australia but a good part of the interview was concerned with that afternoon's football match. Eventually we got around to the quality and diversity of food in this great State. Interesting how stereotypical misconceptions are perpetuated. The BBC interviewer cheerfully referred to his hunt for 'possums in the rainforest' and wanted my opinion on the eating or not eating of kangaroo, as if this was the most important food issue in this State. Both Louise and I got in a few sentences about multicultural influences and how in this country the good things are available at prices that *everyone* can afford (unlike Britain, in my experience).

Dinner tonight at Stephanie's. Two members of staff congratulated me rather timidly and both said they were not sure if this was the appropriate response. I said that I thought it was and it was good for me to know they felt positively about the new directions. Two former staff members rang to offer hearty congratulations.

7 JULY

*T*he phone rang at 5.00 this morning. It was Holly's Amtrak reservations being confirmed by fax. She has achieved all this by applying her impressive grasp of technology, but nonetheless I confess to a moment of glee when I read in the fax that she could have done it all via a local agent and a local phone call!

At the Cafe today I poached John Wilson's pork and pistachio sausage and we put together a hot salad 'lyonnaise-style' of sliced sausage, boiled potatoes, quickly tossed cabbage and fragments of duck confit, all tossed in a mustard vinaigrette. I preferred this to the earlier version with lentils. If I manage a weekend with Holly in Lyon, I will be intrigued to note whether such classic bistro dishes are still on offer. And do the *bouchons* of Lyon still exist? *Bouchons* are small bistros devoted to traditional and very hearty Lyonnais specialities – tripe, potatoes, sausage salads, platters of head cheese or potted meat as we call it.

And Justin made an outstanding *ribollita*, a twice-cooked vegetable soup. I enjoyed such a soup two years ago in Florence and no doubt will sample others in a few months. The soup has to be as thick as porridge with a generous drizzle of fruity olive oil.

One other new dish is to be a simply sautéd chicken breast sliced onto a bed of peas and artichokes, dressed with lemon butter.

And yet another dish is a grilled loin of lamb marinated with Middle Eastern flavours and served with a trio of sauces – baba ghanoush, a red pepper and almond dip, and a tabbouleh that includes a little preserved lemon.

1 0 JULY

Yesterday I went to our National Gallery to see the current exhibition of Amish quilts from Lancaster County in Pennsylvania. My interest in the Shakers was first stimulated by my friend Betsy, who became interested in their philosophy while on study leave in New England. She brought home with her simple Shaker-made wooden boxes in which she stores her embroidery wools and threads. I was fortunate that my visit coincided with a tour of the exhibition conducted by one of the gallery guides, which added so much to my understanding of the quilts.

When Lisa was very young she and I were both addicted to Laura Ingalls Wilder and her stories of a mid-nineteenth-century American pioneer family. *Little House in the Big Woods* was followed by eight more titles, which we read and re-read. While Lisa was entranced by the doings of Ma and Pa and Laura and Mary, I was just as delighted by the details of domestic life in their many different homes and especially the way in which Ma sustained her family, displaying exemplary resourcefulness, never wasting a crumb (except to give to the birds), and always coaxing the best flavour from the good things she set before them. The whole family was engaged in meal preparation, whether it was Pa, who shot the wild turkey, or Laura, who gathered the cranberries or ground-cherries, or Ma, who made the sourdough bread. An ideal picture is drawn where the girls willingly helped Ma plant, pick and peel. Activity was not confined to the kitchen – Ma also stitched dresses for Laura, Mary and their dolls, and made rugs and quilts.

In the eighteenth and nineteenth centuries virtually all North American women took up their needles to create curtains, tablecloths and, above all, bed coverings. These quilts are a recognised art form and different communities favoured certain styles and colours. I cannot remember reading detailed descriptions of the quilts that Ma made but I imagine she would have incorporated scraps of sprigged or patterned fabric left after making something for one of her girls.

Not so with the Amish, however, which brings me back to the exhibition. The Shakers were originally Swiss Anabaptists who fled Europe to avoid persecution for rejecting what they saw as the luxury of the Roman Catholic Church. Their guiding principles were to live a simple life, serving

God and the community, to seek continuity with the past and respect all the traditions of family and community. They disdained excess and valued hard work, discipline and fine craft. There were and are several Shaker communities in the United States, the Amish sect being geographically located in Lancaster County, Pennsylvania. This group continued with little outside interference from the early part of the eighteenth century until nearly 1950, before its intriguing if anachronistic lifestyle and dress resulted in it becoming a tourist attraction, with all that this implies. One can still buy a quilt in Lancaster County, but it is most probably not one of the classic designs.

There are five main designs used by the Amish quiltmakers. All are strongly geometric, and to see so many quilts hung in proximity reinforces the similarity between them and the work of early abstract painters. Bands and bars, diamonds and squares of lovely jewel-like colours, rich blues, greens, purple, rust-reds. Without yellows, whites, scarlets or pastels, the effect is rich, sombre and substantial. Our guide explained that the Amish are quite a wealthy community and able to afford fine wools for their modest garments, always loosely pleated to disguise the body, but again in these lovely mid-toned colours. Their quilts were made from large pieces of these same wools, whereas the patchwork quilts that we are more familiar with indicated less affluent households, as the quilt had to be constructed from all manner of bits and pieces. (Such as Ma would have made, I am certain.)

I was quite uplifted by this collective hit of 'goodness'. No egos on parade, no victims, or obsession with angst or mysterious symbolism, or competitiveness – just a sense of strong, steady light. 'Lit from Within', the exhibition was called – a most appropriate title.

I cannot resist a last word from Laura Ingalls Wilder. The following extract and recipe from one of her later books, *Farmer Boy*, is included in one of my most treasured books, *The Little House Cookbook* by Barbara M. Walker.

Early in the afternoon the bushel baskets and all the pails were full, and Father drove home. They were all a little sleepy, soaked in sunshine and breathing the fruity smell of the berries.

For days Mother and the girls made jellies and jams and preserves, and for every meal there was huckleberry pie or blueberry pudding.

HUCKLEBERRY PIE

FOR A 9-INCH PIE (18 CM)

Common Family Paste for pies	*brown sugar, ¾ cup*
(Substitute your favourite	*flour, 2 tablespoons*
shortcrust recipe)	*pinch ground nutmeg*
Blueberries, 2 dry pints (5 cups)	

Line pie pan with half the pastry. Reserve the rest in the refrigerator.

Pick over berries, eliminating any bruised ones. In a bowl mix sugar, flour and nutmeg. Put half the berries into the pie pan and strew with half the sugar mixture. Add remaining berries, mounding them towards the centre and top with the rest of the sugar mixture.

Preheat the oven to 220°C. Roll out the top crust, place it over the fruit and pinch the edges. Vent the crust with a small slash and put the pie in the oven. Reduce heat to 200°C and bake for about 40 minutes, until nicely browned.

Serves 6–8

Barbara Walker explains that true huckleberries contain hard seeds unsuitable for pie-making but that many Americans call wild blueberries 'huckleberries'. We will have to use cultivated blueberries, increasingly available in the southern States of Australia.

12 JULY

Stephanie Dowrick and I are now investigating Fidelity and exploring the narcissistic personality. It is fascinating and illuminating.

Narcissism tells you *other people's needs are a drag . . .*

Narcissism tells you to *follow your emotions*. Doing something because it needs doing is not the point. Your feeling state is your only valid point of reference . . .

Narcissists are unable to tolerate and learn from a view about themselves that differs from their own ... Offered such a truth, they will attack, deny, withdraw, sulk. They will shout and blame . . .

Somewhere, far inside themselves, narcissists know truths about themselves that are far worse than any unpalatable truths someone else could come up with. This is why they react to a pinprick as though it were a dagger.

There has been a good response to publicity for The Cook's Companion Workshops after three days. The classes on fish are the most popular. Many who call wish I were giving the classes in the evenings. I'll see how this first series goes. There is a great deal to organise and I shall work with a different chef for each class so that everyone at Stephanie's can feel involved.

A new initiative post-July 4 has been to request the pastry cook at Stephanie's to make baked goods for sale at the Cafe. Pastry cook Liz made the cornflake meringues that I rediscovered in working with Mum's manuscript and mentioned in my entry for 16 June. They sold very quickly. Today I delivered bags of oatcakes that we cannot get enough of. They are perfect with the mellow cheddar cheeses we stock in the cheese room.

The oatcake recipe was given to me by Sally Clarke, owner and chef at the delightful Clarke's restaurant in Kensington Church Street, London. Anyone visiting London should try to lunch or dine at Clarke's. As at Chez Panisse in Berkeley, California, this restaurant offers one carefully planned daily menu, providing a choice of two or so dishes. I have always found the menus to be delicious, beautifully balanced and reflecting the best of British produce. The cheeses served come from Neal's Yard Dairy, near Covent Garden, and, together with Sally's oatcakes and the breads made on the premises, they are not to be missed.

On my last visit to Clarke's I rang to book and when I sat down and the menu was presented the first item read 'Prosciutto on leaves with Stephanie Alexander's watermelon rind pickle'. Such generosity and acknowledgement is rare indeed and I was astonished and, of course, delighted. And the pickle was as perfect as any batch I have made myself.

I had a long discussion about Christmas with Anna, who is now being shared between me and the Cafe. It seems crazy even to be thinking of Christmas in July, but every retailer I meet assures me that all should be planned by the end of August. We started talking about carry bags and decorations, tissue paper and quantities and budgets. It was good to get all the ideas onto paper and to have scheduled a meeting when all relevant personnel will have to submit costed ideas for their Christmas projects. I am utterly seduced by efficiency! To work with someone who not only has ideas and a sense of humour, but who quickly and calmly carries things through to a conclusion, is so satisfying. It permits all those ants in my head to run even faster.

13 JULY

A rare day to myself. The Cafe is not yet open on Sundays, but it will be soon. I organised all the recipes for the cooking workshops and started collating information relevant to my tax return. And I wrote the presentation I have been invited to give in Sydney at Government House in a week's time. The event is entitled 'Food and Ceremony; a celebration of food and eating in Australia . . . in delicious surroundings'. I am a little embarrassed that I am to speak yet again on 'The Importance of the Family Table', a topic I have addressed on several public occasions. Having so recently finished work on *Recipes My Mother Gave Me*, I think I will dwell on the breadth of influences I experienced at my own family table.

Not only were the culinary horizons wide at our family meals but the important rituals associated with eating dinner together were never ignored. The table was always set properly. The embroidered linen tablemats demonstrated Mum's prowess as a member of the Embroiderers' Guild. Wine and water glasses were set automatically. The bread was usually homemade and the meal would always consist of two courses, sometimes three. We had a round table and the circle was not broken until, with the advent of television in 1956, a little gap was made in the circle so that we could watch the evening news.

From my father and grandfather I absorbed the belief that mealtimes were times of social intercourse; that debate was healthy and that it was OK to disagree. I also learnt that it was important to listen to all sides of a question and I soon realised that for my father totalitarian thinking was unacceptable. My grandfather, a very radical ninety-year-old, had exchanged the rhetoric of the lay Methodist preacher for belief in the new world order he felt was being established in the Soviet Union.

But from my mother came a different passion. As an artist she worked with various materials – paints, pastels, embroidery silks and sometimes a gardening fork. In the kitchen her passion was even stronger. Her delight in working with these raw materials, many of which she had grown herself, and her unfailing ability to create small miracles to set before us nightly, was inspirational. I spent many hours sitting at our kitchen table watching, listening, helping and confiding. When I was well and truly grown up, with children of my own, my mother told me that sometimes she had to bend her head low over the mixing bowl to hide either a smile or a blush as I poured out my totally uncensored confessions.

My mother taught me to cook. She taught me how, and why; I helped her grow things and pick them, and learnt to understand the relationship between careful husbandry in the garden or orchard and quality on the table. She introduced me to dishes that originated in cultures – usually non-Anglo-Saxon cultures – that had long understood that what one eats is of paramount importance. Meals at our table were always interesting; some dishes were very simple, some complex. The preparation of sauerkraut or bread rolls and the pickling of chicken feet were considered topics of conversation at least as worthy of note as the politics of the day.

Mum delighted in beautiful things and with a very limited income she had collected plates, bowls and serving platters she particularly loved. They would be set for birthdays, or when friends came to share our table. She was an enthusiastic gardener and the tiny posies on the table were quite eccentric, just as likely to include shivery grass or culinary herbs as 'regular' flowers. So Mum communicated personal style without it ever being articulated. The way she handled her pots, the lacquered tray she treasured, or the pink and white Spode teaset she bought with her first earnings as a food writer – all had significance for her, which she was happy to talk about if asked.

Entertaining friends was something both my parents loved. The family circle opened to include an extra one or two or four, and we all tucked our elbows in and beamed. My university friends loved to be invited for a weekend, and they were always astonished by the food. Forty years later they still tell me that they had never seen or tasted anything like it.

When friends came to visit, such occasions were treated as performances by my mother. There would be special dishes, and plenty of them, with maybe a theme to the dinner – I remember a Japanese evening of sushi rolls (this is the late 1950s, remember), when Mum was persuaded to don the lovely kimono she had bought on her trip to Japan in 1936, when she and my father met on board ship. Special music would be organised by Dad, sometimes as a mini-concert after dinner, and of course to complement the food he would choose the wine, which he bought from Jimmy Watson in Lygon Street, one of Australia's first wine merchants. Jimmy's bottles came almost exclusively from the Rutherglen area and big reds they were, too.

As I grew older there were always parties for special days. My twenty-first birthday, graduation dinners, my welcome-home-from-Europe party, the birth of a new grandchild and so on. Always a special dinner had been planned, with thought given to the extra touches. With this background it is not at all surprising that I decided to stage my own nightly performances. I just chose a larger stage. Like my mother, I am a very shy person, and with cooking one can hide behind the dishes.

14 JULY

*B*astille Day – had I remembered in time we might have considered a celebration menu at Stephanie's. Too late!

Today I tasted the sublime fruit jellies being made by Medlow, a small company in the McLaren Vale, which we are now selling at Richmond Hill Cafe & Larder. They are absolutely wonderful. Several years ago I made some myself – the memory is of a huge pile of apricots, many hours' labour and a very few squares of intensely flavoured fruit jelly. But the texture I achieved was coarse in comparison to these discs of pure joy. They explode with flavour on the palate. One is quite speechless for a few seconds. The pink grapefruit is quite out of this world. Passionfruit comes a close second. They also look like fairyland, the pastel colours juxtaposed in cellophane packs, and are proving to be irresistible to the customers also.

Former head waiter Andy has contacted me and wants to talk about re-employment. Things have not worked out for him and we agreed that the timing of his departure was unfortunate. The wide world can be a harsh shock after the supportive warmth of Stephanie's Restaurant. Andy has no desire to reclaim his position, knowing that the moment is past, but he is interested in experiencing life at the Cafe.

16 JULY

We have new artwork on the walls at Stephanie's. In the Burchett room hangs a pair of Chinese block prints, depicting a butcher with cleaver and a farmer driving buffalo, which were chosen by my parents in China. The remaining works are by my friend and former waitress Julie Patey. Julie has chosen well. Her dramatic yet romantic pastels blend wonderfully with these stately Victorian rooms. When the upstairs rooms were redecorated nearly nine years ago, an art historian scraped at the walls to ascertain the original paint or paper colours before recommending the present colour scheme. At the time we were all a bit astonished. Having just come out of the era when all Victorian homes were painted white, to accept strong turquoise in one room and deep peachy pink with gilt cornices in another required great confidence in the expert. But it has proved a success and is an excellent background for these thoroughly modern works.

I often think of Stephanie's Restaurant as an ocean liner. Not an altogether fanciful idea, if one has ever driven up Cato Street at night to the huge house, apparently suspended or 'sailing' on the hill, with all its lights twinkling in the darkness. To continue the metaphor, then, the liner faltered and lost power over the last two months and must now regain its momentum so that it will be steaming along strongly in six weeks' time when I leave for Italy.

At the staff meeting today we discussed abandoning the fixed price structure. This is revolutionary talk! I was the first person in this State to operate a serious restaurant on a totally fixed price structure, and probably the only other operators doing so in the entire country in 1976 were Gay and Tony Bilson at Tony's Bon Gout, continued later at Berowra Waters Inn. Having been seduced by the fixed price menus I enjoyed all over France I loudly championed the concept of a meal having a beginning, a middle and an end. I still believe that the best way to eat is a series of smallish courses that complement each other and result in a balanced and delicious meal. The original decision was also a reaction to the dining ethos in the mid-1970s that judged a restaurant by the size of the main course. If the plate wasn't full to overflowing the diner felt he had not received value. By offering a fixed price I felt we were allowing the diners to select three courses, and they perceived this as good value. The structure has served us very well up until now.

My reasons for considering its abandonment are entirely economic.

The public stomach and purse are shrinking and there is an understandable reluctance to go to a place where one is required to eat a lot, or not eat it and pay anyway. Somehow there has to be a way of offering wonderful food, produced with due care and attention, that still covers the considerable costs of making it happen in such comfortable surroundings. The nightmare scenario is two people occupying a table on a Saturday night and eating one entree each, without any wine, then sharing a dessert. Which brought the discussion back to minimum charges, something none of us likes. Tentatively we have agreed to give unrestricted à la carte a trial for one week and see where the problems lie. I am actually hedging my bets and also offering a Celebration Menu on Fridays and Saturdays, which will be a no-choice, four-course option for a fixed price. Our first day for these changes will be 5 August, after a careful advertising campaign and a newsletter. 'Stephanie goes it alone . . . And farewells the fixed price' will be the new cry.

I am gaining strength and comfort from these much more constructive staff meetings. Discussions are frank and open; no one feels belittled or unable to develop an idea. Proposals are examined properly, and different senior staff members volunteer to take on the investigation of particular issues. Having firmly set us on the path to smartening up systems that had become sloppy, I am getting speedy action from everyone. We have no time to lose! Five weeks before I leave for Italy, and a battle for the hearts and minds of the public to be won. The challenge is still to overcome a belief that the Restaurant has closed.

17 JULY

Mary Walker, our maker of preserves, visited Richmond Hill Cafe & Larder for the first time today. We made sure the shelves were fully stocked and all her jars glowed beautifully – the apple and crabapple jellies as lovely as the Medlow fruit jellies, the amber of the pickled quinces alongside the richly red sweet pepper relish and the olive-green tomato relish. Not to mention the peach marmalade and pickled cherries and the golden apricot jam. I have always enjoyed the backlit displays of jams, jellies and preserves that one sees at agricultural shows and we have created just such a display here. Mary had samples of her first fruit pastes to show me – damson plum, apricot, grape and blackcurrant. We will definitely stock those at Christmas-time.

As far as costs and speed of transportation go, Tasmania suffers a disadvantage because of its isolation from the mainland, but it has the advantages of a relatively small community. Mary, who has lived in Tasmania all her life, has developed a personal network of farmers and growers who supply her with high-quality fruits and vegetables. She has picking rights to some very unusual crops. For example, she is producing a small amount of medlar jelly for our Christmas market. And we discussed pickling some D'Agen plums in the late summer (these are the small, pointy plums that are dried to produce prunes and which I enjoyed eating fresh earlier this year). They are an excellent size to pickle and enable us to overcome the problem of not being able to fit many larger plums into our small jars. I mentioned how much I enjoyed golden mirabelle plums, which I have not seen in Australia, but remembered in delicious tarts when I lived in France a long time ago. Mary was confident that she could find a few trees in Tasmania and promises to make us some golden plum jam. Or even greengage jam. She is waiting for the Seville oranges, which should be available any day now, to start our citrus marmalade.

Nick from the cheese room gave me a recipe called Baghdad Marmalade, and with such an irresistible name we just have to try it. Apparently the recipe was collected by someone from the British Museum of Archaeology. The very idea of marmalade in Baghdad is bizarre – it reminds me of Elizabeth David's account of making Christmas puddings on the Greek island of Syros, recounted in *Spices, Salt and Aromatics in the English Kitchen*. Stephanie's Restaurant is about to launch into making 500 Christmas puddings, sufficient for both establishments and for retail sale, a project sure to take at least several weeks, so I enjoyed looking up the paragraph in Elizabeth David's book.

> Now, all those with their fine talk of the glories of Old English fare, have they ever actually made Christmas pudding, in large quantities, by Old English methods? Have they for instance ever tried cleaning and skinning, flouring, shredding, chopping beef kidney suet straight off the hoof? Have they ever stoned bunch after bunch of raisins hardly yet dry on the stalk and each one as sticky as a piece of warm toffee? And how long do they think it takes to bash up three pounds of breadcrumbs without an oven in which they could first dry the loaves? Come to that, what would they make of an attempt to boil, and keep on the boil for nine to ten hours on two charcoal fires let into holes in the wall, some dozen large puddings?

We do not expect to encounter these difficulties, although the preparation of probably close to thirty kilos of beef suet is still a formidable task.

18 JULY

*T*oday was our first Foodie Friday at Stephanie's. I have coined this phrase to draw the attention of the marketplace to the fact that Friday is now our only lunch day. I was very pleased with the response. We had two full rooms of lunch customers and the atmosphere was very buzzy. The kitchen team had contributed ideas to the menu and I was pleased with the dishes, although less pleased that so many customers ordered the steak. Few ordered my personal favourite – a chicken boudin blanc, partnered with thick slices of grilled boudin noir, with apples and a marvellous layered potato and bacon cake created by second chef Michael de Jong. The black pudding sausage is made by Angel Cardosa, a Spanish sausage enthusiast from near Geelong whom I hope to meet some day. Angel also cures his own hams, makes chorizo, and is apparently a mine of information and delighted to share it.

For reasons of nostalgia, and to please Jodie, who has a very sweet tooth, we included golden syrup dumplings on the lunch menu. I consulted friends and the CWA cookbook to see if I had missed something in this incredibly easy and ever-popular dish. My contribution was to put a nugget of angelica tart mixture inside each dumpling so that fragments of almonds and angelica added interest to what is a rather solid dish!

Golden Syrup Dumplings

2 tablespoons butter	*2 eggs*
2 cups self-raising flour	*enough milk to mix to a soft dough*

Rub butter into flour and add eggs and sufficient milk to make a soft – but not sticky – dough. Take small portions, flatten slightly, add half a teaspoon of the angelica mixture and then roll the dough in the palm of your hand to make a ball or a cylinder.

Drop into simmering syrup and poach dumplings, covered, for 10 minutes, or until they float to the surface.

Serves 4

ANGELICA MIXTURE

3 sticks candied angelica (substitute other glacéed fruit if angelica is not available), roughly chopped	*150 g unsalted butter*
	½ cup castor sugar
	2½ tablespoons light honey
1 tablespoon slivered almonds	*2 tablespoons kirsch or brandy*
½ cup mixed dried fruits (apples, currants, apricots etc)	*2 tablespoons cream*

Place angelica, almonds and dried fruit in food processor and process briefly using the pulse action. The fruit should be quite finely chopped. Melt the butter in a pan and combine with sugar, honey, kirsch and cream. Cook, stirring until the sugar is dissolved. Add chopped nuts and fruit and stir very well. Allow to become cold before using.

Any extra can be spread on a precooked pastry base and baked until the filling is well caramelised. Cut the pastry into slices or squares.

SYRUP

2 cups water	*3 tablespoons golden syrup*
1 cup sugar	*2 tablespoons butter*

Put all ingredients into a pan and bring to simmering point, stirring until the sugar has dissolved.

The evening was much quieter than lunch and we were disappointed that our first Celebration Menu was ordered by very few. And it is an incredible bargain. I cynically wondered whether it might have sold better had it been more expensive. I sipped the sparkling oxtail consommé, tasted the shellfish ravioli, looked at the poached salmon with its caper and lemon sauce, and ate half a portion of the cinnamon poached pears in a tokay sabayon and decided that the customers had missed a treat. Maybe next week.

19 JULY

*N*o glitz! No gambling! Great food!

I am unashamedly attempting to capture some of those out there who are as horrified as I am at the gambling culture that appears to have seized our city. Some months ago (13 May) *Age* columnist Janet McCalman wrote a trenchant criticism of casino culture, arguing that Australia did not become a prosperous developed industrial nation because its people gambled until the cows come home. Rather our prosperity derived from the application of old 'Victorian' values, 'prudence, self-discipline, thrift, foresight'.

Gambling, like the drink, is harmless in moderation, but when it becomes life itself, it is just as destructive. The casino will not enrich us, it will impoverish us. It produces nothing, it just consumes. It exports nothing, it creates nothing. It is a parasite.

But it seems irresistible for extraordinary numbers of Victorians at the moment. I ate at one of the restaurants sited in the complex to see for myself. At 11.00 at night there were children everywhere, children of five and six and older, as well as babies in prams, accompanied by parents who presumably had no problem with their choice of a late-night stroll through these glittering spaces as suitable family entertainment.

On the two occasions I have visited the National Gallery recently, I have paused to lean on the parapet above Princes Bridge and look down the Yarra along the Southbank Boulevard towards the Casino. A solid phalanx of humanity moves slowly along. I cannot dispute the appeal of the place. I can only mourn the inevitable lessening of support for the many other cultural and entertainment destinations that deserve a share of this enthusiasm. And of course I am not disinterested – Stephanie's Restaurant and all other formal or quasi-formal restaurants are suffering a great deal.

I am struggling to recall Stephanie Dowrick's words and to remember that it takes courage to face a new version of my old life, to which I must now adjust. Like any separation after years of familiarity, there is grief mixed with other emotions – such as relief, and there is also anger; anger that I recognise as destructive. It burns hotly in my body like the worst heartburn. I have to get past it and I will.

But it is important to acknowledge its existence at the moment. I realise what the word 'dreadful' means – full of dread. I am feeling dreadful today. Time to stop and hang out the washing or pack my bag for Sydney tomorrow morning. Some physical task often helps the dreads.

20–21 JULY

A delightful weekend centred on Government House in Sydney. As is suitable for a weekend celebrating food and ceremony, some part of the programme concentrated on the house itself. The dining room displayed its fine cedar table, extended to seat fifty guests and set with exquisite silver, crystal and plates, of patterns and periods that would have been used by the various governors of the colony. Each governor and his wife brought furnishings with them from England, and other furniture was commissioned from local craftsmen, resulting in an eclectic mix of styles. Research, conservation and reinstatement of the decorative ceilings in Government House were carried out by the New South Wales Public Works Department between 1983 and 1984 and were based on the 1879 design. The delicate friezes are a delight, and in the dining room the central motif in the ceiling has a light-hearted depiction of a rabbit, a wild duck among reeds, some wheat stalks and bunches of grapes, and the carpet offers an overall design of passionfruit flowers with entwined tendrils on a rich aubergine background.

Early menus were handed around. It was not difficult to imagine the occasions that had been celebrated in this grand room. While the menus included too many courses for modern digestions, this parade of classic dishes offered nothing too ostentatious, and most were put together with an eye to balance and seasonality. The menus noted what decoration would be displayed, and detailed the music to be played and the toasts to be offered.

For a dinner in November 1897 the flowers were 'sweet peas'. The menu read:

CONSOMMÉ
POACHED SALMON
CHICKEN WITH CREAM SAUCE
SADDLE OF MUTTON WITH GREEN BEANS
'BECASSINES' WITH ASPARAGUS
CHERRY ICE-CREAM

If one removed the saddle of mutton, or the chicken with cream sauce, and translated the becassines as squab pigeon, I would be pleased with such a dinner today. I love the idea of cherry ice-cream and will try it myself in November.

There were parallel sessions all weekend, so one could not hear and see everything. Very tantalising. Highlights included chef Cheong Liew, who was introduced by writer and food historian Barbara Santich as a 'master of flavours', discussing the importance of the tea ceremony at a Chinese wedding. Sui Ling Hui, banker turned food writer, guided her audience through the Chinese culinary calendar, indicating the importance and ceremonies given to certain ingredients (regrettably I missed her session due to banked-up Sydney traffic between the airport and Government House). Writer Colin Bannerman spoke of the insights awaiting anyone who shares his passion for early Australian cookery books, and I recognised quite a few titles from my own collection.

Cheong, Sui Ling and I enjoyed a delicious dinner and good conversation that evening at Bistro Moncur. Cheong has a dream to develop a finishing school for the best young chefs, who will come to be inspired by the best practitioners. We all feel that training in techniques and business management, while fundamentally important, does not give the full story. The passion that we have for flavour, for balance, for the ingredients themselves, for the culture and history and myth that surrounds eating, for enjoying a great meal and knowing why it is great, for all of these things and more, is largely lacking in present vocational training. We were all sufficiently practical to acknowledge that such a dream would be difficult to realise. Bureaucrats are unlikely to allot funding for something with such hard-to-quantify outcomes. But the best young Australian chefs would be the better for it. After all, only a handful are able to work with our inspirational practitioners and the influence of these people is being sorely under-utilised.

And the andouillettes and guinea fowl terrine at Bistro Moncur were both outstanding!

The major speakers on Day Two were Gay Bilson, currently consultant to Bennelong Restaurant at the Sydney Opera House, and Barbara Santich.

Gay described her involvement in what sounded like an extraordinary food ceremony. It was a winter solstice dinner, a performance entitled 'Food on Fire' and sponsored by the Sydney City Council as part of their Life in the Streets programme. Apart from the compelling description of roasting clay parcels in giant fires, enough to feed 300 people, Gay's main point was that she believes that there is a hunger for spirituality as we near the close of the century, that there is too little ritual and too little magic in our lives. She went on to claim that formal dining as we know it today contributes ceremony and should not be so readily pushed aside by those who persist in promoting only the very latest thing, the 'grill and garnish' school of cookery. That at the carefully set table we are capable of self-forgetting, of engaging in communion with other people, other minds, and that we need to remember that good food inspires good talk. And that the rituals and small ceremonies implicit in well-mannered eating and communing with others provides food also for the hungry soul.

Barbara spoke of the importance of the carver in medieval society, her major field of study. It was the carver who underlined the hierarchy of the table, presenting food to the highest-born first of all. Barbara suggested that these same hierarchies are still observed in traditional Aboriginal society and that when a kangaroo is killed there are important meanings in the manner in which the meat is divided among the tribe. Behind these decisions lies respect for family, respect for the group and respect for the food itself.

This paper was a very clever and erudite introduction to lunch, which was to be a kangaroo steamer. The word 'steamer' used in this way is uniquely Australian and refers to a dish of chopped kangaroo, salt pork, pepper and onion packed into a metal container (Barbara fancied a billy; I wondered also about a heavy iron camp oven) and left to steam in its juices for about four hours on the side of a camp fire.

In Barbara's latest book, *Looking for Flavour*, she expands on this outline and convinces the reader that the kangaroo steamer is the direct descendant of jugged hare, following the instructions given by Hannah Glasse in 1747. There is plenty of evidence that kangaroo was thought to approximate to the flavour of hare or venison, and the substitution of the metal billy, or enclosed camp oven, for the earthenware jug is early evidence of Australian resourcefulness. This is how we all chose to regard it, anyway, as we soaked up the winter sunshine before taking our seats at one very long table on the magnificent sandstone verandah.

As our conference closed an audience was gathering for a late afternoon

Monteverdi concert to be held in the grounds. The Cultural Committee has the pleasant task of deciding on suitable activities that will offer members of the public the opportunity to experience Government House and that do not conflict with the necessary care of the building and its contents.

22 JULY

First Cook's Companion cooking workshop today (on vegetables) and I was pretty nervous. Strange, really, as I have given so many cooking classes, but one is never sure that there are enough interesting things to say or do, or even worse, whether one will run out of time. Neither of these things happened. I sailed through the practical part of the class and then sat down with the students and enjoyed the lunch. Everyone handled and peeled an artichoke, and few had ever thought of peeling and using the stem. I was lucky to have some salsify delivered, which I added to a braise of potatoes and artichoke hearts. I prepared a gratin of silver beet stems and again was pleased at the students' positive response – most of them confessed that usually they threw away the stems. We made chestnut soup and grated celeriac, sliced fennel, and fried thin slices of lemon until they were caramelised and shaved parmesan cheese with a potato peeler. I made chicken stock and vegetable stock, and encouraged the students to cook with water if nothing else was available but to add flavour with extra-virgin olive oil, fresh herbs and lemons. And I baked Beurre Bosc pears for nearly three hours with butter, sugar and a vanilla bean.

All the recipes were from *The Cook's Companion* but the students seemed to enjoy the opportunity to ask questions and I enjoyed thinking of alternatives or variations to the recipes. My aim, as ever, is to reinforce constantly that to cook well is within everyone's grasp.

25 JULY

What a week! Three cooking classes, the second Foodie Friday at Stephanie's Restaurant today, and then a restaurant packed with people over

to see the Bledisloe Cup, a rugby game between Australia and New Zealand
to be attended by 100,000 tomorrow evening!

I crawled home after service this evening feeling absolutely exhausted,
yanked at in every limb – even my toenails ached! But the exhilaration was
marvellous. We have not had a week like this for probably four months.
The Restaurant powered through all this activity and it came up trumps.

At each cooking class the students were enthusiastic and interested.
The timing was impeccable. They arrived at 10.00 a.m., the practical work
finished at 12.00 noon and by 12.15 we were all eating a beautifully cooked
four-course lunch with appropriate wines. The rest of the classes are full.
I have decided that fourteen is the maximum number of students to have so
that everyone can have a proper look at what is going on in the relatively
small upstairs kitchen, originally designed to service private functions taking
place at the same time as a full restaurant downstairs. Sophie assisted with all
the organisation, including collating the recipes, offering morning tea and
later serving the lunch.

Meanwhile, downstairs, Foodie Friday was happening with a vengeance!
We had 'borrowed' Andy from the Cafe for the day. Sixty for lunch and
once again some delicious dishes were on the menu. I repeated the sausage
medley, but described it differently. 'Chicken sausage' and 'blood sausage'
evoked a much more positive response than 'boudin blanc' and 'boudin noir'.
Logical, really, but I had wondered about confronting the customers with
the word 'blood'. The ravioli of brandade in fish soup was also a winner, but
the triumph of the day was Michael's exquisite chicken liver, leek and
pickled tongue terrine. It looked so pretty, all pink and green and spring-
like. Immediately I decided it should go on the spring menu.

This is an outstanding terrine and the preparation is long and reasonably
complicated. Experienced cooks and those who love a challenge will enjoy
making this (and later on eating it!). At Stephanie's Restaurant it was served
with a small salad of peeled broad beans, black-eyed peas and asparagus tips,
and alongside a slice of toasted brioche topped with foie gras.

MICHAEL DE JONG'S CHICKEN LIVER, LEEK AND TONGUE TERRINE

The terrine is best assembled with warm ingredients so time the various cooking preparations so that all ingredients are still warm when you are ready to assemble it.

LEEKS
10 long skinny leeks, chosen with as much white as possible

TONGUE
1 pickled veal tongue
1 large carrot, sliced
1 leek, sliced
2 onions, sliced

2 stems celery, sliced
100 ml dry white wine
1 teaspoon black peppercorns
2 bay leaves

CHICKEN LIVERS
2 kg fresh chicken livers, to yield
   1.8 kg when trimmed
1 tablespoon brandy
2 sprigs of thyme, the leaves stripped
   from the stems
2 shallots finely chopped

2 cloves garlic, roughly sliced
20 g salt
2 tablespoons freshly ground black
   pepper
1 teaspoon nutmeg
½ litre clarified butter

ASSEMBLY
olive oil for the mould
plastic film
1 cup clarified butter

½ cup chopped flat-leaf parsley
salt
pepper

To cook leeks   Remove green part of leeks, wash leeks well and cook in plenty of lightly salted water until tender. Remove, drain well on kitchen paper and set aside.

To cook tongue   Place tongue in stockpot, cover with cold water and bring to boil. Boil rapidly for 5 minutes, remove scum, then reduce heat so that liquid is just simmering. Add sliced vegetables, wine, peppercorns and bay leaves. Simmer for 1½ to 2 hours or until quite tender when tested with a fine skewer. Cool in liquid and when cool enough to handle, peel off the skin. (Strain the stock, reboil it and taste. If it is delicious and not too salty, use it for a soup or a sauce. If too salty, throw it away.)

To poach livers   Marinate livers in brandy, thyme, shallots and garlic for 2 hours.

Remove livers from marinade, drain on paper towels, pat dry, season with salt and pepper and nutmeg. In a shallow pan heat the clarified butter and gently bring to simmering point. Reduce heat so that a thermometer registers 85°C. Place enough livers in the warmed butter to form a single layer and poach for 2–3 minutes. The livers should feel firm on the outside but still yield when pressed with the fingertip. Scoop out livers with a slotted spoon, allowing the butter to fall back in the pan, and reserve livers on a flat tray. Adjust heat to return butter to correct poaching temperature and continue until all livers are poached and drained. Discard this butter.

To assemble   Lightly oil the base and sides of a 1.5 litre cast-iron terrine mould. Line the mould with two layers of plastic film, leaving a good 8 cm overlap on each side. Chop the tongue into batons or slices.

Ladle a ½ cm layer of clarified butter into the mould and sprinkle with some of the chopped parsley. Now put 2 leeks side by side lengthwise in the mould, positioning them to one side of the mould. You may need to cut the leeks as it will probably take more than one to match the length of the terrine. Then add a layer of chicken livers, each liver overlapping the next to complete this bottom layer. Tuck in a few batons of pickled tongue in any little gaps. Season with salt, pepper and scatter with more parsley. Ladle over a little more clarified butter. Repeat this process, reversing the position of the leeks and livers in the next layer.

Continue to build the terrine using clarified butter to moisten each layer and plenty of parsley and seasoning. Press down on the layers lightly with your fingertips. The excess butter will ooze through to the top but all the ingredients will be nicely moistened.

The final layer should be mounded out of the mould by about 1 cm. Fold over the overhanging plastic film and make a few holes in the plastic with a skewer. Place the terrine on a tray with sides, and press it with a 2 kg weight or a couple of tins from the pantry. The excess butter will be removed from the terrine by leaving the weights in position while the terrine is refrigerated overnight.

Ease the terrine from the mould and cut with a very sharp knife. It is sometimes easier to leave the plastic film in place and to remove it from each slice as a separate exercise.

Serves 12

This evening we had three separate functions, all as a result of the rugby match. One group was belligerent and difficult and some in the party had obviously been drinking heavily before they arrived. It is disappointing when this happens and usually results in an unwinnable situation. Some antagonism was expressed early, so staff were changed in that room, and we did everything we could to speed up the food. Frankly, we were too busy in the kitchen to do more than register their petulance.

This week the Celebration Menu performed well. It started with a parmesan bavarois served with a pear sauce, was followed by the beautiful terrine, continued with our version of Janni Kyritsis's famous dish of poached beef fillet wrapped in a bone marrow dumpling, and the menu finished with a crème brûlée. (Janni was one of the very first chefs at Stephanie's Restaurant and had cooked this beef dish at a dinner we held in 1996 to celebrate our 20th birthday.)

I found the colourful banner painted for me by former Stephanie's chef John Flack, who now lives in New Zealand. John painted it one year when the Restaurant was to participate in the Harvest Picnic. The banner was wrapped around our marquee on the day, its stylised poppies the shape and colours of those on the china we use in the Restaurant. The painted strip of canvas was turned into a proper banner by a flag-maker and it is shameful that it has been bundled away in a cupboard for several years. But not any more. Anna has organised to have an extra panel made for it to advertise Foodie Fridays and it will be formally erected on the front lawn next Friday. The banner is about forty feet long and is so brilliantly coloured it will not go unnoticed!

Sophie and I are refining the wording for our important newsletter and checking our mailing list. Priorities next week are to do another round of cooking classes, send out the newsletter, price the new à la carte menu, and liaise with sommelier Brian and administrator Mark to ensure that all staff know how to produce bills. It will be a bit of a shock after twenty years to have to list individual items rather than write 'Food × 2'. The change will be handled by our computer system in a couple of weeks but we prefer to do it manually for a while, to be comfortable with the change and to be better able to brief whoever is to enter the new codes. Technology again. How much longer can I hover at the edge?

I am very eager to see how our positive week has been reflected in the bottom line. If the new buoyancy continues past the Bledisloe Cup invasion we will need more staff, but I cannot move in that direction yet. I would like to report all good news at next week's staff meeting.

27 JULY

We have had a lovely lunch party given by Gianna Trinchi, the Italian mother of one of the waiters at the Cafe. She invited all the staff. They took her at her word and more than thirty turned up. Such generosity. We all feasted on fried *baccala* fritters, chick pea soup, a splendid casserole of *stoccofisso* with black olives, capers and garlic, and marvellous fresh salads. (*Baccala* and *stoccofisso* are salted or dried codfish, available at good Italian or Greek delicatessens as either plump salted fillets, or as dried slabs of fish that look rather like cardboard shapes to the uninitiated.) When I left at around 4.30 a huge fire had just been lit in the garden fireplace and the young ones looked as if they were settling in. They were determined to enjoy their second-last free Sunday. In two weeks' time the Cafe will open seven days a week, due to overwhelming popular demand.

I asked Gianna for the recipe for the fish casserole and she was pleased to oblige, and included useful tips on how to recognise and prepare the fish. The recipe came with this note.

What I prepared for you that Sunday lunch was *stoccofisso* (stockfish) and not *baccala*. Both are similar (both are cod), but the base preparation of the cod varies. The *baccala* is par-boned and salted. *Stoccofisso* is whole and dried. In Italy the best quality of *stoccofisso* is the *Regno*, which in English is translated into 'spider'. This type of *stoccofisso* is regarded highly because its flesh is tender and odourless.

In Italy, *stoccofisso* is sold dried or soaked. If bought dried in Australia it has to be soaked in fresh cold water for a minimum of eight days. (Never use hot water.) After four/five days the fish is soft enough to be opened like a butterfly. During the eight days the water must be changed two to three times a day.

In Italy, *stoccofisso* is prepared widely, according to each region, so recipes are many and varied. My recipe is commonly prepared on both sides of the Stretto di Messina: Sicily and Calabria.

GIANNA TRINCHI'S STOCCOFISSO ALLA MESSINESE

1 kg stoccofisso (presoaked)
1 medium onion, chopped
1 clove garlic
a good olive oil
5–6 tomatoes, peeled, seeded, chopped
a handful of pine nuts
a handful of sultanas
2 tablespoons salted capers (soaked
    in warm water and dried well)

1 large handful pitted black olives
2 medium-sized potatoes, peeled and
    quartered
1 cup dry white wine
pepper to taste
a little salt (if necessary)

Cut the fish into large pieces, taking out the main bones. In a large pot on a moderate heat, sweat the onion and whole garlic clove in plenty of olive oil. Once the onion begins to caramelise, discard the garlic. Then add the tomatoes and cook for a further 5 minutes until the tomatoes begin to reduce to sauce. Add the fish, pine nuts, sultanas, capers, olives, potatoes, wine and pepper. Cover the pot tightly and bring to boiling point. Taste for salt. Reduce the heat and simmer for one hour. Check regularly to ensure that the liquid is always just covering the ingredients. If not, add a little water.

Serves 6

28 JULY

I took Dad to the doctor today to hear the results of his earlier CAT scan. It was confirmed that he did suffer a small stroke, probably when he had his major fall last year, which has left him weak on the right side. There is nothing to be done except watch his blood pressure and for him to take his time when moving around. Another serious fall is to be avoided at all costs. He is still in such good spirits after the cataract operations and cannot believe how brilliantly coloured the world has suddenly become.

Dad spent many of his adolescent years in the Victorian country town of Ballarat. I have arranged to spend a weekend there with him at a very comfortable hotel. We will drive around and look at old landmarks, and have a good dinner in front of a fire and a relaxed evening of conversation. This is a treat before I fly away. I am very anxious about how he will cope without me. I have arranged for his essential services to be taken care of, but eight weeks is a long time without tender loving care.

I unpacked a few of his boxes of books and papers that have been pushed into a corner for years. Now that I have a new bookshelf I can sort them all out. I marvel at his organisation. There were envelopes full of important birth and death certificates of present family members as well as long-departed relatives, carefully folded legal documents, bank statements pinned together, and folders of carefully captioned photographs. I am reasonably organised but I cannot claim to be in the same league. To collate all this primary material will be a fascinating retirement project for someone – brother John, perhaps?

As mentioned earlier, John works as a senior public servant in the Northern Territory's Department of Education. Darwin is so far away that we see each other very seldom, so it is inevitable that I feel isolated from his concerns and interests, and I think he feels the same about his family Down South. Once I have conquered e-mail, which really only means organising a phone line and obtaining a modem – neither a very difficult thing to do – we can perhaps try to catch up on the last fifteen years!

31 JULY

The Stephanie's Restaurant newsletter is finished and Sophie has done an excellent job with its formatting. It includes a calendar of events that continue while I am away and takes us into November. There will be gardening lectures followed by lunch, wine tutorials for women only also followed by lunch, and a guided cheese tasting by Will Studd and much more.

I am really getting into the swing of these classes, which is probably just as well. Tonight the Channel 9 'Getaway' team aired a programme they had filmed at the Restaurant a month ago. The show regularly includes a segment where viewers choose a fantasy wish and the team obliges. Two viewers had requested a chance to cook with me as their 'fantasy'. I was happy to do this and at the end of the programme it was announced that I was holding a limited series of cooking classes. Tomorrow we shall await the reaction.

Also tomorrow I fly to Sydney to attend the annual dinner of the Australian Booksellers' Association at which they announce their Book of the Year. The book selected is to be the one that they had most success with and had most enjoyed selling. I have been sent a plane ticket so I believe that there is something in the wind.

So July finishes with a huge input of energy, initiative and positive morale. The staff are smiling again, the bottom line is improving slightly, and I have come up from the depths and am now in full stride.

August

1 AUGUST

The Cook's Companion was voted equal Book of the Year, together with Robert
Dessaix's *Night Letters*, by the Australian Booksellers' Association at dinner
this evening! We each received a generous cheque, which I shall spend in
Italy on something just for me. *The Cook's Companion* has been a milestone
in my life. I never thought it would be so successful or be welcomed so
warmly by so many people. It continues to be a humbling experience to
have people stop me in trams, in the supermarket, in shops, on the street,
wherever I go, and thank me for writing a book that has changed their lives.
Overwhelmingly the responses reinforce my belief that it is anxiety about
'how to' that prevents many from even trying to cook for themselves. I have
succeeded in gaining the trust of my readers and they, in turn, feel liberated
and able to 'have a go'. It seems inadequate just to say thank you. I feel my
face pleating into my Cook's Companion smile, and wish I could think of
something more original to say.

The assembled booksellers all assured me they expect it to be big again
this Christmas. Penguin have produced a sumptuous limited edition that I
have not yet seen, although I have received the 500 special bookplates that
I am to number and sign.

We had nearly one hundred phone calls this morning from members of
the public who had seen the 'Getaway' programme on Channel 9 and
wanted further information regarding the cooking workshops at Stephanie's
Restaurant. I am scratching my head as how best to accommodate this
massive number. The existing dates are full so I shall have to open up new
ones. And they will have to be on my return from Italy. Sophie and I have
now set aside six more sessions and they are filling up fast.

New menu next Tuesday. We did a bit more testing before service on
Saturday night, and I was delighted with my duck breast rolled in cumquat
butter and parsley, seasoned with a fine scattering of *fleur de sel* and freshly
ground pepper.

Leigh has taken on the challenge of cooking the duck breast over rock
salt. This procedure gives an incomparable flavour to the bird but is a tricky
and dangerous technique. We use our very heavy black cast-iron skillets and
heat a layer of rock salt to very hot. The duck breast is cooked skin side

down until it is golden and most of the fat is rendered out. It is cooked for less than a minute on the flesh side and is then scraped free of salt crystals and laid to rest in a warm dish with melted cumquat butter, parsley and a little reduced duck stock. We then slice it very thinly and serve the accumulated juices as the sauce.

Once several ducks have been cooked in this manner a lot of duck fat accumulates in the salt and it sometimes catches fire. A heavy metal bucket in which to gently discard the fat-soaked salt is always at the ready, then a fresh layer of salt is added and the process starts again.

(A less hazardous method for home cooking is to place the duck breast skin side down in a preheated, very hot and heavy frying pan and leave it alone for five minutes. Do not prod it or shake it. The fat will render in the same way as in the rock salt method but you will not have to worry about jumping grains of red-hot salt that leap and sometimes stick to one's face. Turn it for one minute and then finish the dish as described above.)

On the same plate goes a small salad of torn radicchio and fennel.

3 AUGUST

*M*y life is improving on all fronts. Anna is a part of this. Today she helped me clean up my computer. As we removed old manuscripts and first drafts of published work, and stored speeches, and trashed letters relating to long-discarded projects, I had a wonderful sense of starting a new page in my life. Now I have plenty of hard-disk space to write on with abandon in Italy.

5 AUGUST

*T*he end of an era at Stephanie's and the beginning of something new. Tonight was a successful debut for à la carte pricing and a new menu.

The food was lovely with very few glitches. Jeff goes on a week's leave today so it is the first chance for Michael to head up the kitchen team. I will be hands-on this week (no cooking workshops until next week) to ensure the menu is well-launched and that all members of staff have a good opportunity to work with me. It is interesting that it takes only a few words or a rearranged plate to understand the concept of a dish more fully. For example, I had left the recipe for an espresso coffee semifreddo to be prepared. The cook conscientiously followed my published recipe but interpreted it in her own way. I suggested larger chunks of biscuit and a more flamboyant swirl with the caramel.

We serve a square of this semifreddo sandwiched between chocolate wafer biscuits alongside a scattering of chocolate-coated coffee beans.

STEPHANIE'S CHOCOLATE, COFFEE AND AMARETTI SEMIFREDDO DESSERT

This ice-cream will never set really hard so make it a day before serving it.

THE SEMIFREDDO

12 amaretti biscuits
70 ml (2½ fl oz) strong espresso
coffee mixed with 50 ml (1¾ fl oz)
Amaretto di Saronna liqueur
6 egg yolks
few drops vanilla essence

150 ml (5¼ fl oz) milk
260 g (9 oz) castor sugar
750 ml (26¼ fl oz) cream, whipped
1 tablespoon coarsely crushed
chocolate-coated coffee beans

Crush the biscuits and soak them in the coffee and liqueur. Beat the egg yolks and vanilla until thick and lemon-coloured. Heat the milk and sugar and simmer until the sugar has dissolved. Simmer for a further 2 minutes and then pour onto the yolk mixture and beat until the mixture is quite cold.

Fold in the whipped cream and biscuits with any remaining coffee and liqueur and the crushed coffee beans. Line a tin, 18 cm (7 in) square by 4 cm (1½ in) deep, with parchment, pour in the mixture. Swirl the caramel through the creamy mixture, then put it in the freezer. Just before serving cut the semifreddo into nine squares 6 cm (2¼ in) square. (Note: There will be eight slices to serve; one to test.)

THE CARAMEL

½ cup castor sugar   ¼ cup cream

¼ cup water

Boil the sugar and water until you have a dark caramel. Stand back as you pour on the cream. Stir until smooth.

THE CHOCOLATE BISCUIT WAFERS

110 g (3¾ oz) plain flour   125 g (4½ oz) unsalted butter at

15 g (½ oz) Dutch cocoa powder   room temperature

100 g (3½ oz) castor sugar   3 egg whites

150 g (5¼ oz) dark chocolate,

    melted over hot water

Mix together the flour, cocoa and sugar. Place the mixture in a food processor and add the rest of the ingredients in this order: chocolate, butter and egg whites.

Line a flat baking sheet with parchment. Make a template from cardboard or plastic so that your squares are precise. Paint on the mixture quite thinly using a spatula, to form biscuits a little larger than the squares of semifreddo. Bake at 200°C (400°F) until crisp. Cool for a minute and then remove to a cake rack to cool completely. These biscuits are very fragile so make a few extra. You will use 2 for each portion.

TO FINISH

On a cold plate, place one of the biscuits, topped with a square of semifreddo, then another biscuit. Scatter around a few chocolate-coated coffee beans.

Serves 8

6 AUGUST

*T*he extra cooking workshops are now completely full. I know that when I have some unpressured brain space (in Italy perhaps) I must deal with this message being given to me so strongly. The general public is very eager for me to teach and if I am to do this I have to find a way that is compatible with everything else I am responsible for. I will plan a new series for 1998, but not yet!

Dinner at the Restaurant tonight to test out the new dishes was very pleasant and was the first time John and Jean, newly returned from their posting in Frankfurt, had caught up with our mutual friends Helen and Bruce. What with Jean and John having just returned, Helen and Bruce about to leave for New York on study leave, and me about to leave for Italy, a good deal of the conversation revolved around travel and new horizons. It is a time of change for all of us and I would have to say the mood was very UP!

7 AUGUST

*H*olly leaves for her travels on Tuesday morning, less than a week away. When I remember how anguished I was at her last departure in 1992, it is interesting that both of us are taking this parting very much in our stride. Her father is collecting her at 4.00 a.m. We will say our farewells the night before!

On that last occasion I felt that a part of me was being wrenched away. When Holly was three months old she and her father and I had a long European holiday. Lisa, aged eight and a schoolgirl, was left behind with dear friends but I think, in retrospect, this was a mistake. We should all have been together. During the holiday Holly mostly travelled on the chest of one parent or the other in a green velvet pouch and it does not seem too fanciful to date our close bonding to this experience. Her departure for a year in France as a seventeen-year-old exchange student was our first real separation. Both Lisa and I successfully held back tears until Holly turned from those big doors at Immigration and ran back for one last hug. That, of course, was my undoing. I can still feel and see her clenched fingers and blue fingernails digging into my shoulder, hanging on until she was able to break away and step into the world alone.

Five years have passed since then. Holly is now a mature adult (twenty-two, in fact), very independent and capable. An eight-month separation seems much shorter than a year, especially as I shall be away for two of those eight months. Holly has completed a major sort of her bedroom – possibly the first since that other departure – and the pile of discarded paper to be put out for recycling is astonishing. She has been very reluctant up until now to give up a single exercise book or folder that had been part of any one of the fifteen years she has been a student!

I have to temper my impatience with this attitude, and my relief at seeing the stacks of paper moving at last, with the memory of how angry I was with my own mother, who obviously shared my dislike of accumulated 'stuff' and who, on my return from Europe after a two-year absence, informed me that she had sent most of my childhood books to an op shop and had got rid of a lot of old papers. Including, I remember, a 'novel' I wrote when I was thirteen. My book was about 'Someone in the Fourth' and was closely modelled on the English school stories I was addicted to at the time. I did not know then, and I still do not know, what The Fourth meant in terms of progress through the English secondary school system, but it seemed to be the age for wonderful goings-on in the dorm, with late-night escapades, and tuck boxes, and remits.

Much later Helen and Jean disillusioned me about the imagined delights of boarding school. They had both been boarders and had not found it altogether as fabulous as had 'Jen at the Abbey'!

But to this day I regret the disappearance of my complete set of the Billabong books. I also remember that it was from one of these wonderful books – *From Billabong to London*, when Nora and her father operated a Home for Tired People during the Great War – that I learnt that the correct way to serve a soufflé was with two hot silver spoons. The hot spoons were presented to Nora and she had to slip them into the soufflé, which was still a little creamy in the middle, and not wince as she burnt her fingers. Did I make all this up? I don't believe so. I am certain that the cook was described as having been French-trained and that she knew about proper food. I would have been about twelve when I read this. Already any food snippets caught my imagination.

8 AUGUST

Our fourth Foodie Friday and the best yet. More than sixty for lunch and a big house this evening. The food at lunch was great and we all enjoyed a busy and buzzy day. I must say that I do enjoy a day in the kitchen and I feel that I am super-charged with energy at the moment.

9–10 AUGUST

I am taking Dad to Ballarat tonight for our planned night out of town together. It will be my last chance for a while and we are both looking forward to it.

It has been a true voyage round my father. I heard stories I had never heard before. Dad lived in Ballarat for thirteen years from the age of nine. We drove past his old school, now rebuilt on the same site, past the smart Victorian bandstand in Sturt Street, and then down historic Lydiard Street. He pointed out the office in which he had once worked as a junior clerk for an estate agent. His early duties included collecting funds for the Methodist Babies' Home and collecting back rents. Dad described touring with his employer, Edgar, 'in an old Essex' (means absolutely nothing to me), when he and Edgar slept in the car with chaff bags on poles slung across the front seat to the back, while Edgar's 'intended' and a friend shared a two-man tent. Dad said they once went as far as Brisbane – an incredible distance for two country lads – and as they were unsure how to dress for 'the tropics', they wore pith helmets and loose khaki shorts. They were affronted when a Brisbane trammie leant out of a tram and yelled, 'Where are the tigers then, mate?'. A lovely story.

My grandfather was always a romantic and enjoyed thinking of unusual ways of tackling problems. As a builder during the Depression he was undaunted by a lack of building materials. He used scrap iron from the abandoned goldmines in the district and built reinforced concrete houses with a rough-cast finish. These extraordinary structures are still standing today. As Dad said (with a certain degree of satisfaction, I thought), while we gazed at the old family home in Durham Street and two others in Tennis Street, 'It'll probably take a bomb to blow them up'.

These houses are not beautiful but they are certainly different. Grandpa was fascinated by the plastic nature of concrete; he sculpted curved window boxes and window nooks and arches, built round leadlight windows in surprising places, and included spacious attic rooms, topping it all with a high-gabled roof. A sort of rustic, antipodean Gaudi, one might say!

We had a delightful evening at the Ansonia Hotel. Dad ordered borscht and kangaroo. I thought that there would not be many eighty-nine-year-olds who would be so adventurous.

Next day he directed the tour to the Botanic Gardens. Ballarat is famous for its begonias but they were not, of course, to be seen in the winter. Ballarat is also famous for its chill winds and here it did not disappoint. It was rather marvellous to walk against the wind and admire high Victoriana in the shape of the statuary pavilion holding larger than life-sized marble statues depicting the flight from Pompeii. The building, originally unveiled in 1888, has been restored recently. I loved its coloured glass, tessellated floor, the ghostly gleaming figures, the impeccably polished brass railings, and its bullnosed roof in corrugated iron. From inside the pavilion we looked out on carefully planted beds of pansies and poppies. It was very reminiscent of an English public garden of the same era. On to Lake Wendouree and Dad told of steamer rides on the lake and Sunday school picnics. Black swans, long-legged wading birds and seagulls were the only signs of life on this Sunday morning.

It is quite difficult to find accommodation suitable for someone using a walking frame. I have already mentioned the need for level surfaces, but we encountered a new problem in Ballarat. As both rooms had a shower within a bath Dad could not have a shower. There is no way he could manage to step into the bath, even if there had been a grab rail. He dislikes being so restricted and longed to have a bath. I was too frightened to encourage him, though, in case he could not get out again. The weekend was a great success nonetheless and will be long remembered.

11 AUGUST

$\mathcal{A}$ quiet, last day with Holly. She packed her bag and backpack and handbag and did a few practice marches down the hall, and then declared she could manage the lot up and down escalators and stairs.

As Holly is to leave before dawn tomorrow, we had an early dinner of her favourite meal (still!) of lamb chops and mashed potato. She gave me a cheerful hug and retired to bed.

At 4.00 a.m. Holly tiptoed into my room for a goodbye kiss. 'See you in Italy', she said. I hope so.

I then went straight back to sleep.

12 AUGUST

$\mathcal{T}$he messages are consistent from the cooking workshop students. They love the structure of the classes and the fact that they are able to ask me lots of questions and that I am so accessible. In my kitchen there is not much space but the students can touch or stir the food and taste the sauces before they are seasoned, observe the various stages of a process that may be difficult to describe, nibble at some raw fish paste to understand seasoning, or have a salt tasting or any one of a thousand things.

I shall offer a new series early next year. One important side benefit has been that I am much less anxious about Italy now. In many ways the structure of the Italian classes will be very similar to these classes and there will be more assistance. Also there will not be such a timetable to stick to. If lunch in Italy is half an hour later than anticipated, well, so what! *Male!*

Julie Gibbs has been an important friend through thick and thin and, as she knows only too well, there has been quite a bit of both this year. Tonight was her first visit to the new Stephanie's. We drank a little toast and then settled in. Julie was thrilled with her first à la carte meal and we had a relaxed and peaceful evening. We did some sums and noted that it now costs at least $10 less per person for a three-course meal. The staff have a new spring in their step and they have all stated how much they are enjoying the renewed buzz in the dining rooms.

Over dinner, Julie presented me with a parcel. In it was an advance copy of *Recipes My Mother Gave Me*, irresistible with its starry blue cover on which sails a Sunbeam mixmaster, a bit like a magic carpet, I thought. Probably how it appeared to many a housewife. It is always a very special moment when the work becomes a reality. I shall leave the advance copy with Dad when I go away so he can show it to his friends at the old folks' home.

Both Julie and photographer Simon Griffiths will join the Italian party for two weeks. There will be some serious work to be accomplished amid the fun. We are all hoping for great copy, great shots and a great book!

14 AUGUST

At the Cafe today. We are still mulling over Christmas trading. How much extra to order? For some items it doesn't matter much if we over-order as they have a long shelf-life. For other things we are not so sure. Simone has left to join her fiancée in the United States. Amanda has taken over the management of the shop, leaving Angie with more time to concentrate on the bigger picture. Amanda is efficient, a good communicator and a true food lover. We are more and more convinced that the shop should concentrate on selling those things closely connected to our areas of expertise and consequently we specialise in accessories that relate to cheese – boards, knives, bags, graters – or that are connected with Richmond Hill Cafe & Larder, such as our sunny yellow teapots, our hand-knitted egg cosies, our handmade pepper grinders and so on. Our range of preserves is exceptional and should be allowed to grow. The cookery books sell very well and we shall expand this area. But we are not grocers – our general grocery items just do not sell, and they take up undue shelf space in what is quite a small shop.

We have now introduced the continuous brunch menu on Saturdays and Sundays, which has resolved another problem. There is no longer any need to tell customers that breakfast has finished. If they want scrambled eggs at 3.00 p.m. they can have it!

Justin has made the stuffing and the dough for the *panzarotti* that Maggie and I shall offer as a first course at our joint cook-up in the Hunter Valley this weekend. *Panzarotti* are squares of a thin dough stuffed with a mixture such as cheese and ham and deep-fried. At Stephanie's Michael has made and bagged up two litres of jellied game stock. We agreed to this weekend away many months ago, believing it would be an invaluable opportunity to work together and to rehearse one of our intended Italian meals. The dinner is for Brokenwood Winery and we are off tomorrow afternoon. Julie and Damien will entertain us at their Sydney home on Friday night and they have invited Tony and Peter, our intended Italian assistants. As I have already mentioned, Peter will not be there for the classes but may come later for the holiday bit.

15 AUGUST

We have been thoroughly spoilt tonight by Damien. He prepared a wonderful crayfish salad with celeriac remoulade, followed by stuffed guinea fowl that was meltingly tender, served with Australian wild rice, some fine and smelly cheeses purchased from Richmond Hill Cafe & Larder, and a final act of devotion – a pear and green peppercorn soufflé! Not to mention outstanding French chablis and burgundy.

I remember the guinea fowl dish from many years ago and I also remember marvelling at the time at how moist and delicious it was. I asked Damien for the recipe. He is such a fine technician that any recipe he writes will be meticulous.

DAMIEN'S GRILLED BREAST OF GUINEA FOWL WITH SAGE AND BACON FARCE

Begin the day before serving.

3 guinea fowl, each about 1 kg
  dressed weight

FOR THE FARCE

200 g fat bacon (belly bacon
      preferred), diced
4–6 sage leaves

1 small clove of garlic, crushed
finely grated zest of 1 lemon
lemon juice and pepper to taste

FOR THE SAUCE

Stock

olive oil to roast the fowl and meat
carcasses of the guinea fowl,
      drumsticks, necks and wings
300 g chopped gravy beef
250 g chicken necks
200 ml dry white wine
1 large onion, peeled and chopped
1 carrot, peeled and chopped

1 stalk celery, chopped
water to cover the ingredients
2 cloves garlic
bacon trimmings from the farce
2 strips lemon rind
a bouquet of thyme, 1 bay leaf,
      some parsley stalks

Sauce reduction

1 small onion, peeled and chopped
60 ml port
60 ml red-wine vinegar
the reduced stock (see method)

50 g cold diced butter
½–1 tsp freshly ground black pepper
a few extra drops of red-wine vinegar

Bone the fowls by removing the drumsticks and thighs in one
operation. Then remove the breasts, chop the wings back to 2 cm from
the breast flesh. Remove the skin from the thighs and drumsticks and
cut off the drumsticks. Cut away the flesh from the thigh bones and
reserve the meat to use for another purpose. (Damien makes a delicious
little crepinette, a sort of high-class hamburger, using this reserved
meat, seasonings and minced pork belly.)

Chop up the carcass in small pieces.

The farce   Combine all the ingredients in the food processor and work
to a coarse paste. Taste for salt and keep the farce sharp to taste with
lemon juice and spicy with pepper.

The stock   Heat some olive oil in a baking dish and add the chopped carcasses and brown carefully.

Remove carcasses to a stockpot and continue to brown the beef and chicken pieces until all are done. Add these to the stockpot. Pour off the fat from the baking dish into a bowl, passing it through a strainer. Add the wine to the pan and boil for a few minutes while scraping up all the sticky sediment. Add this liquid and sediment to the stockpot. Return the reserved fat to the baking dish and heat. Add the peeled and chopped onion and carrot as well as the chopped celery and cook slowly to brown them. Transfer to the stockpot with a slotted spoon. Discard the fat, add a cup of water to the pan, boil and scrape up the sediment and transfer to the stockpot. Cover the contents with cold water, add the garlic, bacon, lemon rind and bouquet of herbs and bring to the boil. Skim well and reduce to a simmer for 4 hours. Skim from time to time and replenish the liquid removed with fresh cold water. Strain, skim the fat and reduce the liquid to 300–400 ml.

The reduction and sauce concentration   Bring the onion, port and red-wine vinegar to the boil and reduce to half the original volume. Add the reduced stock, return to the boil, skim and simmer for 10 minutes. Strain into a small pan. The butter, pepper and extra red-wine vinegar are not needed until the moment of service.

Filling the breasts   Place the breasts on a board. Using a piping bag filled with the farce, fill the breasts, piping between the skin and the flesh. Try to keep the skin attached on the breast bone (the top) and the wing joint. Pat the farce evenly across the breasts and refrigerate until needed, skin side up and uncovered to dry the surface.

At this point almost all the work is done, except for the garnish and cooking on the day of service.

Cooking the breasts   Heat a ribbed cast-iron grill or a roasting dish with a solid base. Brush the skin side of each breast with a little olive oil. Seal the breasts on the skin side. Reduce the heat and continue cooking principally on the skin side. Turn them over to finish off.

Approximately 10 minutes in all. Remove to a warmed dish and rest for 5 minutes before serving.

Reheat the sauce and when it boils, work in the butter with a whisk, add the pepper. Taste, adding a few drops of red-wine vinegar to sharpen the sauce.

Serves 6

After dinner Julie modelled the dressing gowns Tony and Peter have made for the students, and very fetching she looked too. In fact, we may have to increase the order! Each gown has an embroidered pocket with the words 'Stephanie and Maggie in Italy, September 1997' superimposed over the map of Italy. A great souvenir for each of our students – and necessary too as we will all share bathrooms.

16 AUGUST

𝒜 slow start to the Hunter trip as Maggie and I detoured to my favourite clothes shop, Reads, conveniently close to our hotel in Woollahra. A few purchases later we went to have a good look at Jones the Grocer. They buy Maggie's products and cheese from Will Studd, and I noticed they also had a few of the Stephanie's Restaurant items. The owners had recently visited Richmond Hill Cafe & Larder so we were able to mutually congratulate each other on our very different enterprises. It is a most attractive shop and it takes its brief as 'grocer' seriously. The stock is a mix of tinned and preserved foods, with a big section for dried fruits, nuts, pulses and so on, a small selection of fruits and vegetables, plus a great delicatessen counter with food to go, as well as sausages and cheeses. Something for everyone, and on this Saturday morning business was brisk. I took note of the neatness of the snap-locked plastic boxes, as we are finding that our cellophane bags with stapled paper labels look tatty after several customers have handled an item.

On to the Hunter.

Cessnock still has a few of its original wide verandahs shading the main shopping street. The surrounding countryside was drought-dry, the sky boldly blue without a wisp of cloud. There were few animals to be seen, just leaning corrugated-iron sheds in various shades of rust. And then we started to see the Hunter Valley vines, the rows looking very stark in their winter bareness. At Brokenwood we were greeted warmly by winemaker Ian Riggs and shown to the kitchen.

The first surprise was that the kitchen was no more than a metre from the first dining table, so this was to be full-frontal cooking and serving. No hiding or skulking possible. And no blood and guts on display, I thought, contemplating the pigeons we had intended to roast and then carve from the bone.

No matter how one anticipates and prepares there is always the unexpected to contend with when working in a different environment. And everything takes so much longer, when even a search for a pepper mill can occupy a few minutes, whereas in your own space you know exactly where it is. Or where to clamp the pasta machine. Fortunately the adrenalin also flows in such circumstances, and after a few desperate minutes we got down to work.

The most difficult things we had to deal with were wrongly calibrated ovens that refused to heat up sufficiently, no exhaust system, so searing pigeons on the hotplate filled the room with smoke that we had to hope would clear in time (it did), and worst of all, two new baking trays, in one of which we cooked pears and in the other, artichokes. The pans looked pristine as we added olive oil for the artichokes and butter for the pears, but they had a residual coating that was not obvious and it caused severe discoloration of the artichokes and had a similar but less worrying effect on the pears. We trimmed the artichokes and transferred them to another pan and thankfully they still tasted very good. The food mill only had one disc and it was the finest one. Thank goodness for our two assistants, Steve and Brett, volunteers from neighbouring restaurants. Maggie had great difficulty rolling and filling the little pasta *panzarotti* as it was 28°C, and with the additional heat being generated by the hotplates, the dough dried to a biscuit texture in seconds, so she could only roll out a small piece at a time, rather than one long strip.

As I mentioned, the method of cooking and serving the pigeons had to be changed from our original plans. I seared them on the hotplate and then removed the legs and breast fillets. The legs went back into the oven on baking-paper-lined trays, and the breast fillets were arranged flesh side down in a series of sauté pans between which I divided the beautiful stock that I had infused with extra roasted pigeon trimmings and garlic. Steve undertook the herculean task of forcing potatoes, celeriac and garlic simmered in cream through the devilishly fine sieve. By the time the piper piped in the guests we stood ready – benches wiped, and smiles on our faces.

Brett stayed with us through the service and was still there smiling at midnight, by which time Maggie and I were almost swaying, and it was not due to the glass of Bollinger or the beautifully aged 1985 Brokenwood Semillon that we had imbibed by then.

The assembled thirty guests had a marvellous time. And we decided that as we had coped so well with thirty, our Italian dozen would be a breeze!

The next day we tried to find a spot for brunch. Robert's restaurant was apologetic – they had a function due at noon. At Peppers Guesthouse the lunch menu was not available for another half an hour and we had planes to catch. But we could have a bowl of pasta. So we sat on their delightful verandah, enjoying the sunlit view of elegant eucalypts and, further away, a winding creek edged with peppercorn trees, and felt at peace with the world, fully rested and relaxed, enjoying the glow of virtue that results from a job well done.

19 AUGUST

*A*nd now I am writing a new list every morning. 'Things to do today.' Many of the items are ongoing projects that must be left in someone else's hands.

~ Copy and ideas for a new newsletter for Stephanie's that must go out a week after my return.

~ Streamline the production of the puddings and shortbread for the Cafe and for Stephanie's.

~ Set aside three days for publicity for *Recipes My Mother Gave Me*. Anna has produced a schedule of events for me that stretches until April 1998!

~ Tomorrow a photo for *Stern*, a German magazine, and a 'typical
   Australian recipe'. As I know that Germany imports some kangaroo
   I have decided to give them a recipe for roasted fillet of kangaroo with
   a note for their readers that they could substitute hare or venison.
~ Photo for *The Age Good Food Guide* awards night. With the change of
   ownership at Stephanie's has come the need to change the photo they
   have in their files. The awards night is the night after I leave. Valerie will
   represent the Restaurant and Lisa and Angie will represent the Cafe.
~ I have also had to nominate someone to possibly accept an award for
   The Cook's Companion at the New South Wales Food Media Club awards,
   also to take place several days after I leave.

Yesterday I forgot to attend a publicity meeting with Penguin's senior
publicist. Fortunately she knows this is unlike me and has made another
time.

Even before I get on this plane I must plan my re-entry. I am encouraging
communication by fax rather than mobile phones. We are hoping that the
fax at our villa will work efficiently.

20 AUGUST

*L*ast cooking class today. My energy levels are way up and I am charging
into each day. I am always hungry, too. Up early, exercising, working, then
socialising, probably drinking too much wine and sleeping fitfully. And
I spring out of bed, ready to add to the current list.

Anna is marvellous. She is able to keep up with this manic energy, and is
such a doer. The perfect personal assistant and so multiskilled. I have
accepted an invitation to go on a cooking trip to Christchurch in February,
but have regretfully refused a week-long trip to Avignon with the Olive Oil
Council. And tomorrow I am off to Perth for more doings. Perth stages its
own Masterclass weekend (as does Brisbane) so there is a Masterclass circuit
developing, always hungry for talent. A class with Maggie and a session with
Will, each one given twice. The labna balls in olive oil have been carefully

vacuum-packed, as have bags of spiced cherries, green tomato relish and oatcakes.

Jean and John have already moved into my home and we are all pleased with the arrangement. Rosie the poodle adores Jean, and Jean is very taken with Rosie. Rosie has not had as much attention since Jean was last here. Long walks, early dinners, brushes, a lap to snuggle into. They are going to get on famously. Lisa has agreed to emergency dog-sitting.

In the garden, spring is almost here. The street trees are prettily pink. In my front garden I admire the juxtaposition of the white daphne blossom set against the *Azalea fragrantissima*, with snowdrops and white narcissus at ground level. In the side garden I have a pink daphne near a small-blossomed camellia sasanqua and knots of winter roses, their floppy green and rose petals like old-fashioned sunhats. In the back garden the flowering currant has bunches of pink flowers. There are growing buds and shoots on the bluebells and new shoots on all the roses. I am pleased to remind myself that I will be back in time for the roses.

My bedtime reading has lately been *Night Letters* by Robert Dessaix, my co-winner of the Australian Booksellers' Association Book of the Year. In his book Dessaix reminds me that not all of Italy is one romantic landscape of smoothly rounded green hills, thrusting cypresses and weathered stone villas. He is aghast at the dirt and the crowding, the pollution and the ugliness of its mass housing. I recall staying with Jean and John one summer when they lived in a large house on the outskirts of Rome. The walk to the station was along a winding road edged with trees in fluttering new leaf. There were rounded hills in the distance and the blurred dome of St Peter's, but in the foreground was an astonishing flotsam and jetsam of discarded possessions abandoned to rot. Among them on this day was an old fridge, a broken chair, and casually tossed plastic sacks of garbage.

Night Letters is captivating. Dessaix skilfully weaves his stories and travel anecdotes and the mood dips and rises between sadness and acceptance, gentle humour and acute observation.

21 AUGUST

An American wine and food writer, Dan Phillips, dropped into the Cafe yesterday to give me a copy of a newsletter he had spoken of on an earlier visit. This particular issue of *Simple Cooking* reviews some specialist books that I may order from the States. These personal newsletters are intriguing. I subscribe to *The Art of Eating* by Edward Behr and subscribed to our own Michael Boddy's newsletter. Michael's newsletter has since sadly been suspended and is sorely missed, Edward Behr's is a very academic publication, while *Simple Cooking* seems to be aimed at a broader market.

Off to sunny Perth and, amazingly, Maggie was on the same plane. She had expected to arrive some hours later.

22 AUGUST

The Masterclass does not start until tomorrow, so today we could pursue a few other connections. Maggie and I visited The Grocer, a Perth wholesaler of good things, and Maggie signed several of her books and I browsed. I picked up a flyer telling me that this very same weekend there was a cultural and scientific symposium on the olive, to be held at historic New Norcia and to be presented jointly by the Benedictine Community of New Norcia and the University of Western Australia.

I know that it is irritating when an outsider presumes to comment on local arrangements, but it does seem a pity that the Perth Masterclass and this symposium were organised at the same time and yet are located at about 130 kilometres apart! Perhaps it is an example of no communication between groups who ought to be in touch with each other. As a Masterclass visitor I would have liked to have been given the option of visiting the monastery to listen to some of the speakers, or, if that was too difficult, surely some of the speakers might have been asked to present their papers at the Masterclass. There is no doubt that for Perth food lovers the timing and location of these two important meetings would pose a dilemma.

I should mention, though, that Kingsley Sullivan, who has re-established the original wood-fired oven at New Norcia and bakes bread there in commercial quantities, was at the Masterclass to explain some of his secrets.

The olive oil from New Norcia is delicious and we will be using it in our demonstration. It is in very short supply as the revival of the olive press and the husbandry of the trees have gathered momentum only over the last few years. The monastery itself has been located in New Norcia for 150 years, founded by Dom Rosendo Salvado in 1846, and I would love to visit it. I read in a magazine article about its Spanish architecture, richly decorated interiors, Old Masters' works of art and extravagant furniture and furnishings. It will have to wait until another time, as the programme over the next two days is very full.

We lunched with the inimitable Jim Mendolia, the sardine and anchovy king, and his wife, Lyn, at the Indiana Teahouse, a pavilion right on the beach at Cottesloe, looking through cane shutters to the blue of the Indian Ocean. Gabrielle Kervella, the queen of goat's cheese, and Will Studd were also at the table.

Jim brought along samples of his sardine fillets smoked over Western Australian jarrah wood and his lightly cured sardines that are then soused with wine vinegar and herbs. They were delicious and the chef had prepared a finely chopped salsa of preserved lemon, capers and parsley, which went very well with both, I thought. I particularly like those smoked sardines and can see them as a salad item on one of our Cafe menus soon.

Jim also had a sample of anchovy butter for me. This will be a new item at Richmond Hill Cafe & Larder from next week after a long delay due to problems with tins and lids, too frustrating to go into but part of the endless saga of Australian packaging.

We are in the midst of a surge of interest in small-scale production of preserves, especially pickles, jams and sauces. No matter how original the contents, the range is mostly packaged in one of the same three or four containers that are produced by the Australian giant ACI. Only a few other shapes are imported and handled by distributors and wholesalers, and these shapes can disappear overnight if a decision is made not to import any more.

It is very frustrating when one views the exquisite packaging that sets many imported products apart. Chargrilled eggplant pickle from Italy, sold in a smoothly rounded jar that permits the slices to display their curves most beautifully, adds appeal (and dollar value) without a doubt. And yet my eggplant pickle tastes at least as good but will always look more pedestrian in its straight up and down, 'short back and sides' jar.

ACI points out that it is prohibitively costly to manufacture the 'die', or mould, for a new shape and that the minimum numbers that would make a new shape possible are very high. The only other alternative is for an individual or a company or a wholesaler to import packaging. In the case of jars, there are plenty of beautiful examples available, notably in Italy, where a developed sense of aesthetics seems to be a part of everyday life. But to do so one must import a container load, which is approximately sixteen palletts. Depending on the size of the jar a pallett may contain around 2,000 jars. So to import 32,000 jars will require a minimum outlay of $25,000 – an enormous amount of capital for a small company, and almost always an impossibly large amount. So the vast majority of Australian-packed produce looks pretty ordinary. We all do our best with label design.

23 AUGUST

*T*he first session of the Masterclass weekend introduced Will Studd and Grant van Every to discuss matching wine and cheese. Confessing to special interest I found this fascinating. Seven cheeses were tasted and only one was considered to be best matched with a red wine. And in Grant's opinion the worst wines to have with cheese are cabernet sauvignon and pinot noir.

Cheesemakers have long known that for many cheeses, white wines, and frequently sweet white wines, offer the most perfect pairing. And it follows that it makes little sense to present three or more vastly different cheeses and to expect a single style of wine to show either the cheese or the wine to its best advantage. This leads to interesting implications as to how we should be presenting cheese in our restaurants. At the Cafe we have introduced a cheese menu, with explanatory notes, but after this session maybe we will suggest that cheeses be offered singly with a glass of one particular wine.

This session offered seven pairings and I have listed my three favourites.

1 FRESH CHEESE

Fromage de Chevre, made by Julie Cameron at Meredith Dairy
in Victoria
Pascall Jolivet Sancerre 1995

Will points out that this style of cheese is characterised by fresh
acidity and a lingering creaminess that leaves the palate unconfused.
Grant comments that this wine, with its steely, crisp acidity, has
the structure to break up the chalky texture of goat's cheese, and
the subtlety of its fragrance does not overwhelm the perfume of
the cheese.

2 INTERNAL BLUE MOULD

Cropwell Bishop Stilton
Mount Horrocks Cordon Cut Riesling 1996

Will points out that all good blue cheese has immense flavour
strength with a touch of ammonia. It needs to be high in salt to
control the growth of unpleasant moulds.
Grant comments that, in general, blue cheeses are best with
sweet white wines and that red wines can taste tannic or like
varnish if taken with blue cheese. The sweetness of the fruit and
the unfermented sugar in this preferred wine offers a perfect
counterfoil to the salty tang and the volatile mould components
of the cheese.

3 HARD COOKED CHEESE

Heidi Gruyere
Campbell's Liquid Gold Tokay

Will describes this cheese as having a concentrated, slightly
sweet flavour and a pleasing smooth texture.

Grant says that this wine is a fine example of the great and
unique style of wine northern Victoria produces. The wine has
luscious toffee and malt characters with a long finish. Its nutty
flavours go superbly with the baked custard flavour of the
cheese, but remember to sip the wine as it is strong and can
overpower anything else in the mouth.

Maggie and I enjoyed our own session and it went very well.

Western Australia is the only state commercially farming white rabbits at
this time. We prepared this splendid ingredient in two ways. Maggie jointed
the rabbit and cooked it with verjuice. I boned the rabbit and stuffed it and
roasted it as a ballotine. We sautéd the superb rabbit liver and presented it
on the plate alongside a purée of dried broad beans that was also part of the
demonstration. We told the class that the purée was more delectable if
the broad beans were skinned and that this can only be achieved by either
laboriously skinning each bean after it has been soaked, or by soaking,
cooking and then passing the purée through a food mill to hold back the
skins. A young woman in the audience then said that she and her family sell
skinned dried broad beans from her business, Kakulas Sisters in Fremantle,
and on the second day of the class she presented us with a packet each.
What a find! We were so delighted and have asked Eleni Kakulas to let us
know if these beans are imported from the Middle East or whether they are
grown (as she suspects) in the Ord River area in the north-west of the state.
Discoveries such as this reward those prepared to ask questions, or willing
to travel to new horizons and meet other food lovers with exciting tastes to
share. (In fact, we later found that the beans are imported by a firm in
Brunswick, a suburb of Melbourne!)

In the second part of the demonstration Maggie made a simple sauce
agresto, her Italian herb and nut paste, its sourness coming from verjuice,
which we paired with fresh goat curd from Gabrielle Kervella as a simple
and refreshing starter.

Once again, we are really rehearsing for Italy – the rabbit dish is on the
menu for Day Three of each cooking school!

Later in the day Will and I attempted to describe our concept of a 'food
destination' in a session entitled 'The Richmond Hill Mob'. I had samples of

some of our products to show – green tomato pickle, labna balls, spiced cherries, oatcakes and Maggie's quince paste – and Will offered tastings of selected cheeses. The thrust of our presentation was that excellence is what we are striving for. The ability to choose a great loaf of bread is as important as the ability to taste and choose from a range of fine olive oils. We believe that high quality appeals to a wide range of people of both sexes, all ages and from all walks of life. Often the best response comes after a customer is offered a taste or is otherwise helped to understand the products. Friendly, accurate information in language anyone can understand is proving to be very effective.

In between the sessions there is socialising, book signings and many cups of tea. Tonight we are to dine with butcher Vince Garreffa and his wife, Anne, at his home, where no doubt Vince will be joined by his friend and equally passionate cook John Maiorana for what I imagine may be an extravaganza of Italian food. Vince's business card says 'Vincenzo Garreffa – Prince of Flesh'!

24 AUGUST

*A*n extravaganza was an understatement. The guests included fellow chefs Chris Manfield and Cheong Liew, broadcaster Alan Saunders, cheesemaker Gabrielle Kervella, staff from the Hilton and John and Eve Maiorana. Vince and John did the cooking and Anne served the wine and was a relaxed host.

Our first Italian dish was a magnificent frittata with lightly sautéed sliced new season's artichokes. This was followed by a risotto of stinging nettles.

In *Recipes My Mother Gave Me* I commented on my mother's recipe for nettle soup and it made me realise that I no longer see clumps of luxuriant nettles as I did when I was a child. (I well remember the pain of a few nettle stings on one's bare calves.) Presumably most have been sprayed out of existence. However, John has been carefully protecting the stand of nettles in the bottom of his garden for just this occasion. The risotto was excellent – creamy, olive-green, very grassy and herbaceous. (After all, one describes a wine like this, so why not a risotto made from a wild grass?)

Next came more fruits of the garden. Young broad beans still in their pods, chopped and braised with extra-virgin olive oil. They were partnered with braised and stuffed artichokes and a small piece of the exquisite White Rocks veal that I have been buying from Vince for Stephanie's Restaurant for some years now.

The two cooks dashed to and from the kitchen, rarely joining the guests, which was a pity as they are both great raconteurs. Vince has installed an extraordinary kitchen range with a 1.2 metre-wide oven large enough to hold a whole lamb. He designed the kitchen range himself and it was handmade to his specifications by Giovanni Agostini in Perth. It is called a Gianfranco. The milk-fed lamb of about eight kilos was rubbed with oil, seasoned and slowly roasted, and basted with pinot noir from Margaret River! Eventually the roasted lamb, all golden and shiny, was brought to the table on a board that could have come from the famous Breughel painting *The Peasants' Wedding*. Vince carved with impressive accuracy. The lamb melted in the mouth.

As a digestive, and in the way one might more usually offer a green salad, a platter of garden-picked fennel was passed around. The bulbs were left whole and we just pulled a layer or two as we wanted and ate them quite unadorned. How often we talk about freshness. How rarely are we able to eat something picked only minutes before. And what a difference there is.

The evening looked set to go on for hours, but I was about to fall asleep at the table so we made our farewells, leaving Vince and Anne's daughter Marisa cheerfully washing a mountain of dishes.

What generosity, and how privileged we have been to be part of such an evening. Will we find such splendid cooking in any Italian *ristorante*?

JOHN MAIORANA'S STINGING NETTLE RISOTTO

60 shoots of nettles, the youngest and most tender possible	1 small white onion, finely chopped
	60 g prosciutto, finely chopped (optional)
1.5 litres chicken stock	300 g arborio rice
60 g butter	150 ml dry white wine
2 tablespoons olive oil	60 g parmesan, freshly grated

Carefully wash the nettles and remove any stringy stalks. Boil the stock and keep hot for future use. Simmer the nettles in 2 cups of the stock for 3 minutes and then drain. Keep the stock. Chop nettles very finely and set aside.

In a heavy-based pan melt the butter and the olive oil over moderate heat. Add the onion and prosciutto and cook on moderate heat until the onion is golden. Now add the rice and stir thoroughly so each grain is well-covered with the oil and butter.

Raise the heat to high and add the white wine. Stir thoroughly until the wine is reduced completely. Lower heat to moderate again and add about ½ cup of the stock and continue to stir. Continue to add stock as it is absorbed and cook the rice a further 15 minutes. Add the chopped, soaked stinging nettles and reserved stock and cook for a further 5 minutes, stirring thoroughly to get an even, green colour. Add the parmesan cheese, stir and serve immediately.

Optional variation If you have access to male zucchini flowers (flowers that are on a thin stem, not attached to the fruit), shred or chop them and sweat them in a little butter or olive oil. Stir them into the risotto at the same time as the parmesan cheese.
Serves 6

25 AUGUST

*O*n the way home from Perth I detoured to Maggie's Adelaide apartment so we could spend a few hours checking on last-minute arrangements for Italy. Everything seems in place. Final recipes have gone to Caroline for editing before they are included in the student booklet.

The wines and their delivery details have all been confirmed (but not yet paid for). Our new credit cards seem to work. The extra dressing gowns have been made and packed. We have a list of every student and his or her hour and mode of arrival in Siena. Our tickets have arrived. Time to think about packing! I haven't bought the Vegemite, but I think I might.

Back home to find a long e-mail from Holly faxed to John-in-residence, who is an enthusiastic 'surfer'. She was surprised to see Melbourne trams in the streets of Seattle and took herself for a nostalgic tram ride. The tone of the letter was very cheerful. She is now starting her tour of the United States, moving every day or so to a different city, and will be more difficult to contact. I shall send her an e-mail (thanks to John again) just before I leave and she will pick it up in Toronto before she heads off to France.

26 AUGUST

Today I interviewed Craig, a prospective new pastry cook, and I think he will be a fantastic addition to the Stephanie's Restaurant team. Enthusiastic, fast and competent, if today's workout was a sample. I have also promoted Leigh to the position of third chef in recognition of his loyalty, hard work and commitment. I am leaving the kitchen with a strong brigade dedicated to preparing good food and I am as confident as it is possible to be that they will uphold all that Stephanie's Restaurant stands for. I am very fortunate to be able to move away for so long with such confidence.

Administrator Mark Bowdern, Brian, Valerie and I walked through the building and I commented on various details I would like to see attended to in my absence. I have very good people and they are all wishing me a fantastic Italian experience with not a trace of resentment that I will be away so long. Sophie has the Restaurant marketing in hand and she and Anna will work well together. At the Cafe the team is in such full swing they may not even notice that one of the partners is not around. I have every confidence there too.

I met with the Penguin publicity people today. I have chosen the menu for the launch of *Recipes My Mother Gave Me*, which is to be on Remembrance Day, a few days after my return. The recipe for Lorraine soup included in my mother's original is a much-diminished version of a richly luxurious soup that she had discovered in one of her old cookery books (*The Cook and Housewife's Manual*, by Meg Dods [Mistress Margaret Dods], published in 1837). We will make the original version, thickening the broth with a paste of pounded chicken breast and almonds rather than the flour, milk and almond thickening Mum has recommended for reasons of economy.

And now I must get to the suitcases!

Late this evening I was rung at home to inform me that one of the editors of *The Age Good Food Guide* was dining at Stephanie's. Rita Erlich has always been very positive about the Restaurant and I have felt that she understood my cooking better than some. I decided that she would not have expected me to get out of my baggy pants and cease my suitcase sorting to go and greet her, so I sent warm wishes instead and instructions to offer her a complimentary slice of Michael's exquisite chicken liver, leek and pickled tongue terrine.

As *The Age Good Food Guide* is well and truly printed now and will be released next Monday I assume that this was a private visit, maybe to share a well-deserved quiet evening with a friend, rather than to pass public judgement. Although I suppose if one is a food critic one can hardly put one's critical faculties in a back pocket even when not officially on duty.

27 AUGUST

I am not so sure now as I had a photocall this morning from *The Age*. One fascinating thing about writing a diary is that I can wonder about certain things and later all is revealed.

When the tumultuous events took place at Stephanie's (two months ago now!) I sent a newsletter to *The Age* and the *Herald Sun* and was rather hurt that there was no printed acknowledgement in *The Age* of the change from fixed price to à la carte, or of the cooking workshops or any of the other initiatives I set in place at such dizzying speed. There was a mention in the *Herald Sun*.

I had thought that I'd contributed enough to the industry to deserve four lines at least in the newsy column that appears each Tuesday in *The Age's* 'Epicure' pages. But nothing was printed. Oh well, I said to myself as I drove along (I often converse with myself in the car). I don't have any friends there! Obviously the press has decided that I have had too many centimetres of newsprint this year. I would have thought the fact that I introduced fixed price to this State and it is being abandoned after twenty years was an important story, but apparently not. Surely it is news, though. And are they not there to report news?

Now I wonder if they intend to acknowledge it in a more lengthy way next Tuesday at the book launch and awards night. I will be arriving in Rome airport about that time. But Lisa, Angie and Valerie will be at the ceremony and have booked a table at the Cafe afterwards to celebrate or commiserate.

Today is my last day working at Stephanie's, so Jeff, Michael and I have gone over the production plans for Christmas produce, possible dishes to include on the lunches throughout December, possibilities for Christmas Day luncheon and emergency plans if there is a staffing casualty. Sophie and I have discussed the November newsletter, the Spring Racing Carnival, and the next series of cooking workshops. I am now leaving this to Sophie and Anna. Valerie and I have chosen silver teaspoons and some extra coffee cups. Mark and I have agreed that a fortnightly faxed bulletin from the secretary to me will be quite sufficient.

That's it for work here, although I will return for dinner on Thursday night with Angie and Duffy and on Saturday night with Julie and Damien.

28 AUGUST

Today is my last day working at the Cafe. Nicky and I have reviewed the menu and discussed a replacement for the quince pancakes (we've decided on pear and blueberry) and I have stressed that she must taste, taste and taste again. I have chosen some attractive packaging for our oatcakes and shortbread. Anna is still working on a box for the puddings.

Mary Walker's display gets better and better. She seems to be able to keep up with our demands. More and more books are arriving. The outdoor seating will finally be installed while I am away and an extra two or three tables are now regularly set in the shop in the evening after the shop has ceased trading for the day. With these initiatives as well as Sunday trading, we will be doing capacity. And still the customers queue at the door.

Lisa has blossomed in a wonderful way. She is excelling at her work and is rapidly becoming known as a personality. She is enjoying the challenge, is mixing with so many different people, and is just so happy! She has sailed through some very sticky patches. Once when Lisa hit a difficult situation, her reaction would be to shrink from it. Not now. Now she turns it over in her mind and considers ways of dealing with it. Lisa admits that the management course she did a few months ago has helped.

And so I am done here too! Another team wishes me well and hopes I have a stimulating and fun time. I have too much to do to feel nervous or even excited.

29 AUGUST

I am at home, supposedly packing.

Anna and I are on the phone to each other several times today.

My computer is being serviced.

I am having lessons in mobile phone use, as I will have Lisa's phone while I am away.

Things have to go to the dry cleaners and my sandals need new heels.

The disk from Caroline is causing problems at the printer but I am not to worry as Rob (the printer) says he will work all weekend if necessary to get the recipe booklets finished! Caroline drops in scented lavender bags for Maggie and me. We wish she was coming too.

I put novels in my bag and take them out. Books are so heavy. Finally I decide on my holiday reading. A Minette Walters for the plane, *Judy Cassab Diaries*, *Italian Days* by Barbara Grizzuti Harrison, *Pleasures of the Italian Table* by Burton Anderson, Elizabeth David's *Italian Food*, and two paperback novels that I know nothing about. I wanted to take a copy of *The Cook's Companion* but I am not sure whether it will fit.

The garden smells intoxicating – of warmed runny honey. It is a perfect spring day and the scents drift from the wall of jasmine and from the flowering prunus.

The printer drops in at 6.30 p.m. with the boxed booklets and one for Maggie and me to read on the plane. They look fantastic.

30 AUGUST

*H*olly has just rung from Montreal. She is staying with one of her Melbourne friends who is studying there. She sounded well and happy and was enthusiastic about the three days she spent in Quebec city. Who knows if we shall meet, but I do have a French visa should I decide to go.

Singer Helen Noonan has also just called from Auckland, where she is singing in *Phantom of the Opera*. The show does not finish in time for her to sing at the Tuscan evening we are planning on my return. But we are talking of a regular Friday event at which Helen will sing cabaret songs in the billiard room. We will probably bring in a piano … Plenty to think about. Anna will have to pick this up and fine-tune the proposal.

I cannot take on any new projects now. I absolutely have to pack.

When I acquired sole ownership of Stephanie's I knew that I had two months to put things in order. I have achieved almost all of this. I have altered the public perception that the Restaurant is closed or has been sold; changed the structure of the Restaurant to make it more user-friendly and more affordable; instituted a very successful teaching component into the Restaurant; I have planned a series of guest lectures; consolidated staff; and created excitement about Fridays; and I have improved the bottom line. And I am filled with energy and excited about being able to chart my own course. Now seems a good moment to move on to the next stage in my life.

To be continued from Tuscany …

Settembre

September

1 – 2 SEPTEMBER

*T*he luggage! An ignominious beginning to the Italy experience. At the airport I was required to repack my suitcase as union regulations decreed it was too heavy to be handled. Once I had moved some of the books and notebooks into another box it was accepted. What with my share of the cotton embroidered dressing gowns, fifty sets of booklets, a small suitcase full of knives, enough medical supplies to stave off the plague, and my own personal effects, I had a huge amount of stuff. Maggie will no doubt have the same problem.

We met in Sydney airport's transit lounge, both feeling flat and flustered by all that had happened and hadn't happened. Then on to Kuala Lumpur for an overnight stopover. This scheduling was unavoidable and had the hideous side effect that we were required to collect our luggage and deal with it once more. But we had a whiff of Asia, and I had a congee for breakfast, with black beans, astonishingly fresh peanuts and lots of finely shredded ginger. It was so delicious and I was reminded how sad I was to remove our congee from the Cafe menu due to lack of interest. At the dim sum lunch at the Hotel Concorde I particularly enjoyed the braised chicken feet and yam dumplings, and the slippery rice pancakes with prawns.

We each had a massage in the afternoon and it was about then that we heard of the accident in Paris in which Diana, Princess of Wales, and her companion Dodi Al Fayed were killed, along with the chauffeur, apparently attempting to escape pursuing photographers. Like everyone else I was shocked, and I thought about the effect on Diana's two sons. They have already had to deal with the very public details of their parents' private lives, and at this most vulnerable time of their own lives they now have to cope with a shattering loss. Looking back on this a few days later I felt the public response of overwhelming sadness may in time be some sort of comfort for the princes. It must surely cause the British monarchy to wonder about the wisdom of continuing to project an image of distant superiority that appears increasingly irrelevant and expensive.

We flew out at night and I woke early as we passed over the mountains. Below me an unearthly landscape of jagged peaks of a watery, inky blue cocooned by fluffy cloud. As we descended into Rome the reflected early morning sun cast a wide, rippling sash of gold on the sea.

Once again the saga of the luggage, the difficulty of finding trolleys, and then we were out and met at once by Tony (with his own smaller mountain of luggage) and Maggie's friends Ichiko and David Noonan. Ichiko and David live in a stone farmhouse they are renovating in Umbria – two hours away. David is an airline pilot and knows every lift and stair at Rome's airport. We collected our hire-car and divided our luggage. David was to drive our smart Peugeot minibus (well done, Colin: a very good choice) and Ichiko their Land Rover. Everything in Italy takes time, but eventually we set out for our villa, too tired to notice anything much but the inevitable trucks on the highways. A pause for coffee woke us all up. My nostrils started to twitch at the smells of coffee, salami and sugared pastries. Yes, we were in Italy.

3 SEPTEMBER

*O*ur villa is quite wonderful, even though jet-lag has dulled our responses. Last night I cooked a simple meal of chicken breasts deglazed with verjuice and a green salad, and then we all crashed. Everything could wait for the morning.

Today we realise how fortunate we are. Parts of the villa date from the sixteenth century, with many changes having been made over the years. Some rooms have exuberant late nineteenth-century frescoes painted on the walls. The floors in the main reception rooms are terracotta flagstones that are worn and uneven. They are polished to a dull gleam from more than a hundred years of use. It takes a bit of getting used to as one slips and dips across them.

The furnishings are traditional, as are the shuttered windows that open onto gardens and courtyards, and beyond to distant views of Siena and olive groves. Some windows have narrow curtains of fine white cotton embellished with intricate drawn-thread embroidery. Staircases are stone. Each bedroom has its own charm. One even has a bathtub in it! Another has a pair of four-poster beds. Mine is on the ground floor and has one of the

shallow sinks that are typical of Tuscan farmhouses. There are several of
these stone and marble sinks in the villa and they are cool to the touch. Each
has a third tap that delivers spring water to the villa. The city of Siena, we
learn later, is fed by a twenty-five-kilometre aqueduct, which has brought
fresh water into the city from the hills since the fourteenth century.

The main dining room has a magnificent traditional fireplace. The villa's
owner, Anna Rosa Vasconetto, tells us that this is the largest working
fireplace in Tuscany. I don't know if this is so, but it is very impressive. More
than four metres across and just as high, it holds a collection of grills and
racks that promises all sorts of delights. It even has a door where the family
could enter and sit at the back of the fire to keep warm. We met our landlady
last night very briefly. She read us the house rules and is definitely
accustomed to being in charge.

We discover a cavernous cellar with buttressed arches. It is cold, clean
and empty, other than for a sole bat. With the door to the cellar left open in
order to store wine, one quickly notices pungent cellar breath of damp, cold
and ancient stones. Some of these stones and foundations date back 1,000
years, says Anna Rosa. Just the spot for the extraordinary amount of wine
that has been delivered. We explore the pool and its surrounds, noting the
herb garden that we are encouraged to use. The villa has a tall windbreak of
bay trees. We will never be short of a bay leaf!

Late in the afternoon Peter Lortz walked up the driveway laden with
a pack and not one, but two, surfboards! Apparently he created quite a
sensation in Siena, which is not that close to a surf beach. Peter had
travelled to Italy via the Maldives, where his boards were put to great use.
They are now parked in the cellar for the next few weeks.

The kitchen is small but efficient. We plan to use the courtyard as a flow-
over work space. Tony Phillips has a designer's eye and can see how to
rearrange furniture to best effect. We need to create a separate space for a
breakfast room on the first floor, where there is a suitable room. On the
second floor is another excellent kitchen (all these refrigerators will be
needed), and this will be staff quarters, where Tony, Elena Bonnici and Peter
can retreat to, and where we can set up the ironing board.

This is all great fun, rather like grown-ups playing house!

And then I read a fax from Melbourne, a copy of the review of
Stephanie's that appeared in *The Age* following Rita Erlich's visit. It was very
unpleasant and in no way represented the new initiatives fairly – the review
implied that the Restaurant is boring and overpriced, despite the reality that
a three-course meal is now at least $10 cheaper than it was two months ago.
I am devastated and also very angry.

Rita Erlich asked no questions and engaged in no dialogue on the night,
I was told, and made little attempt in this review to present the big picture of
a restaurant that is finding a new path, one which includes teaching, special
occasions, and spontaneous cooking one day a week, along with altering its
pricing structure and offering wines in a different way.

I am frankly disgusted that this is the best our most serious newspaper
can offer. I am also sad to know that I am not there to deal with the
disappointment of the staff who have shown me such loyalty and were so
very willing to execute the many changes at the breakneck speed that I
believed was necessary to mark the new ownership. Losing one hat in *The
Age Good Food Guide* doesn't bother me a bit (and Richmond Hill Cafe &
Larder has been given one). In fact, it eases the pressure a little and,
considering the uncertainties of the last year, is understandable. But this
unfair and selective overview of the present operation is inexcusable.

I understand that if one performs in the public arena, and charges money
to experience the performance, then one should be prepared to have that
performance evaluated. Sometimes the judgement will not be to one's liking.
Sometimes those who offer the judgement inspire no confidence. And on
many occasions the judgement is offered as infotainment to armchair
viewers/gourmets who prefer this distant experience to the real thing. But
those who sit in judgement must remember that they need the performers
in order to have a job and that they have a responsibility to be fair and to
understand context. And to acknowledge their own subjective preferences.

I have to get past this belt in the guts quickly as we have an unbelievable
amount of work to do before our students arrive on Saturday.

4 SEPTEMBER

I have sent faxes to my staff. An added frustration is that Maggie and I are both experiencing problems with our mobile phones, with the unfamiliar fax machine and with the modem on Maggie's computer. All in all, we are confirmed in our belief that we are unable to deal with the modern world and are probably better suited to a sixteenth-century villa and all its charms. And maybe it would be a good idea to forget all these problems and go shopping for food.

Setting up house for seventeen people is quite something. Given the unusual hours kept by most shops in Italy, one has to mobilise early. We have made a six-page shopping list. The next task is to obtain money. First problem. Many ATMs are out of order. Others have low maximum limits, which is unhelpful when we knew our major shop for equipment and dry goods would come to over a million lire (about $1,000)! And the suppliers only take cash. And then we have to find the nearest Co-op. Here we are in deepest Tuscany, with not a neighbour in sight, and yet twelve kilometres away is a modern shopping complex. Mind you, our first attempt was via the scenic route. In other words, we became hopelessly lost and wound around some very pretty country roads, admiring scattered villas and church towers, but we did not find the Co-op for more than an hour. Came back like homing pigeons, though, with bulging boxes and bags.

I felt partially cleansed of the ugly review by the act of buying long, slender zucchini with blossoms attached, perfumed peaches, firm, crisp fennel and gloriously red peppers. Anna Rosa says that the tiny *alimentari* (general store) at the bottom of our hill includes a butcher who sells excellent meat. We have ordered the boned loin of pork for Day One of the course from him. And at the same shop we also ordered pastries for our guests' breakfasts.

5 SEPTEMBER

*M*aggie has some wonderful friends who have made this adventure possible. First is Ichiko Noonan, whom Maggie first met at a cooking school in Melbourne several years ago. Ichiko was intrigued by our project and volunteered to look at the properties on our shortlist over a year ago. Her husband, David, took a video camera to these viewings, helping us to make our choice. And then they drove for more than two hours to collect us at the airport and the same again to deposit us here at the villa. We have invited Ichiko to join the second school as a gift from us.

Our next ministering angel was Ann Parronchi. Ann is an Adelaide girl, married to an Italian, and she lives near Florence, but she is very friendly with the distributor of Maggie's products in Sydney. 'Adelaide people are like that', says Maggie. Ann has been amazing. She interviewed Anna Rosa on our behalf months ago, and she organised our three intended excursions to the Florence market with the students, including hiring the minibus and arranging for Italian-speaking guides. She also lent us high-quality cooking equipment, and escorted us to a wholesale warehouse, Metro, on the outskirts of Florence, for both equipment and food, which are only accessible to those who hold an Italian entry card. Ann does, so we were in.

The last excursion I had to Florence was to visit the Uffizi Gallery. This time it is to buy baking dishes and knives. Life is full of surprises.

Shopping at Metro was very satisfying. The equipment was all there and we negotiated good deals for an espresso machine and grinder, a pasta machine, a food processor and a spice grinder, as well as trolleys full of small stuff, from spare knives to food mills to simmer mats. But the food section took our breath away. It was a miniature wholesale market. Purchases are by the case but the quality was outstanding. We bought cases of fresh borlotti beans, cannellini beans and eggplant, and wished we had the space to buy cases of tomatoes, baby beans and porcini. We bought giant tins of the best tuna in extra-virgin olive oil, sacks of rice for risotto, and bags of dried pasta. We bought whole cheeses. Ann told us that one can use a whole Parmigiano-Reggiano as security for a bank loan here.

The fish were so fresh and included elegant and leggy scampi, brooding blue-black lobsters, cuttlefish, calamari and octopus shining in their velvet-black ink, and giant swordfish, to mention just a few. I wanted to grab bags of small crabs for fish soup, shiny mussels and tiny red mullet and bundles of seaweed. But our Peugeot has no airconditioning and we had one and a half hours of driving ahead. If we visit Metro again we will organise chillers.

We enjoyed our drive home, food stacked to the roof. Here and there the last of the sunflowers blazed in a field. Corn stalks waved in the light breeze. Everywhere were silvery olive trees, columns of poplar or thrusting cypresses, and the more distant patchwork of a combed, newly ploughed field, alongside one growing greenly, alongside another left fallow. The traditional two-storeyed villas that one sees on the farms have shallow-pitched, square-topped roofs, the shape seemingly unchanged for centuries and recognisable in the background of so many Renaissance paintings.

Back home Elena has arrived and Tony has created miracles by moving furniture around. We now have an elegant and spacious breakfast room, with fresh flowers and a cream-footed cake platter piled with red grapefruit. Tony has removed and stored the chintz bed covers, and each bed now has a plain white self-patterned cover, on which is folded one of our lovely cotton dressing gowns, a similarly embroidered green apron, the booklet of recipes and a small gift of specially selected *bomboniere* and biscotti.

Tony told us that the smart refrigerator in the main kitchen is too cold and had frozen all our food! The most immediate consequence of this was that I used the frozen tomatoes to make a sauce and we had pasta and fresh tomato sauce for dinner and went to bed, to deal with this tomorrow.

Every new day has challenges when one is a traveller. The replacement refrigerator part has to come from Bologna, which will take a few days, and the students arrive tomorrow. Anna Rosa is horrified at the number of towels we want from the laundry. And the fax machine is still difficult to operate. But all the wine has arrived, the rooms look wonderful, the shopping is distributed among the other three refrigerators, and the pork has been collected ($100 for two large pork rib roasts – around four kilos).

6 SEPTEMBER

*O*ur first students are safely installed, many very tired having flown direct from Australia. We needed to change one room allocation in order to allow two smokers easier access to the courtyard. Probably Anna Rosa would not mind, but we have made a rule of no smoking inside the villa. Other than that, everyone was thrilled with their rooms, with the villa, and simply to have arrived and settled in.

Maggie has had two computer experts from Florence here for four hours to solve her fax/modem problems. She has to send a story each week to *The Australian* newspaper and must get the system up and running. They have reassured her that it is not uncommon for software to misbehave when one travels to a different country, particularly in rural areas, and that such frustrations can happen 'even to rocket scientists'.

Our team of three helpers worked wonderfully well and we all felt pleased with our first experience. Maggie and I sat with the students for a simple dinner of antipasto followed by corn-fed chickens in a garlicky tomato sauce, followed by a chunk of Parmigiano-Reggiano and half a pear, and then Tony's apple tart. Tony decided to finish the tart with the splendid thick honey given to us by Ann Parronchi, which was unfiltered, not heat-treated and richly flavoured, and he infused it with a stalk of pungent dried lavender. Ann tells us that one day, ten years ago, an old man named Alfredo turned up just after she and her husband had moved to their new home at the restored farmhouse in which she and her family live and informed her that they needed a hive and that he had always made the honey for this farm. And he has done so ever since.

TONY'S APPLE TART WITH ANN'S HONEY

DAMIEN'S PÂTE BRISÉE

180 g unsalted butter	pinch of salt
240 g plain flour	3 tablespoons water

FILLING

5 firm apples (such as Granny Smith)	60–90 g butter
¾ cup local honey	100 ml brandy, Cognac or eau-de-vie
2 sprigs dried lavender	

The pastry   Remove the butter from the refrigerator 30 minutes before making the pastry. Sieve the flour and salt onto a marble pastry slab or the workbench. Chop the butter into smallish pieces and toss lightly in flour. Lightly rub to combine partly. Make a well in the centre and pour in the water. Using a pastry scraper (and being mindful of the technique you have observed of mixing cement), work the paste to a very rough heap of buttery lumps of dough. Using the heel of your hand, quickly smear the pastry away from you across the workbench. It will combine lightly. Gather together, then press quickly into a flat cake and dust with a little flour. Wrap the pastry in plastic film and refrigerate for 20–30 minutes.

Preheat the oven to 200°C. Roll out the pastry and line a 24 cm loose-bottomed flan tin. Bake blind for 15 minutes, then remove the foil and beans and return the pastry to the oven for another 5 minutes until it is golden.

The filling   Peel and core the apples, then slice them into rings. Toss the apple with the honey in a bowl, ensuring the pieces are evenly coated (this prevents discoloration and prepares the apple for the caramelising process). If honey is very thick, first stand in hot water for 15–20 minutes. Marinate/infuse honey with dried aromatic lavender.

Melt some of the butter in a frying pan and sauté a small batch of the apple over a medium heat, turning the pieces as they caramelise. Remove the apple to a plate to drain, then repeat this process, using a little more of the butter each time, until all the apple is cooked. Arrange the cooked apple decoratively over the pastry case, reserving the accumulated juices.

Melt a knob of butter in the pan, then deglaze with the brandy. Tip in the reserved juices and the lavender and reduce over heat until a thick syrup has formed. Pour the syrup over the apple and serve.
Serves 6

We are discovering how fleeting is the moment of perfection and that when one is surrounded by produce picked when ready to eat this is exactly what one must do. Perfection, gauged in terms of juiciness and glossy unblemished skins, quickly gives way to slightly fermented and wrinkled softness. Daily shopping seems a necessity. This is the next challenge to be met. We cannot drive to Florence every day for supplies, but the local markets are not able to supply the quantities we need for each meal. Further research will be required.

7 SEPTEMBER

SCHOOL ONE

Day One   So far so good.

The rhythm of each day begins with breakfast at 8.00 a.m. Class assembles in the courtyard for the day's briefing at 10.00 a.m. We all cook until 1.00 p.m., and then spumante is served in the garden before sitting down to lunch. Siestas begin at 3.30 p.m. and by 7.00 p.m. the students assemble for an aperitif and to plan their evening activities. The understanding is that Maggie and I also do our own thing in the evenings.

We divided the students into three groups, two working outside in the courtyard and one in the kitchen. Parsley was plucked, garlic was chopped and the students were introduced to the *mezzaluna*, that boat-shaped, two-handled knife that rocks across a heap of garlic or a pile of parsley with impressive efficiency. One team shelled the fresh cannellini beans from their raspy, creamy pods.

The impressive pork roasts were seasoned and went into the oven without delay.

Maggie made pasta by hand and the students got into the kneading, rolling, stretching and, later, the cutting. Two broomsticks were suspended across two stools under the kitchen table to hold the drying pasta. (A near-disaster was averted when one of us automatically went to pull a stool out from under the table for a moment's rest. Immediate shrieks – only a few strands of pasta slid to the floor.) Sultanas were soaked in red-wine vinegar, pine nuts toasted, and two students spent most of the morning peeling Roma tomatoes. Another two were instructed to halve these sensational tomatoes, ease out the jelly (no squeezing, please) and then slice each half into thin fillets. Almonds were pounded in a mortar, amaretti were crumbled, peaches were peeled with an asparagus peeler, to be halved and stuffed for dessert.

Three hours later we sat at a table under the elm trees and enjoyed the fruits of our first day's labours.

PASTA TWO WAYS
~ PINE NUTS, SULTANAS AND PARSLEY
~ FILLETS OF TOMATO WITH RED ONION AND
ANCHOVIES
Antinori Rosé 1996

SLOW-ROASTED LOIN OF PORK WITH BRAISED
FLAT ONIONS AND FENNEL AND FRESH
CANNELLINI BEANS
Antinori Badia a Passignano Chianti Classico 1995

BAKED PEACHES STUFFED WITH AMARETTI
AND BROWN ALMONDS

We have a good group and they chatted like old friends. The sun was still fierce in the afternoon and the table may have to be re-sited tomorrow. I am not happy with any of the bread we have found so far. The crust is brittle and the crumb dry. How do the Tuscans make their crostini with this bread? (Crostini are thin slices of grilled or toasted bread.) We tried and ended up with shattered slices. We shall ask Anna Rosa for advice.

Almost all the students decided to explore Siena in the late afternoon and evening, and after they had gone Tony, Maggie and I had a refreshing swim in the villa's attractive pool and a quiet dinner of bread and tomato soup – the *pappa al pomodoro* constructed during this morning's classes. Early to bed. Shopping is a big problem for tomorrow's class – Sunday is almost total shut-down in this part of Italy, and already we have underestimated some quantities of the food needed.

8 SEPTEMBER

Day Two   A big day today! But fun. Figs, fig leaves and vine leaves were first harvested from the farm. Fattoria di Corsano means 'farm of Corsano' and this villa is still part of a working farm, producing wine and olive oil.

The students grilled eggplant (no need to salt them as they were so freshly picked), zucchini and red peppers, all to be enjoyed with Maggie's *salsa agresto*, made with her own verjuice; they made lasagna dough and the parsley sauce to be used to assemble it; wrapped quail stuffed with grapes in fig leaves; simmered green figs in verjuice and then wrapped them in vine leaves ready for the grill; and soaked sponge fingers in the sweet *vin santo* for a lemon dessert. Stone fruits were sliced, sugared and splashed with *vin santo*. Maggie gave the finishing touches to our first risotto and crisped the sage leaves in butter while Elena and the students arranged the antipasto. Bundles of green beans were tucked inside some very creamy mortadella, and we sliced the remainder of yesterday's peppers.

We also made *piadini,* flat breads that are very popular in Tuscany, placing the thin, soft discs of dough onto a hot grill. Three minutes on each side and they came off crisp, with burnt bubbly bits. We kept them in a basket between a folded tea towel until all were ready.

Perhaps one of the most important lessons that we want the students to absorb is that no good food need be wasted. Yesterday's cannellini beans will be a salad or a purée for crostini today, the macerated stone fruits not eaten this evening will be breakfast tomorrow, and so on.

Tony lit a fire in the grill which looked spectacular. The quail parcels took about twenty minutes to cook – plenty of time for us to enjoy our antipasto with a crisp Orvieto Classico. Lunch again under the elms. One student said to me that she thought it unlikely that anything better could be served than this lunch. I take this as a challenge.

ANTIPASTO
~ GRILLED VEGETABLES SPRINKLED WITH
BALSAMICO
~ PROSCIUTTO E MELONE
~ PEPPERS STUFFED WITH PORK SAUSAGE

~ GREEN BEANS IN MORTADELLA
~ GREEN FIGS GRILLED IN VINE LEAVES WITH
VERJUICE
~ SALSA AGRESTO
~ PIADINI
Antinori Orvieto Classico 1996

GRILLED QUAIL STUFFED WITH GRAPES AND
SAGE LEAVES AND WRAPPED IN FIG LEAVES
Antinori Santa Cristina 1996

RISOTTO WITH CRISPED SAGE

LEMON CREAM WITH FRESH BERRIES
Antinori Muffato della Sala 1995

We discussed possible excursions, and the students want to book transport
to visit Montalcino the day after tomorrow. Our minibus can only seat seven
and everyone wants to go, so a bigger small bus is needed, plus a driver.
Peter's language skills will be essential for this. Not only is Montalcino
famous for Brunello wine, but Anna Rosa says there is a very pleasant
restaurant there.

Maggie, Elena, Peter, Tony and I had a late swim once again and an even
later light meal of some delicious eggplant lasagne made by one of the few
men at our school. This man has a special interest in wine, but he is rightly
proud of his parsley and bechamel sauces that provided the creamy layers in
the lasagne. I wonder if his new-found interest in cooking will stay with him
once he returns home. Those students who stayed in tonight also loved the
lasagne. The last light of the day was amethyst, which faded, as we watched,
to a soft grey, then to inky black. There were no stars. In the distance the
lights of Siena twinkled.

9 SEPTEMBER

Day Three   *Panzarotti* today, those delectable fried, savoury parcels. After
the difficulties Maggie and I encountered with them at our rehearsal at
Brokenwood last month, we decided to roll and stuff the dough in the
upstairs kitchen, where it is cooler than the crowded kitchen. The stuffing
was fantastic. We used salami instead of ham and some matured pecorino.

The *brodo*, or broth, we have been making every second day is delicious,
reflecting the quality of the boiling fowls we buy.

Today we grilled pigeon over one of Tony's special fires fuelled by bay
leaves. We had planned to use artichokes but they were unavailable, so
I suggested a gratin of large chunks of pumpkin tossed with garlic and
Parmigiano-Reggiano. It looked sensational when presented in one of
Anna Rosa's caramel-coloured, glazed, oval earthenware dishes. The softly
set honey semifreddo was a magnificent dessert, served with figs picked one
hour before lunch then gently stewed in a syrup flavoured with the digestive
liqueur Amaro.

10 SEPTEMBER

Day Four   We are having to substitute a few dishes, as some ingredients
we had counted on prove to be unavailable. Some students are concerned by
this – others understand about 'going with the flow'. Maggie and Peter went
to Siena early this morning to choose fish for today's class.

Today we had a visit from Chris Butler, who is part of the *Movimento
Internazionale per la Cultura dell'Olio da Olive*. Another Adelaide person happily
transplanted to Italy, Chris is passionate about informing others all about
olive oil: from dispelling myths regarding its production (traditional
methods have led to faulty oil whereas modern continuous extraction
methods produce better quality oils); to telling us that very few in the
community (including many Italians) are able to recognise basic and very
common faults in much of the olive oil produced. Chris claims that as much
as sixty per cent of the olive oil exhibits faults of oxidation, rancidity,
scalding, mouldiness and other nasties. As almost every farm in Italy

produces its own oil, the phenomenon of 'cellar palate' – 'this is the oil we have always had and we think it is the best' – is widespread.

Under Chris's guidance we tasted a very fruity Tuscan oil and a mild oil, both without defect. And then, to mark the difference, we tasted an oil bought that day from the supermarket and another unidentified but very bad oil. All were labelled as extra-virgin olive oil. Both of the latter, we noted, were rancid and oxidised, and we also detected the 'scalded' character of one of them. It was an interesting thought that most of us feel confident in recognising rancid or 'fridgy' butter, or milk that has gone off, or wine that is corked, and yet this other basic commodity is rarely rejected and when purchased is often stored in full sunlight, decanted into murky bottles and generally abused. Chris was quick to point out that it takes months to become an olive oil taster and that his hope was that at least now we would recognise bad oil and protest to our supplier. I wonder what response most of us would receive were we to return an opened bottle of extra-virgin olive oil to our local supermarket, declaring it unacceptable? And yet we would expect our complaint to be taken seriously if it was a pack of butter.

After the tasting came lunch and, to start, a *pinzimonio* (like the French crudités) of raw, crisp vegetables and a bowl of fine oil (approved of by Chris) from Ann Parronchi's estates. With this we made crisp grissini (little pencil-thin breadsticks). Next, another of Maggie's wonderful risotti, this time made with radicchio and moistened with a lightly saffroned fish stock, followed by a soupy stew of local fish, mussels and tender calamari. Dessert was a tart of plums baked in butter and settled in a warm crust on fabulous mascarpone.

Each time we have made pastry over here we noted that the unusual texture of the Italian butter makes the process very perilous. The butter is always very soft, and we have to chill the marble bench with bags of ice cubes and work very fast. Next time we will freeze the butter before we start.

This afternoon the students have gone to Montalcino to taste Brunello di Montalcino and to have a light meal. Peter, Maggie, Tony, Elena and I went in search of a farm selling goat's cheese.

We drove along dusty tracks, following very vague instructions, and eventually we found the isolated and ancient farmhouse. Outside was an old lady sitting with her knitting and a flyswat. Yes, they did have some cheese, but it was not the best time of the year for it. Festoons of scarlet tomatoes picked on the vine hung from the roof, as did giant hams. There was a rich smell of manure. After we had paid for our cheese there were smiles all round, and the woman urged us to come back soon. A cock pheasant dashed across the road as we drove back.

This landscape in which we found ourselves looked like a lunar landscape. It is known locally as *Crete di Siena*, sometimes translated rather awkwardly as 'Clays of Siena'. Once heavily forested, the land has been extensively cleared for cultivation over the centuries. Anna Rosa described it as an ecological disaster and maintained that these fields would grow very little were it not for the massive amounts of fertiliser and other chemicals poured into and onto them. After the growing season the fields are burnt and, apparently, in the late summer, the evenings are illuminated by the glow of many fires. The soil is then turned over to expose the heavy clay clods, which lie fallow until the rains come to soften them before planting. Viewed up close, the fields are gouged rows of grey clay. From a distance, one remarks on the shifting patterns created by the sun and shadows on this strange, grey landscape. Here and there is a field striped in bands of black sooty stubble against greenish-grey clay. And then, far away, one glimpses a square belltower, or a villa of pink stone, partially hidden by trees, or one drives past a patch of *Nepitella* (wild mint) in flower, and again one is in Italy. I can imagine the transformation in late spring and summer, when the cornfields will be green and swaying in the breezes and the sunflowers will blaze.

11 SEPTEMBER

Day Five   Another substitution. There were no male zucchini flowers today (surprising, when there were plenty yesterday), so we made fritters from the slender female fruits. They were so sweet and the brief frying left them with a firm texture that I found delightful. We started a minestrone, to be completed tomorrow after our first trip with students to the Florence market. I discussed the Tuscan practice of reheating a minestrone and adding bread to it, the soup thus becoming *ribollita*, meaning 'reboiled'. There were no quinces, so we accompanied the delicate caramel *panne cotte* with poached pears.

But we did buy stunning farmed rabbit, one of Maggie's specialities. The rabbit was preceded by potato gnocchi and followed by an outstanding salad of radicchio and raw fennel, and we all exclaimed over the beautiful Isole e Olena Chardonnay 1995 that accompanied the meal. Already we know we will have to substitute guinea fowl for pheasant for the grand finale dinner. The guinea fowl have been ordered from our very obliging local butcher.

This evening it has been arranged for the students to visit the local aristocracy. They are invited to their lavish apartments and a dinner will be prepared for them. Maggie and I will go next time. We are taking advantage of their excursion to catch up with our notes, check receipts and write the mammoth shopping list that Peter and Tony will deal with in Florence tomorrow. Already some students are worrying about how to catch their planes in three days' time, and once again we bless Peter, who calmly contacts hire-cars, taxis and bus companies for them.

Tony, Maggie and I had a simple dinner of leftovers – grilled eggplant with caramelised onion, raw vegetables and mayonnaise, and cold rabbit and beans. The kitchen smells wonderful. Elena has baked *panettone* (a yeast cake flavoured with candied peel and dried fruit) for the students to enjoy for breakfast before the market and she has also cooked a pan of damson plums to enjoy with yoghurt. There is a laden tree on the edge of the property and we helped ourselves today, noticing that the fruit was dropping.

12 SEPTEMBER

Day Six   To Florence today for our visit to the covered market at San Lorenzo. Peter and Tony left before 7.00 a.m. to meet with the obliging Ann Parronchi and do another marathon shop at Metro, in an attempt to limit the number of daily shopping trips for basic dry goods. They have a long list and more than a million lire to spend. We shall meet for lunch at a country restaurant at Tavernelle – Ristorante La Fattoria – again organised by Ann.

I tried to send an e-mail to Holly last night, using Maggie's computer and following Maggie's instructions. I failed, or rather it failed. Holly would have known what to do! My mobile phone refused to turn off yesterday. It glowed greenly beside my bed until the battery ran out. And now I seem to have mislaid the notebook in which I jot down all manner of vital observations and messages to myself. Next year, 1998, is definitely the year in which I will conquer technology.

I comfort myself with the fact that many of the students are having problems with their phones, and Maggie is still not entirely happy with her modem. After receiving a long fax from the Restaurant, which included details of a few unfortunate incidents, as well as some glowing reports, I started to question the value of being in touch. Especially when one is unable to influence things after the event. I will have to send a few thoughts and suggestions to Anna, who will filter or censor them if I express myself too strongly. I remind myself of my own rule: let two days elapse before reacting publicly to anything unpleasant. I will push all these issues away until tomorrow.

But the market and the produce lightened my mood.

It was quite a shock to drive into a city after such a long time in seclusion. The whine of the Vespas, the honking of car horns, the *bella figura* of seemingly the entire population.

We met up with Ann and Tony, who reported that their Metro shopping had been successful and that Peter was on his way home with the van packed to the roof with food, food and more food.

In the market the buffalo mozzarella is wrapped in strappy leaves 'to keep it firm as it is so fresh, and to look beautiful'. In the delicatessen section the star was the veal. Firmly textured, rose-pink, with a fine veil of silky fat over the loin – I lusted after this veal!

Everyone was fascinated by the tripe stalls – the frilly shapes of unnamed parts, and intestines, spleen and testicles, not to mention something that was explained as being the milk glands of young heifers. I admired the smoothly rounded, shallow marble trough and counter at one particular tripe stall. Across the way, one could buy *panini* filled with cooked, chopped tripe in rich broth – the roll was dunked in the savoury broth before being handed over. I bought a whole *finocchiona*, the Tuscan *salame* flavoured with fennel seeds. It is quite a soft sausage, which we enjoyed later with sliced fresh figs. We negotiated the purchase of some white truffles – these are the first of the season and I had been fearful that our first class might miss out on this treat. They were two million lire the kilo, about $200 for a good taste for seventeen people.

On to the fruit and vegetables. Once again, it is the quality that impresses. We had hoped for porcini, but there were very few, due to the current drought. Most were being imported from France, but eventually we bought some that had been picked in Sicily. We bought salads and round, apple-shaped zucchini; unusual citrus called miagawa that have bright-green rind and are brilliantly orange inside, very juicy and midway between a lemon and an orange; melons so scented that their fragrance filled the air in the bus on the return journey; some early *cavolo nero*, a cabbage with long, dark leaves that have a purple bloom, to add to our soup, and narrow-leaved rocket; and, as a very last purchase, we returned to the fish and meat section and bought some *gamberetti*, tiny shrimp one boils and eats like peanuts, and some very delicate squid. These went straight into chiller bags as we reboarded our bus for the lunch spot. Tony had his arms filled with fresh flowers bought at half the cost they had been in Siena.

My Italian is adequate for market shopping but less useful for general conversation.

Lunch was delightful. We ate in the garden under market umbrellas. Ristorante La Fattoria is set on a hill overlooking an archetypal Tuscan vista of soft foliage, pink villas, vineyards and hillsides guarded by cypress.

SAGE AND ANCHOVY FRITTERS
~ FRIED POLENTA WITH A FUNGHI SAUCE AND
A LIVER SAUCE

COLD TRIPE SALAD WITH TOMATOES,
RED ONIONS AND CELERY
Antinori Bianco 1996

235

RABBIT WITH WINE GRAPES
~ CARTOCCIO OF PORCINI, POTATOES AND
PANCETTA
~ GREEN SALAD
Antinori Tenuta Marchese Riserva 1994
Antinori Chianti Classico Riserva 1995

RICOTTA SPONGE CAKE WITH FRESH BERRIES
Prunotto Moscato d'Asti

It was all good but the tripe salad was the hit of the day, closely followed by the delicate ricotta cake, with its generous scattering of berries, including tiny and intensely flavoured *mirtilli*, or bilberries.

Back home we launched into the big stowaway of the crates and crates of food and prepared a very simple meal, all cooked on the fire. Tony grilled the porcini and parcels of pig's liver and bay leaf, which we enjoyed with an outstanding Antinori Peppoli Chianti Classico 1995, and we finished with spicy *panforte* and a glass of Moscato, the unusual raisiny wine that seems to work well either as an aperitif or, as in this case, with something sweet, in the same way that we might offer a glass of tokay or muscat. It is still warm enough to eat outside in the evening, but today's short thunderstorm did make us think of approaching autumnal days.

The day ended well: one of the students had accidentally picked up my notebook, and the phone worked after recharging. Stephanie's Restaurant remains the only unresolved concern of this morning.

13 SEPTEMBER

Day Seven   Paolo de Marchi is to talk to us about the wines of Chianti today and will stay on for lunch. Paolo's own estate, Isole e Olena, produces some of the most admired wines of the area. Again it is through one of Maggie's friends – Peter Wall, currently managing director of Yalumba – that we have been able to organise this treat.

We started early in the kitchen so as to be free for the tasting. Everyone had an extremely busy morning. More changes and substitutions. We were able to buy male zucchini flowers yesterday at the Florence market, so they will be part of our antipasto. We also prepared for the evening. So we picked parsley and basil, peeled and chopped tomatoes, cucumbers and celery, and finely shaved red onions for the *panzanella* salad. We opened the mussels and mixed them on the half-shell with chopped rocket and olive oil; and dipped the tiny shrimp for one minute in boiling, lightly salted water, then drained and tossed them with a few crushed fennel seeds, pepper and olive oil. The cuttlefish Tony had bought were braised with white wine, onions, olives, chopped tomatoes and olive oil. Buffalo mozzarella was crushed with anchovies and parsley to make a simple stuffing for the zucchini flowers. The smaller porcini from yesterday's shopping were divided between the *sformato* (a soufflé-like pudding that will be twice baked in this case) for tomorrow night's banquet and the spinach and ricotta filling for the *rotolo*, a long pasta sausage wrapped in a clean cloth, to be simmered and sauced with crisp sage and brown butter. Veal was larded with anchovies and simmered for tomorrow's *vitello tonnato*, the mayonnaise made and the tuna sauce for the same dish completed. Even the guinea fowl planned for the banquet were gutted and breadcrumbs made for the stuffing.

Paolo spoke to us about the rapid changes that have taken place in Chianti over the last twenty years. From being an area where share farmers worked small plots of land, producing their own wine, oil and crops, Chianti is now owned by fewer people working larger properties. Many of those who once lived on the land have moved to the towns. Paolo cited his own estate as an example of this – when his father bought the property in the early 1950s the estate supported 120 people, but there are now fewer than twenty.

Those involved in wine production in Chianti have taken on the challenge of making better wines and are becoming more and more successful in finding export markets for their wine. More than half the wine denominated as Chianti Classico and over eighty per cent of the production of Isole e Olena is exported. Paolo helped us understand the difference between the appellations Chianti (which may be a blend of sangiovese and white grapes such as trebbiano and malvasia) and Chianti Classico (which may contain no more than five per cent white grapes). Sangiovese is the essential grape of the Chianti region and, according to Paolo, does well in its relatively difficult soils as it needs a bit of stress. It produces wines that have considerable tannin, lots of fruit, and are relatively high in acid.

Paolo believes that the Chianti of the future may still be a blend of grape varieties but that the blends will be far superior to those in the past, when wine made from indifferent grapes was used in the blending. Not for the last time we heard that the regulations that control winemaking and labelling in Italy are viewed by some winemakers as anachronistic. Some of the most famous wines made in Tuscany do not conform to the regulations of the DOC (the Denominazione di Origine Controllata/Garantita, the regulatory system for Italy's regional produce), and these are known as the Super Tuscans. Probably the best known of these wines is Sassicaia.

Paolo led us on a tasting of his Cepparello, another Super Tuscan, which is a hundred per cent sangiovese, commencing with 1995, then 1991, then 1990 in magnum and finally 1987. These are big wines with many years ahead of them. Paolo looked longingly at our stone fireplace and agreed that a wood-roasted *cinghiale* (wild boar) with one of his Cepparello wines would be a splendid match. The *cinghiale* eats the grapes and has become a feral pest to the vignerons.

Talk of *cinghiale* signalled lunchtime. Another memorable feast, culminating with a fine *vin santo* wine from Antinori.

Two of the group are leaving tomorrow, before the final banquet, so we all gathered later for a penultimate final dinner. Those leaving us had an extra course of porcini *sformato* with shaved white truffles. The aroma was shared by all.

14 SEPTEMBER

Day Eight   We waved goodbye to our two early leavers. The taxi was on time.

It is raining! And we have had a thunderstorm. Anna Rosa has rung to ask us to turn off the refrigerator! Paolo told us yesterday that the most important rain usually falls in September and that sometimes it rains for twenty-five days. We do not wish him any bad luck with the harvest, but we are hoping that this rush of water is temporary.

Two hours later we gathered in the courtyard for a group photograph. The rain has stopped, the geraniums look refreshed and the water is draining away fast. A day for catching up with one's notes, reading or, as many of the students have decided, for a visit to Orvieto. Elena is constructing the *zuccotto* for the banquet tonight. This splendid dessert is made from ricotta cheese, mascarpone, nuts, candied fruit and syrup-soaked sponge. The crusts on the edges of the cake slices lining the bowl are supposed to represent the distinctive ribbing of the famous Duomo in Florence.

Elena, Tony and Peter are the most wonderful, hard-working and talented team one could ever wish to have on such a venture. Their combined skills are astonishing: Honours degree in Italian and German language and literature; ten years' experience as a wine and food waiter; qualified chef; more than fifteen years as a cutter of period costume, with special expertise in corset-making; advanced competence in floral arrangements; interior design; wine knowledge; universal good humour and an ability to deal with a motley group of strangers and the constant up and down on the unforgiving stone stairs. We love them all!

Maggie is creating a new dish for tonight's banquet – guinea fowl stuffed with its liver and heart and cooked with the vivid miagawa citrus, flat onions and witlof.

The banquet was an outstanding success.

The dining room looked magnificent, reminiscent of some sumptuous film set. Tony had worked on it all afternoon, carefully placing richly purple grapes on antique platters and filling vases with scented lilies and glossy bay leaves, evoking the paintings of Caravaggio. Silver candlesticks were polished and the table was set with Anna Rosa's best embroidered cloth. Despite the morning's thunderstorm the power stayed on!

There was a collective gasp as Maggie opened the lid of the glass jar in which our truffles were stored. The aroma instantly filled this very large room. Next came the *sformato* of porcini with a porcini and parsley sauce, then the guinea fowl with its rich and complex flavours in the stuffing, then excellent three-year-old Parmigiano-Reggiano with pears – and the climax was the stunning *zuccotto*, carried in triumphantly by Elena.

The wines were wonderful, including a generous taste of the noble Super Tuscan, Sassicaia 1992, made from one hundred per cent cabernet, and the delicious Muffato della Sala 1995 botrytised dessert wine.

Then it was goodbyes all round, and we had done it! School One was completed and the comments were glowing. And so to bed. Some of the students were being collected at 5.10 in the morning to catch the bus to Florence. We decided not to get up to farewell them.

15 SEPTEMBER

*M*onday, and our First Day Off.

The five of us set off late morning for a day in the country. Our plan was to visit Montalcino, an excursion strongly recommended by our students, taste the Brunello di Montalcino, wander the town and have lunch on an outside terrace. We achieved all this, although at Montalcino most shops had closed for siesta by the time we had parked and started our stroll. Never mind – we continued on and lunched at a very simple country restaurant. The food was not extraordinary but it was honest, and we all felt expansive. As ever, the view over the vineyards was wonderful; in Tuscany one almost takes it for granted. Conversation was good. We have become a very close-knit group, with minor domestic details assuming huge importance. Will there be enough hand towels at the laundry tomorrow? Should we change the used soaps in the bathrooms?

16 SEPTEMBER

*T*o Siena this morning for supplies. I am entranced by the Campo – the famous piazza in which the Palio horse race is held each July. Siena is a very approachable city. One can become familiar with its little alleyways and speciality businesses, and linger, find a favourite corner, even return and be greeted as a regular by a smiling waiter. The town's dusky-pink bricks and stone add warmth to its public spaces, in dramatic contrast to the more imposing and formal striped black and white marble facade of the Duomo.

Our second lot of students has arrived. And so has Ichiko, who will be one of the group. Tony made his pastry in one of the marble sinks, which was at least as effective as chilling the workbench in the kitchen.

Tonight's dinner was fabulous. Local *salame finocchiona* rolled around Elena's grissini, wrinkled black olives and white bean purée crostini to accompany an Antinori spumante. Next, corn-fed chickens roasted with slices of lemon and garlic under the breast. Today was the first day of the harvest and Elena had obligingly picked a few bunches of the tightly packed wine grapes from the villa's own vines. Most were stewed with the leaves and stems of chard (the smaller-leafed version of our backyard staple silver beet). And then Tony's apple tart, this time bathed with chestnut honey.

17 SEPTEMBER

SCHOOL TWO

Day One   We are amazingly well-organised, and the tasks seemed so straightforward this time. We were even able to fit in a few extras. The students helped make bread, and some lemon biscuits to accompany tomorrow's dessert. It is warm and sultry and very pleasant under the trees at lunch. These students are much less extroverted than the last ones. Group dynamics are fascinating.

Maggie, Tony and I took our first walk this afternoon to see a hidden stone tower less than a kilometre away. Interesting, but not so old – 1856 was the date on the carved stone crest. As we pushed through this lightly forested area, I wondered aloud about the likelihood of encountering a savage *cinghiale*. The others laughed at me (a touch nervously, I thought).

The full moon was an astonishing blood orange. It hung low over the trees as we enjoyed a bowl of soup and a last glass of wine before bed. I have found that the only way to move past a messy patch in my life, be it an emotional or a business concern, is to take action that resolves the matter as far as it is possible to do so at the time. I wrote a letter of protest to the editor of 'Epicure' at *The Age* after the review of a few weeks ago, and I have also communicated my thoughts about matters at both the Restaurant and

the Cafe. Why then do I still feel so troubled? There is something still
nagging at me that I have not yet identified.

My dreams are becoming more crowded and more troubled. Once the
lights are out, my subconscious drags me straight back to Melbourne and to
a mess of problems, anxieties and unresolved matters. As the day dawns,
though, I travel quickly back to Italy.

1 8 S E P T E M B E R

Day Two   A very full morning. Looking back through my notes, I see that
this is what I said on the second day of the last school. We even forgot to
make the *piadini* but we managed to finish the minestrone for tomorrow,
make some biscotti and ice the lemon biscuits, as well as achieving all the
other dishes. Elena made *panettone* for tomorrow's breakfast.

For this school, we grilled the quail without wrapping them and then
immersed them in a bath of seeded grapes, verjuice, extra-virgin olive oil
and cracked pepper for about fifteen minutes. The smell of the wood fire is
marvellous, helped by the plentiful supply of dried bay leaves. Anna Rosa's
brother presented us with a basket of small white peaches, so we cut some of
these into tiny dice, tossed them with red currants and spooned the mixture
onto the lemon semifreddo dessert.

Tonight the students opted to stay in to enjoy lasagne, while we decided
to eat in a country restaurant recommended to me in Australia by a visiting
chef from New Zealand. We felt a bit like children escaping as we sped
along the country dirt roads. A hare bounded away from us. Le Torre de
Stigliano was only about twenty minutes from our villa and was a good
example of an Italian country restaurant. Some dishes were better than
others, but we were all pleased with the nettle risotto (so soon after enjoying
it in Perth!), the squid-ink risotto, the fried sage leaves (although the ones
served with anchovy in the middle, like we had at Tavernelle, have extra
piquancy), the baked *spigole* (fish) and the gently fried chicken breast with
a refreshing sauce of green-shouldered tomatoes, basil and oil.

Red, ripe tomatoes were used for bruschetta, and the green-shouldered
tomatoes were also sliced for the salad *caprese*. I have noted this before. We

who are often deprived of perfect tomatoes yearn for those that are deeply red and sweet. And in Italy they are everywhere. But Italians (and Greeks) also appreciate the acidity, juiciness and different sweetness to be found in ripe but not fully coloured tomatoes, especially in salads.

1 9 S E P T E M B E R

Day Three   Market Day again. The produce was even better this week and somewhere in Italy it must have rained as there were plenty of porcini but, alas, no truffles. We particularly enjoyed buying fish for tomorrow's fish stew and the fishmonger couldn't believe his luck as we ordered more and more. We bought whole fish and chunks of fish, all with unfamiliar names, and we bought heads and frames for the broth, small fish, also for the broth, bags of mussels, tiny *calamaretti* and fat sardines. Our bill was 200,000 lire – this fish stew will be a rare treat. Maybe my consciousness had been raised, but everywhere were piles of green-shouldered tomatoes with signs saying 'Tomatoes for salad'. Of course, there were luscious red ones too, of every size and shape. I bought some *cavolo nero*, and Maggie chose some rape, the dark-green, leafy vegetable that is related to the turnip and the flowering broccoli. A stall-holder insisted that the round fennel were the male ones (I had always believed the reverse) and that only the males were good enough to be used for *pinzimonio*. Maggie was excited to see fresh juniper berries. At the same stall in among the herbs was a tiny posy of wild cyclamen. I admired it and the young woman serving tucked it into the parcel of wild rocket purchased.

Back at the villa, we discovered that we had left the basket of porcini and zucchini flowers in Ann's car! Two hours away! Consternation and disappointment, and a hastily rearranged dinner. We chopped the *cavolo nero* and added it to the minestrone and I made a salad from the remainder of the roast pork cooked two days ago, slicing it finely and tossing it with caramelised onions and wild rocket. Dessert was a delicious mix of sliced white peaches, yellow peaches, golden raspberries and tight, sweet, wild blackberries, lightly sugared and steeped in Muffato della Sala for half an hour. This Muffato is more than sixty per cent sauvignon blanc, which is unusual for a botrytised wine, and Peter described it as having a slightly bitter quality – like marmalade.

And then Ann rang to say she had organised for a friend to drive across tomorrow with our special purchases.

20 SEPTEMBER

Day Four   Magnificent lunch today.

PINZIMONIO WITH OIL
FROM ISOLE E OLENA
Antinori Spumante Brut

RISOTTO OF RAPE WITH ANCHOVY SERVED
WITH DEEP-FRIED SARDINES

FISH STEW WITH MUSSELS AND CALAMARETTI
~ GARLIC TOASTS
Scalabrone Bolgheri Rosato 1996

PRUNE PLUM TART ON MASCARPONE
Prunotto Moscato d'Asti

Today was Chris Butler's lecture and olive-oil tasting. Once again the students were most enthusiastic. At lunch Chris told us some wild stories. Do I believe that in Vicenza they eat cat? Or that near his home they still cook porcupine (a protected species)? Chris was very entertaining when he described an annual local dinner where a chef is invited to cook *stufato* for 400 people in the town hall. This beef stew has mythic status in the area, and everyone knows if the seasoning is correct. If it pleases the assembled throng, they stand and applaud the chef. If it displeases them, there is total silence and the chef leaves at once. Chris also described the *contrade* in Siena. Locals are born in one of seventeen neighbourhoods, known collectively as the *contrade*, each of which has its own sign (an animal). Anna

Rosa, for instance, has already told us that she is an eagle. These *contrade* all compete against each other in the Palio and, according to Chris, there is much skulduggery, with many deals being done and large amounts of money being wagered. This year the victorious *contrada* was the giraffe.

In the evening we had a short outing to Siena and chanced upon a part we had not yet seen. The Porta Romana is an impressive gate set in the ramparts of the old town. The Medici crest was carved in deep relief on the gate. As we strolled along narrow streets outwardly unchanged since medieval times we looked up and into lit apartments displaying fabulous painted, coffered and gilded ceilings. We imagined luxurious and beautiful interiors.

21 SEPTEMBER

Day Five   Another sensational rabbit day, this time accompanied by fresh borlotti beans, and preceded by a mixed grill of porcini, polenta and fried zucchini flowers, with an impromptu stuffing of eggplant and parmesan, made when we discovered we had no ricotta or mozzarella and that, as it is Sunday, the local shop was closed.

Anna Rosa arrived to suggest that the men wore dinner suits to the evening with the aristocrats arranged for tomorrow. We all found this notion hilarious, harking back to travelling in the days of the Grand Tour, when presumably every gentleman included evening wear! She also said that the whole village knew we were looking for ricotta and she had some in her fridge we could have.

Tonight we had a barbecue by the pool. It was still warm enough to sit in T-shirts until 11.00 in the evening. We grilled tiny sausages, and made a salad from radicchio, gorgonzola and toasted walnuts. The lights of Siena sparkled and the orange moon hung low again. There was not even a faint breeze to stir the pines.

2 2 SEPTEMBER

Day Six One of the students declared my green olive and radicchio preparation to be 'like a Tuscan landscape'. I was thrilled at such an image. It was very good, if I do say so myself, and just sort of evolved while I was working. I wanted to create a bed of cooked and rather bitter greens to go with the sliced grilled pigeons for today's lunch. It would be just as good with grilled sausages on another occasion.

A TUSCAN LANDSCAPE FOR TUSCAN PIGEONS OR SAUSAGES

1 red onion, finely diced
2 tablespoons extra-virgin olive oil
1 teaspoon finely chopped garlic
1 radicchio, washed, dried and shredded
2 tablespoons red-wine vinegar
250 g large green olives, cut from the
   stone and sliced
12 witlof, wiped and quartered

½ cup extra-virgin olive oil
4 bunches of cicoria (a long, green
   vegetable with bright-green slender
   stalks and saw-toothed floppy leaves),
   washed and chopped into 3 cm pieces
salt
pepper
juice of 1–2 lemons

Preparation A Sauté red onion in the 2 tablespoons of oil until quite soft. Add garlic and radicchio and cook until the radicchio has melted to a reddish-brown. Add vinegar, increase heat to bubble and reduce liquid fast. Add sliced olives. Cook together for 5 minutes. Set aside.

Preparation B Stew the quartered witlof in a heavy-based pan using the half-cup of oil for about 10 minutes, until it starts to take on some bronze tones. Blanch cicoria in plenty of boiling water for 5 minutes. Drain well and spin in a salad dryer. Add to witlof. Turn to coat with oily juices. Bubble together for 5 minutes.

Add green olive preparation, stirring to blend and meld flavours. Cook a further 5 minutes. Season. Finish with lemon juice to taste. Serve hot, warm or cold.
Serves 8 generously

It is difficult to describe our extraordinary excursion to the home of Nanni Guiso. Nanni is a wealthy man, now retired from his profession as a lawyer and in his late sixties, who has devoted much of his life to pursuing his passion for the theatre and, in particular, string puppets. His family originally came from Spain and later moved to Sardinia, where he was born. He now lives in the nearby countryside in a reconstructed sixteenth-century villa, L'Apparita, set in its own sculptured park, designed by Italy's most famous landscape architect, Porcinare.

One can see no roads, no cars, just the towers of Siena from one boundary, and hills and pines, with the occasional church tower, from the other. One can sit on a gentle rise on banquettes, arranged as for a Greek amphitheatre, and enjoy the theatrical performances that Nanni stages here on a grassy stage. Nanni was a delightful mix of the serious and the outrageous. 'A road is like a zip in an evening dress', he declared early on.

Judging from the signed photographs with warm personal messages that abound in his villa, he appears to have known everyone of consequence, ranging from the Pope, to the King of Spain, Joan Sutherland, John Schlesinger, Princess Margaret, Maria Callas, Visconti and Rudolf Nureyev.

Nanni collects theatrical memorabilia from all over Europe, especially miniature theatres designed for string puppets, and maquettes of theatres, including one of La Scala in Milan and another of a theatre in Rome that was destroyed by fire, so only he now knows what that theatre once looked like. His collections also include the puppets themselves (many outfitted in fabulous costumes), theatre furniture, miniature furniture with which to furnish his tiny stages (a sixteenth-century chest made of ebony with silver-gilt decoration, for example), and sculptural detail from theatres and costumes. Nanni addressed us from the stage of his largest theatre, dating from the seventeenth-century, its stage two metres by three metres. He said that he'd had a ballet commissioned for this little space and that it had proved a memorable evening. His string puppet theatres all work – the curtains open, the lights flicker – and we were privileged to view a scene from *Madama Butterfly*, accompanied by a recording of Callas singing 'One Fine Day'. As the boat pulled away, birds fluttered and Madama Butterfly trembled in despair. It was very moving. Nanni himself was pulling the strings.

The entire collection – theatres, sculpture, paintings, costumes and all the memorabilia – is to be donated to the people of Sardinia next year and relocated there. I have never seen such art assembled in a private home: works by Picasso, de Chirico, Henry Moore and dozens of other artists, some modern, many masterworks of the last century. An extraordinary home, an exceptional man.

Nanni told us that every evening before bed he turns on all his theatres and walks through the house enjoying them. 'I do not want to learn one more thing', he said.

His pleasure in sharing his treasures with perfect strangers seemed genuine if rather astonishing. Our thanks were heartfelt and we all signed his visitors' book, wondering what august names we were following.

23 SEPTEMBER

Day Seven   Tony is a bit worried as to the whereabouts of one of the villa's cats, last seen playing in the mountain of laundry he was sorting and counting. We wonder if it went out with the laundry and into the boot of Anna Rosa's car. There are so many cats it is unlikely we will find out.

Maggie and I had a short but uplifting walk this afternoon. It was good to be out in the air and to watch the pickers in the vineyards. Blue-black and golden grapes were all tossed into the one tub (the traditional method used to make Chianti, rather than Chianti Classico, as Paolo had explained to us). Once one starts to walk along these unmade tracks and minor roads, it is obvious that there are villas everywhere, many well-hidden by clumps of trees. Vegetable plots held the last of the year's tomatoes and fruiting trees featured in every garden.

One of the highlights of today's lunch was a gratin of artichoke hearts and quartered fennel, another triumph of leftovers, or impromptu cooking, however one prefers to view it. When finished, the dish looked at once bubbly and crusty, burnished a dull bronze, positively baroque.

Elena went with some of the students to hear the monks singing vespers at a nearby monastery, Sant'Antimo. Peter, Tony, Maggie and I had a quiet al fresco evening, planning details of our second banquet tomorrow and wondering about the personalities of our third and final group of students.

2 4 SEPTEMBER

Day Eight   A big shop in Monterone this morning. We forgot the celery and the Parmigiano-Reggiano, but we did buy fabulous lamb's lettuce, or *mâche* – or, in Italian, *valeriana*. Some adjustments to tonight's menu will be needed. We will not make fettucine, as there are no truffles, but will instead start the banquet with a small salad. And the cheese tonight will be gorgonzola.

A major distraction today was an expedition to a factory outlet specialising in bags and shoes from Prada and other well-known Italian houses. It proved to be further afield than we had been told, so by the time we had all shopped, settled our purchases and returned to the villa, I was concerned about my preparation for the banquet.

I had no reason to worry – Maggie, who had remained at the villa, had organised everything. On my return, the kitchen was as neat as a new pin, Maggie's guinea fowl dish was looking stunning, all the *panzarotti* were stuffed, and she had even braised artichoke hearts and cooked beans for me. What a friend, and what a partner.

We have promised each other we will not do this project again. To move away from our busy lives in Australia for two whole months has been very difficult to manage. But why are we so adamant? What if we changed the structure? One day less? One school only? Fewer students? Someone on the ground one week beforehand?

The final satisfaction is going to come from having achieved a project spread over such a long time and involving so many people. It just wouldn't be the same if it were too easy. Temperamentally, we both seem to need to pour every ounce of ourselves into these adventures. And while this is quite draining, it is also why our students leave saying things like 'This has been one of the great weeks of my life', 'This has been the best experience I have had in the last ten years', and much more. Entries in our visitors' book are heart-warming. Who knows? Maybe Sicily next time, or Ireland, or France? Or, more likely, our lives will swirl us off in quite different directions.

Paolo de Marchi and his wife, Marta, were our guests at tonight's banquet. It was even better than the last one. Each dish had acquired a little extra finesse.

PANZAROTTI
Delicious and feather-light, hot to bite into, gooey, with mozzarella strings, but sophisticated, with the assertive flavours of salami and spinach.
Antinori Spumante Brut

TUSCAN BEAN SALAD
Creamy, white beans tossed with caramelised onion, parsley and braised artichoke hearts, and spooned onto a nest of tender rosettes of lamb's lettuce.
Pra Soave Classico 1996

SFORMATO OF PORCINI WITH PORCINI AND BONE MARROW SAUCE
Superb and complex flavours, clay-coloured, just like *Crete di Siena* – Paolo had spoken of 'reading the landscape', and here I had done it with food! The sauce was bound with a whisper of cream and we slipped a generous slice of poached bone marrow onto each dish.
Isole e Olena Chardonnay 1995

MAGGIE'S BREAST OF GUINEA FOWL ON CITRUS WITH A BREADCRUMB AND TRUFFLE CREAM UNDER THE SKIN, ON BRAISED WITLOF WITH FLAT ONIONS
Delicious served with just a spoonful of the roasting juices.

GRILLED LEG OF GUINEA FOWL WITH
PANCETTA, LIVER AND WALNUTS ON
RADICCHIO
Course Five! But this was a banquet and the portions
were not large.
La Grola Valpolicella 1993

GORGONZOLA AND RED WILLIAMS PEAR

ZUCCOTTO
Elena and Tony had decorated the *zuccotto* with lines of silver
balls and slices of the candied red grapefruit we had prepared
earlier in the week. And Elena had secretly prepared some
'S's and 'M's in chocolate, so each portion had either an
'S' or an 'M' on it.
Antinori Vin Santo

Rarely have I participated in such a memorable evening. It was an absolutely
fantastic dinner. The room once again looked stunning, thanks to Tony.
Not Caravaggio this time – more riotous, with yellow marguerites in huge
quantities, creamy lilies and tuberoses. Peter served the beautiful wines with
a flourish. No one would have known that glasses were in short supply, but
the reality was that a good deal of between-course washing-up and
recycling was essential.

And so the second school ended. Oops – we forgot the group photo!

26 SEPTEMBER

The Famous Five hit the shops! For our day of rest and recovery, this time
we opted for Siena. Maggie, Elena and I browsed in the boutiques in the
morning, and Maggie and I even found items to fit our somewhat generous
bodies. We both commented on how helpful we found the sales staff in
Sienese boutiques. Like the city, they were gracious and warm. Maybe they
saw us coming, but nothing was too much trouble.

Tony and Peter decided to climb the imposing Torre del Mangia, the central monument in the beautiful Campo, all 86.6 metres of it. They returned one hour later, both rather shaken by the experience, and, although uplifted by the view, they declared it not a good idea for anyone at all bothered by tight corners, claustrophobia or windswept battlements without any restraining devices. Not for me.

I had chosen to spend the same hour in the museum that forms part of the adjacent Palazzo Pubblico. I greatly enjoy the frescoes and narrative paintings of the fourteenth-, fifteenth- and sixteenth-century Sienese schools of art, the backgrounds in so many still recognisable and familiar. Two of the most important works in the museum are by the Sienese master Simone Martini and date from the early fourteenth century. The starry blue of the portico reminded me of the glorious Cimabue frescoes that decorate the ceiling of the Franciscan basilica at Assisi. Then, on the news that very evening, we saw the results of the earthquake that had occurred in central Italy that day and we viewed horrific footage of the slow collapse of the same basilica's ceiling, which killed ten people. And no doubt destroyed forever those very Cimabues I had been remembering. We did not feel a thing in Siena.

As readers of *Stephanie's Seasons* may remember, when I visited Los Angeles in 1992 I experienced a city in the midst of appalling race riots. Later the same year I holidayed in France, and the tiny town I was to go to was swept by devastating floods, drowning more than thirty people. This year I holiday in central Italy, and there is a major earthquake, with ten people dead. I suspect that in medieval times I would have probably been burnt as a witch.

But we didn't hear about the tragedy until the evening and before that, still delighted with our day, we chanced upon an exceptional restaurant where we had lunch. The owner of Ristorante Nello La Taverna later joined us to talk about his philosophy regarding fine produce, and letting ingredients speak for themselves, and respecting the traditions of his region while allowing room for a personal interpretation. He could not know that he was preaching to the converted.

We particularly enjoyed anchovy fillets marinated in extra-virgin olive oil, with shaved white truffles, and a torte of chick peas with fresh artichokes. I ordered a *panzanella* (the tomato and bread salad) to see how a true Tuscan puts it together (more crumbling of the bread, otherwise my version was fine). The pasta was freshly made and the eggplant ravioli was lovely, served with a sauce of melted zucchini flowers. We shared splendid roasted porcini, the meaty stalk split into four, roasted and arranged around the cap like a sunflower. I rarely eat dessert, but was persuaded by a bitter orange mousse with fresh pistachios. Simple food, but so delicious.

A new school tomorrow.

27 SEPTEMBER

*P*eter and I had a horrible time at Monterone this morning – Saturday morning will be avoided in future. Every man and his wife and child were shopping for provisions. The narrow aisles are quite impossible, and I received and probably gave a few vicious jabs with a trolley. Predictably, the aisles displaying canned stuff were relatively empty. But the fresh fruit and vegetables section and the delicatessen counter, where every single shopper in the store needed some prosciutto sliced perfectly and got it, were sheer madness.

We tore the shopping list in half, each took a trolley, and ploughed on with grim determination. Three-quarters of an hour and 500,000 lire later, we were out and on the way back to our haven. This time we startled a cock pheasant, which flew low over the bushes. Lunch, time for a quick spruce-up and then Peter was off to collect our next guests.

Maggie is marvellous with the new arrivals. I tend to skulk in the background, and I can never remember the names for a day or two. Again, the students all loved their rooms. Photographer Simon Griffiths has also appeared and was entranced by the villa. His camera was out of the bag within minutes. And we are off once more.

28 SEPTEMBER

SCHOOL THREE

Day One   Inspired by Friday's lunch at Ristorante Nello, we softened some zucchini flowers in oil in a covered pan over moderate heat, and added them to the pasta sauce for lunch today. They have a delightful and distinctive flavour and texture, especially at the point where the petals join the calyx.

Simon's presence adds a new dimension to every meal. We dish up one portion for him to shoot on a beautiful plate and then serve the students and ourselves on our usual white plates. The walls of the villa are decorated with hand-painted plates – most at least one hundred years old and some much older. We handle them with great care. Their faded colours and chipped edges add to the sense of history.

One of our students is a botanist with a special interest in Australian fungi. I asked her to confirm that the *Boletus* mushrooms that are gathered and sold in specialist outlets in Australian cities as slippery jacks and the *Boletus edulis*, the porcini or cèpe of Europe, are quite different, which she did. She also said that she had once found a *Boletus edulis* in Townsville, under a pine tree. We discussed truffles and truffle cultivation. There are many varieties of truffle, I was told, but the majority are not edible, although some of these are still very attractive to animals. Australia produces a wide variety of these non-edible truffles, which are known and classified by American mycologists. Aboriginal Australians have known about the ones that are edible for thousands of years. Significantly, few in the scientific community had bothered to ask them. This student said she has eaten a truffle in the Northern Territory that tasted like hazelnuts. And her other fascinating comment was that there are plenty of chanterelle mushrooms in Queensland rainforests, but that Australian researchers, scholars and gatherers show little interest in mycology, compared with the research effort in the United States, for example. Today she showed us another specimen of the *Boletus* genus that she had gathered in the woods nearby – this time one that must never be eaten – and we saw how it turned blue when pressed.

I read in the current issue of *Cuisine*, a food magazine from New Zealand (picked up at the airport the day we left Australia), that the research efforts of Dr Ian Hall have resulted in the harvesting of the first black Périgord truffles. The photos showed absolutely magnificent specimens.

Elena has made another of her famous bread puddings from leftover sweet pastries. Sliced and warmed in the oven, it is a popular breakfast dish.

29 SEPTEMBER

Day Two   Both Maggie and I love it when our recipes change. We hope the students do too!

Today we cooked and peeled a small quantity of chestnuts and tossed them with diced pancetta and some seeded wine grapes. This mixture was lengthened with a little olive oil and spooned over barbecued quail. An excellent combination of flavours and textures.

At lunch today two of the students declared they were certain that they had already died and gone to heaven. Another is in bed with a migraine, and I must say I have a pounding headache myself.

30 SEPTEMBER

Day Three   We found the green olives we'd bought at the supermarket to be very salty, too much so to enjoy as a snack, so we blanched them for five minutes in boiling water, cooled and stoned them. The best method for this seemed to be to lean heavily on each olive with a cook's knife. The olive flattened and one could lift the stone out easily. Then they could be incorporated in a combined braise of flat onions and shredded *cavolo nero*.

Today's grilled pigeon was preceded by a dish of braised artichokes, this time with the addition of cardoons, a relation of the globe artichoke. Almost every student expressed some anxiety about handling artichokes, so I gave a very thorough and careful demonstration of some of the ways to handle one.

I covered the heavily trimmed artichokes and peeled, trimmed and blanched cardoons with the remains of the tomato and bread soup mixed with some of Maggie's almond sauce agresto, and covered the lot with fresh breadcrumbs. Two hours in a moderate oven and the artichokes were meltingly tender.

Colin Beer has arrived and Maggie's sunny smile is even wider. Lisa should appear tomorrow, so the character of our community is about to change once more.

Uno   Due   Tre

October

1 OCTOBER

Day Four   Lisa has arrived, with a cold, but delighted to be here nonetheless.

Again the radicchio risotto and the fish – the best yet. Maggie bought spectacular *scorfano* – scorpion fish, fierce and scarlet in colour – and *merluzzo*, which seemed close to our whiting.

2 OCTOBER

Day Five   Today Maggie showed us how to deal with octopus. This was followed by beautiful vegetables – flat green beans; eggplant bathed in balsamic vinegar, garlic and chopped thyme; and young zucchini with zucchini blossoms – and followed once again by the *rotolo*, this time made entirely with porcini, spinach and ricotta.

I often puzzle over how to convince readers that to eat fruit and vegetables that are truly fresh yields superior taste. The small zucchini we had today proved my point. Boiled for five minutes, drained, sliced and drizzled with extra-virgin oil, they were sensational. The slices have a slight viscosity due to those just-picked essential juices, and the stem end is almost crunchy.

September has slipped into October. I wake later, as the morning lacks its early sparkle, but still the sun is up by mid-morning. Parsley and sage bunches are still able to be plucked in the courtyard. We will go to Siena this evening for Lisa's first viewing of the Campo. Elena, meanwhile, is making plans to move on to Spain, and Tony has to go to Toronto to view its production of *Showboat*, his next commission. This is the beginning of the break-up of our little community. We have invited Anna Rosa to our final banquet. Julie comes next week. The market in Florence tomorrow, and then two more days of classes. Now that Simon is here snapping away the reality that there will be a book of our adventures truly dawns on us. We have not had a lot of time to dwell on this up until now. This is not just an experience that will live in our memories but is to be communicated to a much wider audience. We start to turn a more critical eye to the food as it settles on the plate, and we direct Simon's attention to details that we find especially beautiful. The book will be sensational, if his preliminary polaroids are anything to go by!

3 OCTOBER

Day Six   Florence market again. The highlights today were the piles of white truffles at the truffle stall (3,000,000 lire to the kilo), the antics of the showman at the tripe stall, the purchase of two pheasants in feather, the rudeness of the formerly charming woman at the specialist herb stall, and the solicitude of a young man at a vegetable stall.

We have our truffles for the banquet, with a discount because one of the three bought on our first visit proved disappointing. Maggie bought some bull's testicles. The students all assured her they wanted to try them (all, that is, except for the only man in the class and Simon). At the herb stall they were tired of people photographing their wares and tried to shoo us away. I was cross, too, as it had been a long morning and I wanted to buy some wild rocket. Yet this was the very same stall where I had been given the bunch of wild cyclamen last week. Maybe the stall-holder had had a bad morning. Then I watched the young man assisting his elderly customer at the vegetable stall. She bought a lettuce (smaller please), a carrot, a couple of zucchini and so on. Each transaction took some time and the young man was unfailingly helpful throughout. He tucked each purchase into the woman's bag. At the end of it all, he helped her extract the correct notes and coins from her wallet. Gently he pointed out that she was offering him a button, not a 500 lire coin, and then he settled her fine wool cardigan on her shoulders before each wished the other a good day.

At La Fattoria our table had been set in a dark inside corner. After all, it was now October! We asked for it to be reset outside and they smilingly obliged. So many things in Italy seem to be solved with a big smile! The summery, cold tripe salad had disappeared. In its place was a more autumnal *ribollita*, thick and burnished bronze with the distinctive colour and flavour of *cavolo nero*. The temperature was still probably 20°C. Ann said that next week everyone will be in heavy clothes, whether the weather has cooled further or not.

Home again, and the panic of unloading and where to put all this food. The testicles were simmered and then fried and tasted with much hilarity. Most of the men refused point-blank to taste them, although Peter and Tony relented and had a nibble. So did I. I don't think I'll bother again. Like sweetbreads that are faintly chewy, but with a taint of urine, I thought.

Dinner was *panzanella*, followed by a wedge of polenta topped with some grilled porcini, baby sausages, and gorgonzola and apples. I stayed up too late, drank too much wine and woke with a thick head and the knowledge that it would be doubly hard to get through all I have to do.

4 OCTOBER

Day Seven We are on the home stretch now! Today was Paolo's final visit and Maggie switched menus so that she could cook her favourite rabbit and quinces for him. Once again he charmed the students. One senses a visionary – practical and capable in the present, but with longer-term dreams, which he will probably make happen.

Lisa and Colin are very cheerful additions to the family. They will help Tony prepare the room for the banquet tomorrow evening.

Elena packed the remains of the quinces and their juice into a small round bowl. That evening all the students went into Siena, while we stayed in and enjoyed a large salad *caprese* – the classic salad of ripe tomatoes, buffalo mozzarella and torn basil – some salami, and a moulded quince jelly that went wonderfully with gorgonzola dolce. We brought out the guidebooks and started planning where we will go next week. Florence on Wednesday, and San Gimignano and Isole e Olena (Paolo's estate) on Friday.

5 OCTOBER

Day Eight   The students visited Montepulciano and Pienza today while we prepared for the final banquet. Both Anna Rosa and her husband were our guests.

Tony excelled himself. The flowers were red, white and green, the arranged still life in the marble sink included a cock and hen pheasant in full feather. We were twenty-two at the table, with Tony, Elena and Peter all sitting down whenever they could to share in the fun. Tonight's Duomo *zuccotto* had a little cupola on top, made from peaches, and the grappa syrup was tinted pink with the juice of blood oranges. The effect was of the dome bathed in the colours of a rosy sunset.

Tony has established a style that we would have found impossible to achieve alone. He has selected linen, bought and arranged flowers, dealt with the eccentric laundry system, counted sheets and towels meticulously, rearranged furniture so that the house has never looked more gracious, laid out coffee and teacups, soaked away stains, done endless loads of washing, and he is the first one to draw our attention to a walled town, or the Medici crest, or the lion of Venice on an old wall. Now that Simon is here, Tony has the perfect plate in mind for each dish as it is photographed. His eye for detail is remarkable and he is an absolute perfectionist in all that he does.

Elena is a splendid and imaginative cook whose flights of culinary fancy are free-flowing. She has special gifts with pastry and bread baking. Her sunny, happy personality 'that is also a bit salty', as she describes it, is a joy, and she relates well to all our guests, especially those who are more withdrawn or anxious. She is idolised by tiny Sarah, the daughter of the Sri Lankan caretakers. Sarah peeps around the door most afternoons and Elena greets her with hugs and, usually, a biscotti or two as well.

Peter has coped with driving a minibus, finding out-of-the-way locations with never a moment of irritation, backing down narrow lanes, endless shopping expeditions with long lists of ordinary and not-so-ordinary ingredients in often surprisingly large quantities, being the cellarmaster in charge of thousands of dollars' worth of wine, chilling it, serving it, talking about it, and soaking off the labels (he is planning a scrapbook as a souvenir). He is also the principal waiter at table with assistance from Elena and Tony.

He is our only Italian speaker and deals with bookings, taxis, unusual requests from students, and he interrogates the butcher on our behalf. While handling all this he lopes through the day looking relaxed and charming.

At the end of the feast, the students gave us gifts and made enthusiastic speeches. No one left the dining room before 12.30, and they went very reluctantly even then.

Well, we have achieved what we set out to do. To offer a special experience of Tuscany to thirty-six fortunate students. We have not presented ourselves as experts in Italian traditions, but as two experienced cooks and food lovers, who respect any landscape we find ourselves in, and who hope to help others gain the maximum joy and flavour from every meal. We know we have changed the way these people feel about everyday ingredients.

Stephanie and Maggie in Italy has been an important experience for us personally. It has confirmed our friendship and respect for each other, it has made both of us realise just how much we love to cook for people, and we have been vastly enriched by the support and friendship of Elena, Peter and Tony. This shared adventure will bond us forever.

6 OCTOBER

*J*ulie has arrived. Exhausted, with a head cold and without luggage. She has had the distinction of losing her luggage twice – three days ago with British Airways and then again yesterday with Alitalia. But, undeterred, she collected her hire-car and by dint of brilliant navigation found us, even in the middle of a storm. We had a hilarious evening going over the stories that are now part of our collective experience. We also ate wonderfully well.

Maggie made some of her incomparable pasta, which was liberally covered with truffle shavings, and Tony grilled us four massive one-kilo *bistecche alla fiorentina*. These steaks are regarded as luxury food but are nonetheless a very popular restaurant dish. The Italian husbands of our two market guides insist on one steak each. Our family has now grown to nine and we were well-satisfied by the four steaks.

The meat was a delightful surprise. When raw, it is quite pink, very dense and fine-textured, with no interior marbling but a significant rim of white fat. Apart from its massive size, it resembles yearling. Traditionally, these huge steaks are cut from the Chianina cattle, the massive white cattle with the distinctive hump one still sees in Tuscany, and which were around this region in Etruscan times. With the steak we had *radicchio di Treviso*, the long and loose-leafed variety, also grilled over the coals, and a whole head of garlic each, blanched and then grilled. Not traditional, but delicious nonetheless, was Maggie's suggestion of a spoonful of anchovy butter to melt over each steak.

Reading one of our bibles, *Treasures of the Italian Table* (or *Pleasures of the Italian Table*, depending on the edition) by Burton Anderson, I learnt that salt and pepper and a splash of extra-virgin olive oil are the traditional seasonings for the steak, and that butter is considered a French aberration. And, further, that often a Tuscan will accompany his *bistecca* with a dish of shelled beans. Apparently it is not at all uncommon for butchers to sell *bistecca* as Chianina when, in fact, it is cut from beef of lesser quality.

Now that there are no students we have spread out. My new room has a metre-high frieze running around all four walls. On three walls the frieze is a repeated pattern of flower-bedecked and garlanded arched trellises, through which one sees gentle hills and cypresses. The fourth wall depicts the Seven Virtues – Temperance, Fortitude, Hope, Faith, Love, Patience and Justice – each one an angel painted in a manner that recalls the work of William Morris. Uplifting to contemplate for the next three weeks! Underneath the frieze is a painted poem written in an old version of Italian that includes quite a bit of Latin. It will be a challenge to translate.

My room with a view has huge windows that open wide so I can look directly onto the garden. No cats can get in, as they could in my downstairs room, so I sleep much better, enjoying the eddies and drifts of cold night air.

This could become a holiday!

7 OCTOBER

*A*n expedition to Siena is planned after a brunch of scrambled eggs with white truffles. 'Truffles again!' sighed Tony. 'Three meals in a row!' The truffle had nestled among the eggs overnight and the shells, as well as the eggs themselves, were significantly scented.

I bought the flag of every *contrada* – all seventeen of them – and the flag of Siena. These will be the central decoration for a planned Tuscan evening at Stephanie's in five weeks' time! We then had ice-cream at one of the cafes in the Campo. After an initial confusion, occasioning much laughter from both the waitress and us when I ordered lemon and FISH ice-cream for Julie, when I meant peach (*pesca* = peach, *pesce* = fish), we made our selections. Mine was an *affogato* – coffee and vanilla ice-cream drowned in freshly made espresso. Absolutely scrumptious, but I did have palpitations and vivid caffeine-induced dreams.

8 OCTOBER

A day of serious retail therapy in Florence.

The start to my day was a long fax from Melbourne, which contained much that was disturbing. Numbers are down in the Restaurant, although there is still constant demand for places in the already full cooking workshops. It is very difficult to gauge the mood of those back home unless they are more communicative. I feel very cut off.

I pushed it to the back of my mind, where it will not stay for long, and threw myself into the joint spending spree. As Lisa observed in the car on the way to Florence, the 'F' word today is Ferragamo! We shopped till we dropped, and by the time we gathered at Cantinetta Antinori for lunch, our combined bags from Ferragamo, Trussardi, Armani, Gucci, Versace, and Prada, to name but a few, were awesome!

The Cantinetta at Piazza Antinori is a delightful lunch spot. So delightful that we booked for lunch again next week. Situated in an old palace, it has existed for a long time as a local *bottega* but now has been given a designer's once-over and is elegant but simple. The wine bottles in the racks behind the bar were draped with bunches of freshly harvested grapes – purple, green, gold and peachy gold. The food was unfussy and good. No surprises here, but the salad *caprese* was generous and the ingredients were first class, and the freshly cooked white beans with extra-virgin olive oil had Maggie exclaiming in delight, as did Elena after tasting her risotto of scampi, and Peter as he spooned his *pasta e fagioli*. I particularly loved the Antinori rosé, Scalabrone Bolgheri Rosato 1996, a blend of cabernet sauvignon and merlot that breathed raspberries.

One of the reasons we were all so abandoned with our shopping is that it is so easy in Florence. Everything is so close, you can stroll from one treasure house to another. Every sales assistant we met was unfailingly polite and smiling, just as they were in Siena, and of course the favourable exchange rate between the lira and the Australian dollar, as well as the tax-free status of most of what we bought, meant that the prices seemed reasonable.

A terrific day and we drove home in high spirits ready for a 'show and tell' over cocktails mixed by Julie – campari and blood-orange juice!

The long, feathery leaves of the false acacia that line the road are a mix of gold and green – from a distance they look as if they are a mass of yellow flowers. The sky was peachy pink, reflecting a rosy light on the ploughed fields, and behind us a golden sun sank in the west.

The closer we came to Villa di Corsano, the more I was dwelling on the business concerns at home. I will have to do some serious thinking in the morning and send a few faxes.

9   OCTOBER

I woke this morning, after a night of astral travelling. I felt that I had hovered over Stephanie's Restaurant in Melbourne and taken its pulse.

It is time to move on. My senior staff are all good people, but they need more of me than I am able to give if the Restaurant is to continue as a pivotal establishment. My talents are now best used in inspiring others, either by writing, teaching, or consulting on projects.

I felt completely calm and resolved when I told Maggie of my decision as we sat alone over breakfast. Fate is extraordinary. To have come to this

huge decision just at a time when I am in the company of someone who has
made a similar one not so long ago in her own life would seem to have been
planned. It was certainly not planned this way, but there is no question that
Maggie is the perfect sounding-board. She understood the gravity of the
decision and its implications that will affect my life from now on. There is
also no doubt that distance has been important in coming to this conclusion.
Away from the necessity of dealing with the daily grind I have been able to
appreciate how rich life can be. I have spoken about appreciating the good
things so often to others but have not allowed myself much opportunity to
do so. Here in Italy I have eaten under the stars, and in sunny gardens,
walked in leafy woods, laughed and read books and had real conversations
about meaningful things with kindred spirits, and I want to do more of
these things.

I shall now plan the Restaurant's orderly and celebratory closure, and
perhaps I shall have no more nightmares. *The Cook's Companion* has sold
nearly 100,000 copies to date and is still selling well. *Recipes My Mother Gave
Me* appears on the bookshelves next month. And Julie expects the Tuscan
cookbook to be published in April 1998. I believe the public values my
opinion and my integrity, and I want to continue to write truthfully and
openly. This journal is the most personal writing I have ever done and I have
found it cathartic as well as revelatory.

I spent this morning assessing the last twenty-one years, and allowing
myself, for once, to focus on achievements rather than insecurities.

What I would like is for the closure of Stephanie's to be seen as an
important milestone for eating in Australia. I have raised and set standards
over these twenty-one years, and asked questions and solved problems that
no one else seemed prepared to do. I have trained staff by encouraging them
and setting an example, rather than permitting brutality or belittlement to
have any place in the kitchen. I have taught kitchen staff about new produce
and how to handle it, and encouraged specialist suppliers and farmers to
diversify or to harvest their produce earlier. I have written and spoken about
all these things to share knowledge as widely as possible rather than keep a
special supplier to myself.

I have also been continually accessible to the media as a spokesperson for
the industry, always prepared to comment, often to inform, and rarely to be

damning. I have always stuck to my belief that no one has all the answers, that there is always more than one way to do something, that there can never be universal agreement in matters of taste, and that to find a new path or a new way becomes less and less likely as global communication increases.

To that end, I find myself totally disenchanted by almost all those who pass judgement on the eating establishments in this country. The basis of their writing seems to be to make subjective judgements and present them as objective truths. Rarely, in my experience, does one find a food commentator willing to put his or her own money (as opposed to editorial money) into participating in the wider concerns of the food industry. I am utterly tired of reading about the 'new trends' identified by a food journalist, who one month wants all food to be in peachy tones and the next month prefers earthy colours, or who announces the latest 'retro' food he or she has discovered – jelly is suddenly in, or out. Bread and butter pudding is out – oh, unless it's made with *panettone* and flavoured with cardamom. What a waste of words, and how deluded if the authors of these columns think what they are doing is advancing the cause of good food. In Australia we are still a community that increasingly does not and cannot cook even the simplest things, let alone a fine jelly!

My most memorable moments have been the happiness communicated by delighted customers and the marvellous friendships and laughs that have been part of the extended family that is Stephanie's.

The closure involves many logistical problems. I spoke at length this morning with Mark and Anna and both feel that I have made the correct decision. Anna said she hoped I could now have a holiday! I feel lightened somehow even though there is so much to be done.

After all this, before 10.00 in the morning, Maggie, Tony and I walked to the medieval tower we could see in the distance. We passed banks spilling with wild cyclamen, juniper bushes with ripe berries, and hedgerows overgrown with nettles. Past old mill wheels and deserted stone houses, and alongside straggling vines. At one point we saw signs of scrabbling in the earth and there was the collection of soft, web-like threads that our botanist student had identified as the hyphae of a mushroom. Had the spot held porcini, or maybe a truffle? Our imaginations raced, but realistically it is still far too dry for either in this part of Tuscany.

Back at the villa, the rest of the group were wild with excitement. They had revisited the farm where we had bought our goat's milk cheese and had been thrilled to see the farmer making fresh ricotta, which he had scooped into a container for them. We ate it, still faintly warm, with borage flowers and wild rocket as the first course for lunch, and followed that with a delicious *vitello tonnato* and salad.

After lunch we all enjoyed the sight of Maggie plucking the cock and hen pheasant we had bought in Florence a few days ago. A great photo opportunity, which Simon did not miss.

My dear friend Betsy arrives from Cambridge tonight, and we will revisit the country restaurant Le Torre de Stigliano.

We did, and three of the group ordered the nettle risotto again. I know that Maggie has her eye on that nettle patch in the garden and will be asking for volunteers to help pick. We will look for some hefty gardening gloves tomorrow.

Peter has made hair appointments for Maggie and me tomorrow morning. Lisa, a much-needed second Italian speaker, is to accompany us. She jokingly said she needed to look up the word for 'bald'. One doesn't see many Italians with bad haircuts, so we probably have nothing much to worry about. Afterwards we are all off to San Gimignano, described in my guidebook as 'the city of towers'.

And so ended a momentous day.

10 OCTOBER

A big day! The haircuts were excellent and very speedy. Slash, slash with a razor, and not only the excess hair but some of the troubles seemed to fall to the floor. We both immediately looked younger and thinner – well, that is what I am saying. I certainly felt better in every way. I wish I had my Stephanie Dowrick book with me. I feel I need to re-read the section on Courage.

And off to San Gimignano, which is rightly regarded as a jewel in the crown of Tuscany's medieval towns. This part of Tuscany is moist, misty and green, quite unlike our sculptured clay hills. The countryside was glorious, the roadside poplars luminous with golden sunlight and golden leaves.

San Gimignano was an important resting place on the pilgrim route from northern Europe to Rome and became wealthy as a direct result of the pilgrim trade. Its fabulous stone towers were built both as fortresses to defend the town and apparently also as symbols of private wealth. Of the original seventy-six towers, fourteen remain, and it is an unforgettable sight to approach the town from the direction of Certaldo and to see the far-off hill bristling with these towering fortifications, which, on the day we visited, were glowing gold in the midday sun.

In the Museo Civico I loved Taddeo de Bartolo's work, *San Gimignano in trono e i suoi miracoli*, depicting the saint holding the town in his lap (all towers intact), flanked by smaller panels explaining the miracles, with little black devils leaping out of sinners' heads, or lying defeated in crushed heaps, very like cockroaches. And the lovely fragmented fresco of a wedding, showing the guests arriving, the wedding couple sitting gravely in a bath together and, in the next panel, the groom turning back the sheets to slip into the marriage bed.

The Collegiata, the twelfth-century Romanesque church that stands in the main piazza, is one of the most frescoed churches in Italy. Its two walls are brilliant with scenes from the Old and New Testaments that are the work of several well-known artists. I find these medieval frescoes very moving. Mostly they are of country people with honest faces and solid bodies, who are simply dressed, occupied in rural tasks, and handling everyday objects. Their emotions are easily read – pain, horror, sorrow, rapture. Their concerns belong to the real world. The colours used, no doubt muted by the centuries, are the same tones as the rural landscape that provides their livelihood – sky-blue, olive-green and ochres.

We lunched at Le Terrazze, a serious restaurant with a magnificent view over the countryside. A pot of delicious olive paste was on the table with some bread to satisfy those who were ravenous! Dishes voted best of the day were the assorted crostini, including one with shaved truffle, the platter of local salami and prosciutto, the carpaccio of veal on rocket with shaved parmesan, and the risotto of wild boar. I also loved the Rosato wine from Pietraserena, which was a golden pink and reminded me of the Domaine Tempier rosé I also love from Bandol in Provence.

After lunch we visited Paolo de Marchi at his estate, Isole e Olena – I wanted to see his *vin santo* grapes drying on their bamboo racks. We drove and drove around winding roads, climbing higher and higher, over stony tracks that must surely be impassable in winter, marvelling at the stands of cypress forest and dense, lush undergrowth. So very different from southern Tuscany, and Maggie and I were speechless at the realisation that Paolo had made this journey six times for us! And then we were there – and so were others. Paolo exports the majority of his wine and he is widely quoted in international wine books and journals. His guests that day included Czechs, Americans, Israelis, Austrians and us Australians. Last night he had dined with some Chinese visitors, also interested in hearing of his viticultural philosophy.

Making *vin santo* is a labour of love – it could not be justified if the holding time were to be calculated or, even worse, taxed, as it is in Australia. The grapes are picked fully ripe and left to dry on bamboo racks until they shrivel and become like raisins. At Isole e Olena the grapes were a mixture of varieties. In the slanting sunlight that filtered between the racks they shone pink, gold and purple. After four months of drying they are crushed and the very small amount of rich, raisiny juice they yield is transferred to oak barrels with its lees, where it rests undisturbed for four years before being blended and bottled. The barrels are never cleaned of old lees. New *vin santo* juice is added and the process starts again. The grapes we saw today will be the *vin santo* of 2001, the wine in the barrel will be *vin santo* in 2000.

It is uplifting to be with people who are passionate about what they do. Colin, Maggie and I will return for dinner sometime next week. Paolo showed us a superior route for the return journey.

We dined on fabulous tomatoes bathed for an hour in a few drops of red-wine vinegar and a generous quantity of extra-virgin olive oil from Paolo's estate, some gorgonzola and salad. Does a genius have to be mad, was the conversation I remember from that night's dinner table.

And Holly is coming tomorrow for the weekend. Her plane and train journey from Lyon will take eight hours, so we will have to pack a lot of information sharing into a short space of time. We have had lots of long phone calls over the last few weeks.

11 OCTOBER

I have to admit to a sore head again today – as do Betsy and Lisa. We collected Holly and Julie's friend Hilary at the station and farewelled Simon at the same time. Simon is to spend a week in Florence but will return for one more day of photography on Monday.

Lovely to see Holly again – so positive, so cheerful, and loving every new experience. She needed to go over every detail of my life since we had last met, and absorb the impact of my momentous decision. Lisa and I had already had a long session on this subject. I found it easiest to give her the pile of faxes between me and Stephanie's Restaurant and all my diary notes to read, and only then did Holly feel that she was in the picture. Both girls accepted my decision calmly and, I suspect, both believe it to be not a moment too soon. And afterwards we could discuss her life and what had been the best bits of her recent six weeks' travelling in North America.

We have a big lunch party tomorrow to thank the Italian connection for helping to make this adventure happen. So major shopping was needed today. Then we all had a siesta. Maggie cooked her wild pheasants this evening and other than the odd bit of buckshot to contend with, they were rich, gamey and enjoyable, although I don't think I can claim to be a true game afficionado. Elena's beautiful eyes swam with tears when someone asked how the birds were killed and she heard the answer. This put a bit of a downer on the rest of the meal, and what with that and my sore head, I decided to retire early!

12 OCTOBER

*I*t is blustery and cold and we are undecided about whether we will be able to eat inside or outside. A decision will be made later. We are to be eighteen at the table. The menu is:

ANTIPASTO DI VERDURE WITH SALSA AGRESTO
Antinori Spumante Brut

ROTOLO DI SPINACI (AGAIN)
Antinori Cervaro della Sala 1995

GRILLED CHICKENS WITH GRILLED HEADS OF
GARLIC, BAKED FENNEL AND POTATOES
Antinori Tignanello 1994
Isole e Olena Chianti Classico 1995

GORGONZOLA AND TALEGGIO WITH MAGGIE'S
QUINCE PASTE

APPLE TART WITH BROWNED BUTTER TOPPING
Isole e Olena Vin Santo 1991
Aldo's grappa

What a party!

It was a riotous lunch. We formally thanked Ann Parronchi, and Diana and Alix from Antinori, and then proceeded to have a really good time. The party moved from inside (where we had finally set the table) to outside in the courtyard, as almost all our Italian guests were smokers! They loved their lunch, and we are now invited for a day with Antinori at their Santa Cristina estates, and a day with Ann and her husband, Aldo, at their home. Elena struck up an instant rapport with Ann's four-year-old son, Lorenzo, and he fell in love with her and insisted that he be seated next to her!

Aldo discussed the Italian 'live and let live' philosophy over lunch. He agrees that often it flies in the face of what is reasonable or sensible but says he would defend it nonetheless. There seems little doubt that it is this quality about Italy which we all find so infuriating and yet at the same time so delightful.

'I take no notice of red lights after ten in the evening. If there is no traffic, I go. In Naples, if you stop at a red light, the driver behind you will honk the horn. When someone is on one side of the pedestrian crossing there is no need for me to slow, only if they are on my side of the crossing. And the wearing of seat belts, while notionally compulsory, is complied with or not, depending on where you live. The highest percentage (of people complying) is for those who live in the north, nearest to Germany,' Aldo finished with a huge laugh.

I wondered about comparable statistics for pedestrian deaths in Italy and the rest of Europe.

The Italians did not want to leave and it was after 6.00 p.m. before they drove away. The two men made substantial inroads into the grappa. I have decided that grappa is most definitely not for me.

Most of us crashed for a couple of hours and I woke at 9.30! It was a ridiculous hour to get up again, but I did, and found Lisa, Holly and Elena engrossed in a giant jigsaw, Julie writing up her diary, and Peter and Colin playing chess and sipping red wine. Maggie, Tony and Hilary were nowhere to be seen. I chewed on a piece of dried bread with pecorino and drank a pot of tea. I have not the patience for jigsaws, so went back to bed to read.

13 OCTOBER

*H*appy birthday, Dad – eighty-nine today!

Maggie, Elena and I worked on the recipe booklet to record all the changes and spontaneous cooking that have made the last four weeks such a challenge and so delicious. Julie needs to take an accurate record back with her to Caroline, our editor.

Then we took Holly to the station. The months will race by and although I will miss her very much, April will arrive soon. In a way I probably don't need too many domestic distractions while I deal with the next stage of my life.

Elena leaves tomorrow morning for Spain and ultimately for Australia. We will certainly miss her huge smile, flashing eyes and, of course, her clever hands and 'salty' tongue. She will be on hand for the Tuscan dinner at Stephanie's and assures me that any time I desperately need her she will be there.

Maggie made a pumpkin risotto using the brilliantly orange *zucca* we bought a few days ago. We take pride in using everything edible, so I cut every scrap of chicken from an extra bird from yesterday's party. The very last of the salsa agresto and the last of the grilled eggplant also went into the pan. The risotto was wonderful and looked great, speckled with rich orange and the black skins of the eggplant and creamy chicken bits. It all disappeared in a flash.

14 OCTOBER

*A*nother trip to Florence – just the girls this time, and we decided to take the train. Lisa was in charge of the expedition, buying the tickets, checking the platform, and reading the maps. What amazing daughters I have.

Betsy and I caught up on each other's life during the one and a half hour trip. So much happens to every one of us that is draining, depressing or confusing. And if one is away from those friends who do care and want to listen, troubles can seem almost overwhelming and it can be difficult to believe that these things will pass or will ever be resolved.

In his book *Friendship: Being Ourselves With Others*, Graham Little distinguishes between social friendships, familiar friendships and communicating friendships. Social friendships oil the wheels of social doings, always with an eye on the exit, he says; familiar friends go out of their way to be indispensable to others but still like some control over them; and communicating friendship is the relationship par excellence for self-discovery, in which one can and does communicate deeply, honestly and sometimes painfully. Communicating friends do not play safe all the time. Betsy and I have a communicating friendship.

I was trying to remember how long we have been friends. Certainly since Lisa was very young – for two years Betsy lived in a tiny flat behind my house, before Stephanie's Restaurant and the household moved to Hawthorn, and she looked after the children in the evenings while I worked. Betsy and Lisa had a special bedtime ritual: Betsy would tuck the blankets in very firmly and tell Lisa she was being 'hammered in' so she was absolutely safe and sound.

We had another outstanding lunch at the Cantinetta Antinori. The five of us shared five appetisers – cheese crostini, *cavolo nero* with garlic on crostini, country truffle sandwich, artichokes in olive oil, and raw *ovoli* mushrooms with celery and shaved Parmigiano-Reggiano.

All were delicious. However, within fifteen minutes I felt very, very unwell. No one else had any adverse reaction, but I left the table quickly and wandered the cool streets, unable to eat and fighting waves of nausea and feeling faint. I was also scarlet in the face. I am convinced it was related to eating the raw *ovoli*, and yet I have had them before. Could there have been a speck of something else in my portion? I will never know. The worst part was that I felt quite unable to eat the rest of my lunch, which was devoured by the others and pronounced magnificent – fresh white beans with tender scampi, calamari and prawns. After an hour I had more or less recovered, but remained weak for the rest of the day.

I still managed to buy an exquisite, delicately sculptured pair of earrings on the Ponte Vecchio: yellow-gold grape leaves, white-gold grapes and a pinprick diamond. And some hand-embroidered table linen.

That night, back at the villa, I went to bed early and Betsy came and 'hammered me in'.

15 OCTOBER

*B*etsy left at 5.00 this morning. I wish she could have stayed longer. And Maggie and Colin have gone to look at pasta-drying machinery in Florence and will not return until tomorrow night.

Elena has left us a beautiful note. It was resting against her farewell loaf of panettone together with a pink rosebud. It was a very personal letter, but she will not mind me quoting one sentence, I am certain: 'I have learnt so much and I have felt an extraordinary range of emotions while learning. In many ways it has been difficult for me, but the more difficult = the more rewarding'.

It was very cold last night and for the first time I closed my windows. There was frost on the glass when I woke. I walked with Lisa and Tony this morning, and the sky was a cloudless blue, the outline of Siena and its towers crystal-clear on the horizon. The rain has washed the leaves clean, and the scent from the bay hedge was wonderful. As we walked under the oak trees through the moist leaf litter, one could almost sense movement beneath it. In a few days, if this weather continues (rain at night, with sunny days), we can be certain of mushrooms. Although after yesterday, my enthusiasm for mushrooms is a bit diminished!

16 OCTOBER

$\mathcal{A}$ quiet day. Julie and Tony have driven to Rome to deposit Hilary and collect Damien. Maggie and Colin are still in Florence. Peter, Lisa and I pottered in the morning and then visited another medieval town, Buonconvento, where we lunched at a very simple and very local restaurant.

Wonderful *ribollita*, and I had *bollito misto*, with its bowl of *salsa verde*. I was interested to see how it would be served, as several years ago I had *bollito misto* served in very grand style from a trolley at the Ristorante Ciccarelli at Madonna di Dossobuono, near Verona, and I am to cook the dish myself for sixty people for a Slow Food Movement luncheon in December. Here it arrived as a slice of veal tongue, unpickled, a chunk of fat chicken simmered in the broth, and some beef brisket on the bone. The broth was not served and the *salsa verde* appeared to contain nothing but very fresh parsley, lots of capers, black pepper and extra-virgin olive oil.

I am the cook tonight and we want the newly arrived Damien to have a wonderful meal.

One of the by-products of the school was two containers of excellent frozen fish soup and a bag of frozen cleaned fish heads. Knowing that two of Julie's favourite foods are mussels and quail, I have decided that the menu will be mussel and potato saffron soup, grilled quail with fresh bay leaves, and Tony's favourite, Grandma's bramble cake, made with the very last of the blackberries and augmented by some of the pears Peter braised with bay leaves and Nebbiolo last night.

Grandma's bramble cake (the recipe for which appears in *The Cook's Companion*, p 122) is supposed to be made with a pastry that uses soft lard. I could not find any here, so I used butter and added some baking powder to the usual flour. The result was absolutely splendid! Its special character comes from the fruit being baked for a long time, encased in dough, and then after it comes from the oven, one prises off the pastry lid, and sprinkles in a generous quantity of sugar and a few chunks of butter.

Peter and I made a desperate dash for a fish shop in Siena and secured some mussels only minutes before it closed. We just had time to get to the station and collect the weary but elated returned travellers. Maggie and Colin had visited a small family company that makes and dries high-quality pasta, and Maggie's enthusiasm was at fever-pitch as she described how the freshly cut strands of spaghettini danced and swayed 'like a belly dancer' under the currents of the air dryers. Within minutes Julie, Tony and Damien arrived also and suddenly what had been a very quiet day became once more full of noise, laughter, excitement and the popping of spumante corks.

I had bought some exquisite green beans and more of the flat onions that we are enjoying so much. They combined to make an unexpected side dish for the grilled quail. The beans were boiled and drained, the onions were braised in some guinea fowl stock and water until tender and the juices syrupy, and then I combined the two and added some fine oil. After most of the vegetables had been eaten, we tipped the rest and every drop of juice over the few remaining quail that will have to wait for another day.

17 OCTOBER

*J*ulie, Damien and Tony are in Florence for a last shop before driving to France for a week's holiday together. Colin, Maggie and Peter are off to Orvieto for the weekend to attend the Slow Food Movement Conference. It is Lisa's last day for sightseeing, buying gifts, packing and saying goodbye. So we are off to Siena again.

Siena revealed another face today. This town has the marvellous ability to surprise one continually. It is not so large and yet it has many different neighbourhoods. The relatively crowded tourist precinct around the Campo is busy with interesting shops and sights, but only a few streets away one finds a Roman wall, a Renaissance church, a quiet local street, an artist's studio, not to mention an extraordinary Gothic cathedral.

Lisa and I went in early to finally visit Il Duomo and the chapel of Santa Caterina. We turned down a different street and soon found ourselves far from tourist Siena. Steep, narrow lanes of brick and cobblestone, perhaps three metres wide, meandered between the stone houses. Creamy stone plaques on the houses listed their dates as 1619 and 1632. In Via della Galluzza, houses on each side were linked by aerial stone corridors. In the Vicolo della Macina, we peeped into the small windows of Ristorante Santa Caterina da Bagoga. It was chock-a-block with Italians, whereas the main tourist restaurants on the Campo are slowing down now as the tourist trade lessens. We entered the cloister of Santa Caterina and were just about to embark on an appreciative visit to the chapel when we noticed that the massive iron gates had been locked, locking us inside! Fortunately a nun came out and explained that it was lunchtime and the chapel was closed until later in the afternoon. We wondered how we would have spent the three hours if she had not noticed us.

Instead we walked on to the Piazza del Duomo and the spectacular unfinished cathedral with its banded black and white facade, said to have been inspired by the cathedral at Orvieto. The interior is overwhelming. There is richness upon richness, magnificence piled on magnificence. I found it difficult to respond to. The extraordinary and justly famous mosaic and inlaid marble floors are almost mind-altering and have a psychedelic effect after one looks too long at the dancing lines and shapes. Wherever one glances there is a masterpiece, stone relief carvings, a polished marble pulpit with its columns resting on carved marble lions, gilded coffered ceilings, stunning inlaid wood in the choir stalls, stained glass, decorated fan vaulting, frescoes, bronzes, engravings and much more. Donatello's bronze work of St John the Baptist was being restored.

It was with almost a sense of relief that we entered the tiny Library Piccolomini, in a side aisle, named for a wealthy Sienese family of the fifteenth-century. Here are displayed gorgeous metre-high illuminated manuscripts and the walls are covered with frescoes by Pinturicchio, which portray the life of Pope Pius II. The paintings are so fresh and animated, the colours so bright, that one might think the works were done not so long ago. This small room is a jewel that one must see.

After culture came lunch and an abortive attempt to visit a wine bar.

No one wanted to serve us so we left and ended up with a mediocre snack. Never mind, tonight Damien is cooking and he has gone to Florence to sniff out truffles as well as visit Armani.

Both were achieved.

Our 'farewell to Damien and Julie' dinner was a delicious simple risotto with zucchini covered with a thick layer of fine beige truffle shavings. Even the next morning when I finished the washing-up there was a memory of truffles in the rinsed-out pot.

18 OCTOBER

*L*isa has gone. I feel bereft! Angie and her husband, Duffy, arrive this afternoon. It has been a changing of the guard at the Cafe – with Lisa gone Angie held the fort; now Angie is here and Lisa is winging her way home to fill the gap.

The pair arrived and, as always, are brimming with enthusiasm, even after thirty hours of travelling direct from Australia. They loved the villa, the views, and the soft autumn afternoon. Both Angie and Duffy bring to life a dedication to making every moment as meaningful, as enjoyable and as positive as possible. One could have no better companions on any adventure.

Tony lit the fire and I asked him to explain his technique carefully. He leaves in three days and for the final week the fire-lighting and grilling skills will have to be passed on to others.

Tony sets the fire with light kindling, mostly dried bay leaves still on their long stems. The bay hedges on the property are very old. The boughs, which are lopped regularly and which form the basis of our grilling fires, are cut into small logs about six centimetres in diameter.

Tony also adds a few pine cones, but not too many, as we do not want a resinous flavour in our food, and a sheet of paper. A few of the more substantial logs are placed at the back of the fire, which is contained in the massive hearth by a U-shaped piece of iron. This has uprights on each side of the U, with guiding lugs where a mesh grill can be settled at various

heights. Tony builds the fire quite high, with some of the bay logs on top.
Once lit, it burns fiercely for about twenty minutes and then settles into a
shallow bed of coals. These are then raked to an even thickness and the food
is arranged on the mesh grill, either directly, or on vine leaves or fig leaves,
and is tended appropriately. The ability to be able to alter the height of the
grilling mesh gives wonderful flexibility. If the quail needs a moment to crisp
at the end of its cooking time, or the already grilled polenta needs a fast
reheat to melt the cheese that has been dotted on top, the grill can be
arranged only a few centimetres from the coals.

Sounds pretty straightforward, but the skill is in knowing how big a fire
to build, which in turn relates to how long one intends to grill. The thicker
logs at the back of the fire are there to provide extra fuel should the heat die
away too quickly.

I had marinated some chunky chicken legs in rosemary, bay and lemon
with extra-virgin olive oil and pepper. Boosted with a few sausages and some
zucchini chunks, this was a light dinner.

I had been reading Burton Anderson in the afternoon and was filled with
a desire to try cooking fresh shelling beans *al fiasco* as he describes it.
Apparently the traditional way is to put the beans and liquid (presumably
water) into a *fiasco*, the straw-covered flask in which Chianti is still sold (one
removes the straw), and to bury the glass container in the coals, after which
the beans would murmur away until cooked. Well, I had no glass Chianti
flask and no likelihood of a fire that would burn all afternoon, so I had to
improvise! I removed an empty flowerpot from the garden, washed it very
well, stopped its hole with a plug of pastry, then half-lined the pot with foil
as an extra precaution, tipped in fresh borlotti beans and a bay leaf and filled
the pot with light stock and put the whole thing in a slow oven two hours
before dinner.

It seems I have created a true fiasco! Two hours later, the liquid is barely
warm and the beans are still hard. I increased the oven heat and when I
inspected just before bedtime the beans were still not cooked. I turned the
oven off, leaving my *fiasco* in it and went to bed. (I did register that one
and a half kilos of fresh borlotti beans in their pods yields 500 grams
once podded.)

19 OCTOBER

*T*he *fiasco* is not a fiasco. In the morning the beans were ninety-five per cent cooked. At lunchtime I finished them off in a pot with olive oil and appropriate seasonings. We enjoyed them with tinned tuna, not of the quality of the Cantinetta Antinori, alas, but the best that the *alimentari* could offer. Maggie says that earthenware dishes of beans are usually left all night in a low oven and that it is not surprising that my beans took so long by this method.

Anna Rosa invited us on a walk to see a very old 'hermit's house'. As we walked, she told us of her childhood in this place. She is one of five children who spent their early years roaming the countryside, discovering mysterious stones, gathering porcini and *ovoli*, and following the running stream to where it opened into cold, clear pools for swimming. She grabbed at a high wire fence along the dusty road and said, with sadness rather than bitterness, 'Foreigners! It breaks my heart to see Tuscany with fences. Once there were no fences in Tuscany. Everything was open. You could walk everywhere. Everyone knew the names of the farmers, and land and crops were respected. There was no need for this. Now the land has been sold, to foreigners for holiday houses, and they immediately put up a fence'.

She told us the history of the hills and of the nearby necropolis of Etruscan origin covered over by forest, and she pointed to the marks of chariots on a narrow path that she says was an old Etruscan (or Roman) road. The medieval tower we have viewed from a distance is one of a series of fortifications, most long since crumbled away, that enabled speedy communication in medieval times. Today black ravens swooped and dipped over the tower. Anna Rosa's stories were from the vantage point of a privileged childhood, and it was only after Mussolini seized property that had been the source of her grandfather's wealth that her family fell on leaner times, and were forced to sell hunting rights and, more recently, to lease out the considerable property they still owned.

We came to the ruins of the extraordinary stone dwelling. Anna Rosa claims it was built around 800 BC – I do not know how she has determined this. Gradually the house is being claimed by the forest. An earthquake damaged the staircase that she says was still largely intact when she was a child; there are now two steps remaining. There is a crude cross engraved on the stone (but this is supposed to be before Christ?), and a man-made ledge, perhaps for a lamp, and an upper storey that is almost gone. We climbed on and around this amazing structure, in awe at being in such an ancient place that is presumably known to other local residents, who are content to let it be. There was absolutely no sign of vandalism or of recent disturbance. The lightly wooded forest and twisting vines grew over and around it. The only sound was the faint murmur of running water from the streamlet below us.

20 OCTOBER

I have a cold and am feeling down. Everyone has decided to have a quiet day. It is misty and there is rain somewhere near. Anna Rosa has brought us some fossils she has just found – sculptured sea shells. Apparently, they are regularly discovered when the clay clods are ploughed. I can imagine that there must be some effect on the psyche from living in a town held snug by medieval walls, from walking along streets that one can span with outstretched arms, from sharing one's space every day with busloads of foreigners. Yet any sense of a limited horizon is offset by the reality of the layers and layers of living that have already taken place here. And beyond the walls, the evidence is on every hilltop, in the ground itself, and even hidden in the forests, of earlier people, some known about, others unknown. What does this mean to the present-day citizen of Tuscany, I wonder?

Maggie cooked a delicious dinner of hand-rolled *cavatelli* pasta (each noodle the shape of a small cowrie shell) made in the small factory she and Colin visited, with *cavolo nero*, sausages and toasted breadcrumbs. Afterwards I fried a few slices of a bread pudding in butter as a prototype for a winter dessert at the Cafe.

In two weeks I will be back home and just for a moment I felt frightened as the prospect of all that awaits me.

21 OCTOBER

*T*oday we returned to green Chianti to visit two specialist butchers and go to a linen shop in Greve. And it is raining – a soft mist that obscures the horizon and any long view, but highlights the changing autumnal hues that are all around us as we drive. I am entranced by mingled gold, bronze, plum and green leaves.

At Panzano we call into Antica Macelleria Cecchini. This butcher's shop is unlike any I have seen. Verdi is playing, there is a contemporary stone sculpture of an exuberantly welcoming naked woman in the shop. Hanging are stalactites of salted and dried split pigs' feet, next to festoons of brilliant chillis. The dried beans of Tuscany are displayed in terracotta pots, a massive terracotta urn holds bold sprays of rosemary, bay and sage to be offered to customers. The butcher is a showman and has an adjacent area where he gives demonstrations and tastings of his pork products. The demonstration bench is a mighty slab of marble, the walls are decorated with contemporary ceramic panels, the floors are pale flagstones. He gives us a list of his products. This is no ordinary list, but a fine work of typography on wonderful paper, with a description of a product and underneath a simple recipe with cooking times. It is twenty pages long and very impressive.

In the section titled 'Stuffed goods', I read of duck stuffed with chestnuts, guinea fowl stuffed with pistachios, chicken breasts filled with white truffles, rolled turkey breast stuffed with sausage meat and prunes, and meatballs made from ham and pork and wrapped in spinach greens.

On another page I read that we must soak the pig's foot we have bought for one or two days before cooking it in soup with beans.

PIEDUCCI DA ZUPPA
(TRANSLATED BY ME WITH HELP FROM PETER)

1 pig's foot, salted and dried　　　*500 g dried beans (for preference zolfini* or bianco valdarnese)* *zolfini* are pale-yellow dried beans of a variety I have never seen before, kidney-shaped, but the shape is less pronounced and they are smaller than cannellini.

Soak the pig's foot for 1–2 days in cold water and for the last twelve hours, add the dried beans.

Rinse well and bring to boiling point in generous quantities of water, without any seasoning, as these trotters have all the flavour necessary.

Check if the beans are cooked in a couple of hours.

Set half the beans aside and purée the rest using some of the cooking water. Add all of the beans to the purée. Cut the meat from the bones of the pig's foot. You now have a soup base to which you can add *farro* (wheat) and seasonal greens such as beet tops or *cavolo nero*.

Serve over Tuscan bread rubbed well with garlic.

Serves 6

We drove on to Greve in Chianti, which is probably visited by every tourist in Tuscany. It is a most attractive and bustling town. Among the antique and souvenir shops were excellent food shops, and in one we bought a flattened disc of very fresh pecorino for dinner this evening and some truffled polenta. At the fish van conveniently parked in the square we bought octopus, also for dinner this evening. And I had the most delectable custard-filled flaky pastry for morning tea. At Antica Macelleria Falorni we admired the extensive range of smoked and cured products, displayed both whole and sliced. The ceiling was covered in suspended hams, the hairy ones indicating that they were from *cinghiale*. Cured pork fat, *lardo*, was sold in chunks, heavily coated with crushed rosemary, spices and salt. Thin slices of this are a favourite crostini topping. We bought some to try later at the villa.

And then on to pretty Volpaia for a simple lunch (we are to have a banquet tonight for Tony's last night). This tiny but enchanting town was rich with the smell of crushed grapes. In the stone tower of the castello there was a pigeon nestled in each available crevice, cooing softly. It was still raining.

Dinner was fantastic. Maggie had selected two of Tony's favourites from the school repertoire. We enjoyed braised octopus with tomato and green olives, followed by the famous rabbit, this time with truffled polenta and flat onions, Tony's favourite gorgonzola dolce, and Peter made chocolate crepes and stuffed them with dried figs cooked in *vin santo* and folded into mascarpone.

Tony is off to Florence tomorrow morning and was ecstatic to read in *Chianti News*, the local multilingual paper, that the Passage of the Princes, the Vasari Corridor that links the Palazzo Vecchio with the Pitti Palace, is now open to the public after more than 400 years. We have all been reading *The Sixteen Pleasures*, a novel by Robert Hellinga, set during the aftermath of the catastrophic floods in Florence in 1966, and one of the most gripping sections deals with the rescue of the paintings from the Vasari Corridor while the waters raged beneath and the narrow corridor swayed and creaked precariously.

22 OCTOBER

*T*oday we visited Ichiko and David Noonan in their Umbrian home. Far-off sailboats dotted Lake Trasimeno, which shimmered in the sunshine. The air was clear after yesterday's rain. We met David at a point off the motorway and then started the real driving. Up and up, the nearest village is tiny Mercatello, but we kept on climbing. Ichiko and David have their home on top of the world, it seemed. They look straight across a deep valley to distant hills, and in today's perfect conditions we could see the shape of the basilica at Assisi. We were entertained wonderfully well and it was late afternoon before we returned to the villa.

Peter told us the hilarious story – hitherto unknown – of how once upon a time, maybe two years ago, he was surfing with some friends in South Australia. He had a few days off but was due back at Stephanie's at 7.00 one night a week or so hence. As he tells it, the swell dropped and his friends decided to move on, searching for the perfect wave, and Peter just sort of went along. When they got to the beginning of the Nullabor he more or less shrugged and said, why not! To cut a long story short, after a few days of fabulous surfing at Margaret River, south-west of Perth, Peter realised that his date with the Restaurant was looming. He and one friend set out for Melbourne and drove without stopping for three days, changing drivers every few hundred kilometres. An hour out of Melbourne, he showered, shaved and settled in for the final stretch. He hit Melbourne with half an hour to spare and rang to reassure everyone that he was on the way, and was more than a little crestfallen to be told that he had been rostered off that night!

And he had never told me before. We laughed tonight but I guess Peter didn't laugh at the time

23 OCTOBER

Today Angie, Duffy and I visited the walled town of Monteriggioni. Tony and I had always been intrigued by its perfectly preserved crenellations and its fourteen towers as viewed from the road to Florence, but this was our first visit. The town is tiny and entirely within the walls. Probably all of its residents are involved in tourism in some capacity, I imagine. It appeared to have little general commerce other than an antique shop, several tourist shops, a luxury hotel and a very good restaurant, Il Pozzo, where we lunched. The buildings looked unchanged since medieval days, although they were perfectly maintained. The only strikingly contemporary note was the bright-yellow Ferrari cheekily parked in the very centre of the piazza. Everyone else parked outside the walls.

An impressive restaurant. A woman in her sixties, probably one of the owners, had one dining room entirely under control. There would have been about thirty customers. She took the orders, carried the food, served the wine, presented the bills, and had plenty of time to pat the head of a little boy eating with his parents, and to cradle a very young baby. The food was interesting and good. Highlights were the salad of raw artichoke with shaved Parmigiano-Reggiano and celery, the chestnut ravioli with a pork sauce, and the *cartoccio* of tortelli with white truffles.

We discussed, among other things, the cult of the presenter – where the newsreader is considered more important than the news, or the interpreter believes he is as creative as the artist. Good talk, good food, good friends.

Back to the villa and to more faxes. The pieces in the jigsaw in Melbourne are being settled into place. It is fantastic to have Anna and Mark working on all the various bits. We will coordinate the announcement of the closure of Stephanie's Restaurant with the launch of *Recipes My Mother Gave Me*. This book, with its emphasis on reflecting a life's work, and its reminders of how we all change and develop, seems a perfect link with my decision to move on from one stage of my life, and to look at some of the new directions that are waiting for my attention.

We had the pork *lardo* on hot garlic-rubbed bruschetta as an antipasto tonight. Just needed a sprinkle of pepper and salt.

24 OCTOBER

I have been reading an interesting book lent to me by our friend Ann Parronchi, *Food and Drink in Florence* by Antonio Villaresi. I may have to revisit Florence next week, even if only to check out some of the addresses included in the book. The author points the reader to the best wine shops and the best producers of bread, cheese, fried chitterlings, *finocchiona* and ice-cream, to name a few. There are also addresses of places one can visit near Florence to view old olive presses and so on. Maybe it will have to wait until next time. Maggie and I are sorely in need of time to sit and read and do very little. In just over a week this will all be a memory.

The book included the recipe for that most Florentine of dishes, *Crostini di fegato di pollo*, attributed to our favourite lunch spot, the Cantinetta Antinori. These crunchy bread slices appear with many toppings, but chicken liver is the most traditional.

Finely chop an onion and brown it in a pot in a tablespoon of olive oil along with three bay leaves. When the onion is golden yellow, add six chicken livers from which the membranes and filaments have been removed. Stew gently over low heat. Stir repeatedly with a wooden spatula as the livers cook. Pour in half a goblet of white wine and cook until it has evaporated. Add half a cup of broth and a pinch of salt. Cook for five minutes more, then remove the livers from the pan and chop or mash them along with four anchovy fillets and a teaspoon of capers preserved in salt that have been washed in warm water. Put the purée back in the cooking pan, add a large tablespoon of butter and cook the purée, without letting it come to a boil. Pour the purée in a small bowl and allow it to cool, stirring occasionally. Smear the liver paste on slices of toasted and buttered home-made bread and serve with a slightly sweetish white wine.

There was also a recipe for an unusual pasta dish, *striscioli*, that includes forty grams of olive paste, 500 grams of flour and six eggs, and recommends the pasta be combined with sautéd cauliflower, tomatoes and crumbled sausages. I think I would like to play with this recipe when I return to Melbourne.

25 OCTOBER

We packed the car with all the cooking equipment lent to us by Ann, which we were now returning, along with various things we hoped she would find useful. Our lunch with Ann and Aldo today was the first real intimation that all this is abruptly coming to an end. I pushed the thought aside and settled back to enjoy the day.

Chianti again and another perfect day. Less than an hour later we were in paradise. Ann and Aldo bought a tumbledown property ten years ago that included a tiny church, San Martino a Sezzate. The building in which they live had been both the priest's house and a farmhouse, with room for animals, including pigeons. There is a long story of how the property was finally acquired.

Ann said that when they were looking for a place to buy, she and Aldo knew that if they could find a church for sale the property would have a marvellous view, as the Church has been very astute at picking good spots. It had certainly done so this time.

One of the conditions of the sale was that the tiny church remained available to the faithful. Technically it still is, although the entrance is now inside Ann and Aldo's house. Ten years on, they have made this into one of the most beautiful homes I have ever seen. The law in Tuscany (and probably elsewhere in Italy) decrees that you can only rebuild to the dimensions and proportions of what went before, and that traditional materials must be used. Not only does this ensure beautiful and *simpatico* houses, but presumably it also guarantees the continued availability of stonemasons and hewers of mighty beams, as their skills are still needed.

In the kitchen was a wonderful woman called Flora, a tough little lady who has helped Ann for many years, and is a real character. Flora was assisted by her niece, Marina, another nuggety and strong woman. Both were in their late sixties but they jumped around the kitchen checking on this and that in a very sprightly fashion. Marina was busy chopping the leaves of young rape with her *mezzaluna*. Only the tender leaves were used and each rib had been discarded (as we would sometimes do with silver beet). A mountain of soft, green, blanched leaves waited to be chopped.

At the other end of the kitchen Flora was impatient to begin making the pasta – 'Do you want to eat today or tomorrow?' she demanded of Ann. So we clustered around and watched her beautiful and very strong brown hands whisk fourteen eggs into a kilogram and a half of flour with nary a speck of flour sprayed onto the flagstones. She slapped the ball of dough with great force several times on the marble workbench, and twisted it round and round like a top before proceeding to roll it out on Ann's dining-room table. It was left to dry, scattered with fine semolina, looking like pools of spilt custard on the white cloth.

Flora is famous locally for cooking porcupine, now a protected species. Having read the grisly novel *Perfume* by Patrick Süskind over the last week, I was intrigued to hear that Flora and her family have grown irises for the perfume trade in Grasse for several generations. The rhizomes are harvested after the flowers have died down and are peeled and dried. Sliced and powdered, they become orris root, which secretes the precious scent. The porcupines eat the valuable rhizomes before they are harvested so are regarded as absolute pests. Just like our rabbits, we all thought.

With the *cinghiale* sauce 'chirping' away, Flora checked the suckling pig in the bread oven. It was a glowing golden brown and smelt wonderful. The butcher had advised Ann that the twelve-kilo pig would take seven hours to cook. 'What nonsense,' exclaimed Flora. 'After that time it won't even have eyes to cry with.' She advised rubbing it with salt, and sticking bits of rosemary twig and garlic slivers here and there in small cuts, and allowing three hours. Flora was right.

To precede the pasta and suckling pig were two of Flora's specialities, *donzelli* and *polpette di cardi*. She stressed that nothing was ever made correctly any more and with ferocious glances of adoration at Ann, tossed at her 'She only thinks of the flowers!'.

The *donzelli* were small pieces of well-risen bread dough that were fried in hot olive oil, drained well and lightly sprinkled with salt. Not dainty food, but very appealing after the long drive and with the smells of all these wonderful things filling the air. The *polpette* – tiny fritters, or rissoles, of cardoons – were wonderful, and could be made with spinach or, more subtly, with spinach mixed with some boiled artichoke hearts.

Cardoons are rarely available in Australian markets (although I have seen them for sale at Cabramatta, a suburb of Sydney), and Ann said that frequently this dish is made by Flora using the long stalks of the artichoke after the flower is picked so as not to waste anything.

POLPETTE DI CARDI

I am guessing the quantities, but the amount of squeezed, drained, chopped cardoons looked like four cups. This might need as many as twenty stalks.

cardoons (or artichoke) stalks
water
juice of two lemons
5 eggs
large handful of dried breadcrumbs

large handful of grated Parmigiano-Reggiano
generous grating of nutmeg
salt and pepper
olive oil for frying

Thickly peel the cardoons. Cut into 10 cm lengths and soak in water acidulated with the juice of one lemon for an hour or so. Discard the water and then boil the stalks in some more acidulated water, using the juice of the second lemon, for nearly an hour until they are completely soft. Drain thoroughly, then squeeze them very well to remove all the moisture, and chop them very finely with the *mezzaluna*.

Place the chopped pulp in a large bowl and add the 5 eggs, breadcrumbs, Parmigiano-Reggiano, nutmeg, and salt and pepper.

Roll tablespoonfuls of the mixture in extra breadcrumbs and fry in olive oil until golden. Drain well.

Serves 6

After offering these as an appetiser Flora must have had some left over. Later in the lunch they reappeared in the *cinghiale* sauce. I liked this – nothing was wasted. A cook after my own heart.

I moved away from the kitchen as I was too tempted by the mounds of *donzelli*. A robin redbreast clung to a leafless fruit tree in a courtyard edged with thick rosemary bushes. Around the corner, and another courtyard where the luncheon table was laid. The garden here was more riotous – old roses clung to the stone walls, and the garden was a mix of herbs and aromatic cottage plants, such as lavender, honeysuckle and bonfire salvia. A third inner courtyard presented a cool, stone-walled space with a sober stone ledge on which reposed a series of weathered terracotta pots, each with a chrysanthemum in bloom. It seems impossible to look on anything ugly in these surroundings of old stone, wood worn smooth with age, and rush baskets for storing almost anything. I felt that one could not have a heavy heart for too long in this extraordinary environment. A magnificent lunch in a magical setting. Ann and Aldo have already contributed so much to our Italian experience, and now even more.

26 OCTOBER

A quiet day for rest, digestion, reading and reflection.

In the evening we grilled calamari over the coals and enjoyed it with some braised *cavolo nero*.

CALAMARI WITH BRONZE SKIN

4 calamari, approximately 16 cm long
4 cloves of garlic
ground black pepper
enough extra-virgin olive oil to barely cover calamari when packed tightly in a dish

Clean calamari but do not skin. Leave tentacles in one piece. Slice garlic finely. Place calamari, garlic, ground black pepper and oil in a shallow dish for several hours, turning once or twice.

Prepare a bed of glowing coals (or heat a barbecue grill). Lift calamari from the oil bath, drain in a colander over a plate to remove excess oil, which would flare up on the grill, and place bodies and tentacles over the coals. Grill about 4 to 5 minutes per side until the tip of a small knife or a skewer can pass through the body quite easily. The skin will have developed marvellous bronze markings. Return the fish to the oil bath and rest for 5 minutes. Squeeze over fresh lemon juice if you like. Slice thinly and serve just as it is, with salad leaves or over delicate pasta. You probably won't need any salt, but check!
Serves 4

27 OCTOBER

I have just discovered that the huge pine trees that edge the gravelled courtyard where we park the cars at the villa are stone pines. Among the gravel can be found pine nuts, some still tightly encased in their very hard outer shell, although most have been opened and the nut eaten by the squirrels that are here in large numbers. The squirrels are very cute – bright-eyed with dark, silky tails.

This evening we visited the abbey at Sant'Antimo, near Montalcino, to hear the monks chant vespers. Our students had all come back entranced with the experience when they went, and we were looking forward to the visit.

The abbey stands quite alone in the middle of a sparsely planted olive grove. At night it is floodlit. It was not difficult to imagine how the sight must have filled the hearts of the faithful with awe and reinforced their belief in the goodness of God's works.

Inside it is extraordinarily beautiful. After so much magnificence in the cathedral in Siena, and in the Collegiata in San Gimignano, this Romanesque abbey is in stark contrast. Said to have been founded by Charlemagne in the eighth century, its shape is that of a simple Roman basilica. The main part of the church was built in the twelfth century.

The massive columns are smooth and decorated in a restrained manner. The only ornamentation is a drawn and anguished Christ on the cross, sculpted from wood in the thirteenth century, and a stern Madonna holding baby Jesus, who resembles a little man, also in painted wood and dating from the same period. The soft, embroidered cloths on side tables are of natural linen, partly illuminated by the tiny glow from several candles in front of the Madonna.

Three Augustinian monks appeared and the Gregorian chanting commenced. The acoustics were remarkable – the voices seem to be pitched quite moderately and yet the round sound filled the space, each note lingering. After twenty minutes it was over and the monks closed their books and walked away. As we left, we wondered about this disciplined life, about whether there are as many recruits for the priesthood these days as there would have been maybe thirty or so years ago. Two of tonight's monks were young men in their middle twenties. The third was much older, white-haired and stooped.

We then turned our minds to more secular pleasures and headed for the Fattoria dei Barbi e del Casato. Attached to this working farm is a good restaurant. Italy never ceases to delight. One turns down a most unprepossessing dirt road, three kilometres fom Montalcino, and after bumping down this road for some time a brightly lit restaurant appears seemingly from the forest! And it was lucky we had booked, as the sign on the door told us it was full. On a very cold Monday evening!

I had the finest ravioli I can ever remember eating. It must be said that it is the quality of the ingredients in Italy that determine whether something is memorable or ordinary. This simple dish of ravioli filled with spinach and ricotta was a poem. The ravioli were quite large – four to a serving. The pasta was strong and yet tender, bright yellow and full of the flavour that comes from country eggs. The ricotta was as light as whipped cream, its texture at once creamy and firm. Not a suspicion of whey or graininess. Just puffed pillows of delectable filling, sauced simply with browned butter and sage.

This was without question the dish of the night. The fattoria makes its own cheese, both the ricotta mentioned and pecorino, its own oil and wine, and it raises the pigs that are used for the house-made *salume* (smoked and cured products) and fresh pork dishes. The owners also claim they produce the charcoal that is used for the grilling fire. With dinner we drank Brunello di Montalcino DOCG Riserva 1991.

Will Studd would have been pleased to taste the aged pecorino, described in the following manner on the menu:

> 'Cacio' pecorino is handmade by the women of the Fattoria dei Barbi using milk fresh from the Montalcino flocks. The ageing is done on beams of fir. Every day the cheeses are turned over, and every week they are washed in lukewarm water. The dry cheese is coated with olive oil and absorbs aroma from walnut leaves.

28 OCTOBER

*I*t is icy cold again. A shopping trip in Siena is planned for the morning and I intend to buy a sweater. And a few last-minute presents. Peter leaves tomorrow and he also wants to have a final stroll around the town. Colin wants to buy a shirt – tonight we are all invited to Paolo de Marchi's home for a grand dinner. The town is busy and we find somewhere to park the van with difficulty. In fact, we parked illegally, but there were other cars there, so off we went.

The shopping was very successful. We strolled back to the car and, lo and behold, it was not there! Nor were any other cars. Yet there was no sign of officialdom, or a notice, or any indication of what had happened. It was perishingly cold, and none of us had a coat. We assumed the car had been towed away and Peter, being the only one with a good grasp of Italian, set out to find it.

It was a long saga, taking two hours, and involving Peter running halfway around Siena, an extraordinary marathon, from one office to another, and then to a car yard. Meanwhile, each of us took shifts at the empty car space in case Peter returned, while the others sought warmth (and limited sustenance) in a nearby *enoteca*. Twenty minutes was all one could tolerate in the bitter cold. We shared jackets and hats. The *enoteca* was warm and a small glass of Chianti was almost medicinally needed to drive out the chill. Three of us ordered *ribollita* and it arrived lukewarm on one edge with frozen crystals in the middle – poor microwave technique. We ate it anyway. We had just about given up all hope of ever finding Peter and had written him a note, leaving it under a rock at the car space, informing him we would take a taxi to the villa, when, just at that very moment, the minibus swung fast around the corner with a grinning Peter at the wheel. He was greeted as a hero, and, 200,000 lire poorer, we were on the way home, needing to thaw out before setting out for Chianti and dinner.

Paolo and his wife, Marta, entertained us splendidly. Marta cooked a haunch of *cinghiale* over the fire and a second dish of *stufato di cinghiale*. Both were delicious and more like veal than pig, I thought. Marta's theory is that as the diet of the *cinghiale* has changed from what they could find in the woods to well-cared-for Chianti grapes, so the flavour has become much milder. Certainly there was no need to wash and soak the pieces, as had been prescribed by Flora when she was making the pasta sauce at the Parronchis'.

The wines were also splendid – Paolo's 1996 chardonnay, his own 1981 Cepparello, and a Nebbiolo from a small vineyard in Trento. We came away realising how fortunate we were to have been invited to the home and table of one of Italy's most talked-about and charming vignerons and his equally charming and interesting wife.

29 OCTOBER

*F*reezing cold again. Well, it isn't actually freezing, but it must be about 6°C. Anna Rosa says the wind is exceptional, that it is blowing from Russia. The heating in the villa is not very efficient, so lighting a big fire is now necessary for warmth. We have started to think of home and warm spring days.

I have spoken to Anna this morning and events in Melbourne are racing along. Instead of having a week to collect my wits on my return, within forty-eight hours I am to be on television, announcing the closure of the Restaurant. The timetable for the announcement and for the book launch will have to be rejigged, as will my meetings with lawyers, accountants and, most importantly, my staff.

Angie, Duffy, Peter and I have decided to visit the *osteria* at Lucignano d'Asso, owned and operated by the Contessa Angelica Piccolomini Naldi Bandini and her sister, Simonetta, and recommended by Anna Rosa's husband. I had also received a call during the first cooking school from an American who was interested in knowing more about our school, and he, too, recommended that I visit this very old town, where he owned a house. Intrigued, we set out on our final rural excursion. Maggie and Colin opted to stay by the fire and catch up with paperwork.

Another treasure. A stunningly beautiful tiny town, very well cared for, with glimpses of fruit trees, vegetable patches and flowering pots over every stone wall. A carved lion brooded on one steep stone balustrade. The stone houses were the colour of honey, some of the doors rimed and wrinkled and smoothed by the winds of at least 400 years. There was absolutely no one in sight – not surprising, as the wind nearly lifted us from the ground.

Inside the only shop, which indeed turned out to be the local *alimentari* as well as the *osteria*, we shed beanies, hats and raincoats and were shown to one of three wooden tables in a starkly elegant small inner room. Three local lads were tucking into a plate of cheese. A roll of paper was brought over by an elderly man and cut to fit the table. This was Eraldo. He brought us a large platter of outstanding prosciutto and his offsider, Rita, explained the difference between the outer, drier slices of a deep rose, and the soft, tissue-paper thin, pale-pink slices that are cut from next to the bone. Thank goodness Peter was here to translate or this interesting detail would have been missed. Two different tastes and textures from the one ham. The second platter held *capocollo* (cured pork neck) flavoured with fennel seed, and a delicious salami; the third, a selection of pecorino cheeses – very fresh, aged, and served with hot pepper and truffles. The fourth platter was a *pinzimonio* of raw vegetables, including outstandingly sweet and stringless celery and chunks of cucumber. A bottle of beautiful oil, il Lecceto (sub-labelled Olio di Podere, meaning 'oil from the holding'), and a basket of excellent bread completed the offerings. How rarely we have encountered Tuscan bread of this quality on our trip. With this we drank two bottles of Brunello di Montalcino: Terre de Priori 1992 and Pertimali 1992. We ate with enthusiasm and delight. Everything was exceptional.

At one point a woman appeared, a scarf wrapped firmly about her head, and gave a swift, appraising look around the little room. By this time we were the only customers. She disappeared after a moment. This was surely the Contessa or Simonetta. When we paid the bill (a very modest sum of 100,000 lire, $100, which included the two bottles of wine), I was handed a note she had left saying how much she wanted to meet us! I left a note for her in return to thank her for the delicious lunch. We roared with laughter when, back in the car, Peter told us that she had said dismissively to Eraldo, after she had surveyed the room, 'It can't be them!'. She could not believe that such scruffy people could possibly include important personages. And I had my best jacket on, too!

30 OCTOBER

*M*aggie, Colin and I are to go to Florence today as we have been invited to lunch at Antinori. Peter will come on the train with us and continue on to Milan. I feel a deep pang of sorrow. He has been wonderful company, gentle, funny, perceptive and hard-working. It is 4°C this morning and Peter did raise a few eyebrows on the train with his two surfboards as well as his pack! He left me a lovely note: 'Your food has always been real, never contrived and never too removed from its original state. This is also, in my mind, the meaning of authentic art as opposed to gimmickry . . .'

Angie and Duffy have packed up their little Fiat and are also off to Florence for a medical conference before flying home. Tomorrow Maggie, Colin and I will set the house to rights, sort out our own possessions, pack and leave for Rome early Saturday morning. Once again we will deal with mountains of luggage – I cannot bear to think about it – and will break our journey in Kuala Lumpur. I arrive in Melbourne early on Melbourne Cup Day. My life is about to change dramatically.

I am fed up with saying goodbye to people. I think I am ready to go home.

3 1 OCTOBER

We have packed, cleaned up the house and eaten the last scraps. Cauliflower and anchovy risotto last night, and today Maggie and I made rissoles with the leftovers and enjoyed them with salad for lunch. Colin has taken the last of the wine to Ichiko.

This is the end of our Italian adventure. I am amazed that our idle and very romantic notion, conceived two years ago, survived its long gestation and developed into such an amazing experience.

However, things Tuscan will not disappear from my life for quite some time. There will be a Tuscan dinner at Stephanie's on my return. There will be all the work on the book (tentatively titled 'Stephanie and Maggie in Tuscany'), there will be its launch, probably at the Cafe, and then there will be a pretty strenuous book tour to promote it. And there will also be a reminder of it all when this journal eventually appears in print.

And now I am about to take a huge step into a very different future.

November

5 NOVEMBER

*T*ouchdown yesterday morning. What on earth was in all those suitcases that was so essential, I wondered, as I unpacked the motley array of grease-spotted T-shirts, lumpy toilet bags still full of untouched potions and lotions, books and a few new possessions.

Off to the accountant and the solicitor today. Both are a little shocked at my decision. Why didn't you do this six months ago, my accountant wanted to know? It was not appropriate at the time, was the answer.

And, perhaps more importantly, these decisions are now mine alone to make.

Thanks to the success of *The Cook's Companion* I now have real choices. There were many reasons that influenced my decision to close Stephanie's Restaurant, but probably the most compelling was having spent two months with friends and food lovers in a delightful environment, with time to think, time to read, time to play and time to plan a less-pressured future. To close the Restaurant down will cost me a great deal of money. I do not believe that my former partner would ever have accepted that half the debt was hers.

It is a fact of life in small to medium businesses that one can tread water for years, juggling accounts, with a healthy overdraft as a cushion (secured, in this case, by my own house), paying all staff, and doing a great job. But when the end comes, for whatever reason, the realities can be daunting: long-service-leave entitlements, redundancy payments, clearing responsibilities with all creditors, making good the premises before handing it back to the landlady, and so on.

If I have to pay for my freedom, I am ready to pay.

As I have already mentioned, I arrived home knowing that a television crew planned to do a story on me and my writing in two days' time. They had no idea yet that there was anything else in the wind. But Anna, Mark and I had conferred about this via fax and we all agreed that it would be idiotic to let this opportunity of a national programme pass without The Big News being included in the story. At this point only Anna, Mark, Lisa, Holly, Maggie and Colin knew of my decision. Anna and Mark had had various rendezvous away from Stephanie's Restaurant to plan tactics, which led to a few raised eyebrows when they were sprung at a cafe table! It was very hard for Mark to continue to manage the business of the Restaurant and not let on to any member of staff that changes were in the air. I now had just twenty-four hours to gather my staff and tell them that their future was about to change in the most dramatic manner.

They were fantastic! Such loyalty, and matter-of-fact planning for their life after Stephanie's. Boulders rolled from my shoulders at the conclusion of this meeting. We agreed to work together and finish with a huge bang on New Year's Eve. I was about to start a four-day publicity tour for *Recipes My Mother Gave Me*, and therefore had access to extraordinary media coverage for my announcement, starting with the televised one. Within forty-eight hours anyone at all interested as far away as Darwin or Perth knew that Stephanie's Restaurant was closing its doors and that I was looking forward to a life with a little more time to smell the roses, not to mention write more, read more, think more and consider new projects.

The Restaurant looked so beautiful as I walked through the dining rooms. Our flower and garden lady, Lorrie Lawrence, had filled the vases with soft spring flowers, blossoms and roses and pretty grasses. The Iceberg roses at the foot of the entrance steps are in full bloom. The display of *Recipes My Mother Gave Me* is a joyous sky-blue against the gleam of the polished cedar sideboard in the entrance and Anna has placed a preloved Sunbeam mixmaster among the books.

11 NOVEMBER, REMEMBRANCE DAY

*T*onight I had a small dinner in the billiard room to launch the little blue book. It will probably be the last time my father ever visits the Restaurant. I had my first intimation of how I might feel in the final days. My heart squeezed and ached as I looked at Dad, coping well with walking frame and a glass of wine. My brother had come from South Australia, and my sister was there, too. Only John was absent, and, of course, Mum. Julie presented me with my very special boxed copy – a special edition of ONE.

1 3   N O V E M B E R

*A*lready half the month has gone and so little recorded.

So much has happened and at such a pace that I have not had half an hour to spare, let alone time to contemplate.

It is my birthday. I was delighted by a call from Holly, and was able to fill her in on the current events, so she will not worry now if she hears little from me for a week or two. My friend Ian also called from Bath, and Betsy sent birthday wishes from Cambridge, together with wonderful diary notes relating to her Tuscan week. She described our villa as 'majestic, humble and alluring' and added that 'for six days I was content, nourished, extended, warmed and happy'. Wonderful Betsy.

Birthday messages on the phone from my best friends. How do they remember? I am hopeless with other people's birthdays.

Dinner tonight with Lisa. We wondered if it would be our last dinner for two at Stephanie's?

1 4   N O V E M B E R

*F*or the first ten days of November I have been running to catch up. Everyone needed my ear! I had to speedily grasp the implications of the Restaurant cooking classes arranged long ago and now almost upon me.

Not to mention the Tuscan dinner, fully booked, with 135 guests expecting a memorable night, and the need to change the lunch and dinner menus in both the Restaurant and the Cafe. The Restaurant menu is now to be titled The Farewell Menu, needing research into my stacks of past menus for those dishes I feel best sum up twenty-one years' work.

I need to ring my most regular suppliers. The phone message needs to be redone, the structure of lunch needs to be changed, and the four phone lines are constantly jammed, so that Sophie's ear is bright pink and hurting from the constant pressure. We must quickly book a band, a dance floor and a marquee for our final party on New Year's Eve, which was fully booked in three days. And then there is Christmas Day to be thought about. Wow! If only I had no need of sleep. Fortunately I am still jet-lagged, and waking at

4.00 a.m. permits a few extra hours to be squeezed into the day. Three consultancy projects have been put to me already! Help! – I cannot consider anything until well into the New Year.

I miss Holly, not just for her bright smile and crazy laugh, but I also need a dog-walker! In fact, I need a wife. There is no time. I haven't made it to the gym yet. Lisa is back into the swing of things at the Cafe, managing beautifully, and all seems absolutely in order over there, although they do want me to change the menu quickly. The new outdoor seating looks good and offers service to smokers, who are outlawed in the interior. But Stephanie's has swallowed me up for the time being.

15 NOVEMBER

*M*ore interviews and a lovely story in one of the papers. A quick overnight dash to Sydney and then back again. The major television interview went off smoothly. I have been so pleased that every journalist has been positive and supportive of my desire to move on to a new stage in my life.

Last night I watched the story of Eddie 'Koiki' Mabo on television and wept. For thirty years, Eddie resolutely fought for official recognition that there had been prior ownership of land on Murray Island before the white man arrived. The programme followed Eddie's life and battle for justice, it emphasised his great love for his wife, Bonita, who was his rock, and it recorded his tragic death and the appalling desecration of his grave in Townsville, and his final journey to be laid to rest on Murray Island. He did not live to hear the High Court's decision in the Mabo case. We know the events that have followed, and the emotional responses of confusion, joy, bitterness, and passionate division throughout the nation. We desperately need reconciliation with all Australians. This moral issue needs resolution; it must come as surely as the republic must come. The deep sadness I feel is but a drop compared with the well of sadness that must be in the heart of every indigenous Australian. And today was the funeral of 'Nugget' Coombs, a lifelong champion of land rights, and an effective and admired bureaucrat through seven different federal administrations.

It is one of the least attractive aspects of much of humankind that the desire for more, be it money or power, effectively wipes out any ability to see a bigger picture, especially where social justice issues are involved. The 'right' decision so often entails some degree of compromise, but the 'haves' already have so much and the 'have-nots' are monumentally disadvantaged in any comparison.

The governor-general, Sir William Deane, has spoken out strongly on the need for Australia to regain its soul by apologising for the past and openly working towards justice for all disadvantaged Australians. Contemporary Australians need not feel blame but they can atone for the past in present-day policies and attitudes. The government is not reading the mood of the people if it persists in its denial of any injustice or inherent racism in its attempt to amend the *Native Titles Act* in parliament. Holly keeps in touch with Australian news via *The Age* website, and mentioned that the few snippets concerning Australian affairs she had read in the *New York Herald Tribune* suggested that Australia was adopting a racist stance in several areas.

I have been reading Thea Astley's book *The Multiple Effects of Rainshadow*. Paternalistic and racist actions and attitudes have dirtied so many pages of our history.

George Biron of Sunnybrae delivered one hundred artichokes from his garden to Stephanie's, including one as big as a bunch of roses. I had always believed that artichokes with a heart as large as this one had were a different variety. Not so, says George, gardener extraordinaire. Just keep on watering and in warm weather this is the result. I cooked it for my lunch and had a solitary meal with a bowl of olive oil and red-wine vinegar as a dipping sauce. It was magnificent!

I assisted at the door last night at Stephanie's Restaurant. Bookings are coming in thick and fast and we are hoping for a full house most nights until we close. As the waiters speed from room to room, an extra person at the door is a very good idea – Dur-é used to fill this role, and she will be warmly remembered by many for her special charm. On busy nights the door opens every minute or so to yet another smiling couple or group. Their names must be checked, coats collected and they must be welcomed and shown to their table. With six possible rooms and table numbers that change every night, depending on the night's configuration, one must be quick to catch on. I must say, I am not yet very confident. Still, most diners are so surprised to see me there, and so ready to share a few words, that I think they happily forgive if I take a little longer than the waiters do to find their name and table number. By 10.30 my feet, in the new Ferragamo velvet slippers I bought in Florence, were much more tired than ever they were when I was wearing clogs in the kitchen. I am seeing the Restaurant from a different angle.

I sank into bed and slept so soundly!

16 NOVEMBER

*T*o the Cafe today for some recipe testing.

Sunday is crazy. Over 300 people were fed between 9.00 a.m. and 5.00 p.m. In between 'hits', I tested two new pasta dishes, a chicken dish and a new steak dish. The berry pancakes I also tried need more work, but the others turned out very well.

Ubaldi Pasta, the local firm who make the pasta we sell, was very receptive to the idea of attempting the olive pasta, *striscioli*, which I had read about in Antonio Villaresi's book while in Tuscany. Ours is a Melbourne variation of this dish.

OLIVE PAPPARDELLE WITH EGGPLANT, OLIVES AND RICOTTA

4 tablespoons caramelised onions

2/3 cup sheep's milk ricotta, crumbled roughly

2/3 cup grated pecorino

1/3 cup chopped flat-leaf parsley

2 cups of diced eggplant (2 cm pieces) that has been pan-fried in extra-virgin olive oil until soft with a golden colour

1/2 cup sliced, pitted Kalamata olives

1 1/3 tablespoons salted capers that have been soaked in water

extra-virgin olive oil for cooking and coating pasta

2 tablespoons balsamic vinegar

500 g dried black olive pappardelle pasta

In a warm, stainless-steel bowl mix the onions, crumbled ricotta, pecorino and parsley.

In a small pan heat the already cooked eggplant, olives and capers, then toss with oil and vinegar.

Cook pasta in boiling salted water. Drain well and add to bowl with caramelised onion mixture. Mix gently, ensuring all ingredients 'coat' the pasta. Finish with more oil and season.

Place pasta in hot serving bowl and spoon the hot eggplant mixture over the top.

Serves 4

Old favourites are very much in my mind as I design The Farewell Menu for Stephanie's. I want to serve a prawn cocktail at the Cafe. I am reminded of how in the old days, in Brunswick Street (site of the first four years of Stephanie's Restaurant), I had recreated an unusual sauce mentioned by Elizabeth David, involving anisette liqueur, pounded prawns and some fennel leaves. We put it all together and it was delicious. I will have to locate a suitable glass dish for it!

PRAWN COCKTAIL

30 medium prawns (or more if they
    are very small)
inner leaves of a butter lettuce

6 small radishes, finely sliced
1 head fennel, finely sliced

SAUCE

5 shallots, sliced
1 pinch salt
2 egg yolks
2½ teaspoons Dijon mustard
2½ tablespoons light soy sauce
½ cup chopped herbs (a mix
    of parsley, tarragon and fine
    fennel leaves)

2 cups extra-virgin olive oil
juice of 1 lemon
Marie Brizard anisette liqueur
    (to taste – start with 1 tablespoon)

To make the sauce, work shallots with salt to a paste in a mortar or a food processor. Add egg yolks, mustard, soy and herbs. Process briefly and then add oil in a steady stream, as if making mayonnaise. Thin with the lemon juice, and add piquancy with the anisette.

Drop the prawns into lightly salted boiling water for 1–2 minutes until they turn pink. Drain well and blot dry on kitchen paper. Toss generously with the sauce. Line 6 pretty glass dishes with the butter lettuce leaves, toss the radish and fennel slices through the sauced prawns, and divide between the dishes.

Serves 6

Note: This sauce is also excellent with all sorts of smoked fish.

Summer eating needs a lighter chicken dish than our present chicken braised with red-wine vinegar. A parmesan-crusted chicken breast is the solution, on wilted spinach with crostini on the side, thickly spread with Maggie's new mushroom pâté.

The fourth dish of the day to be tested was a minute steak. Very loosely inspired by Tuscan adventures, we will serve it with a side dish of grilled radicchio, softly cooked cloves of garlic and baked parsnips. Its topping will be a mustard butter.

In between all these exciting new dishes, the Cafe staff powered through a mammoth service that never seemed to stop – wave after wave of orders. I left at 4.00 p.m. and the Cafe was still full and jumping.

Maggie arrived very late at my place and we enjoyed a glass of champagne and some catching-up conversation. Tomorrow we shall do a little preparation for Tuesday's Tuscan dinner.

17 NOVEMBER

*R*otolo for 140 is no pushover! Maggie, Michael, Leigh and I spent four hours on this dish and wondered why we had thought it would be so easy. Paddocks of spinach had to be stemmed, blanched and chopped; buckets of flat-leaf parsley and marjoram needed to be chopped; boxes of mushrooms required slicing, and the dried porcini had to be reconstituted in verjuice.

Maggie tut-tutted over the ricotta, which was certainly not of the quality we'd had in Italy. And, after complicated sums, Maggie announced that each roll was to contain 232 grams of mushrooms! Eventually we were ready to assemble them. We made fourteen rolls of pasta and each had to simmer, totally submerged, for twenty minutes.

We only just made it to dinner at the Cafe with Angie, Duffy and Lisa. A crazy coincidence had Julie and a mutual friend dining a few tables away. A merger was arranged. Julie will not be with us for the Tuscan dinner as she has to attend the launch of a book in Sydney.

18 NOVEMBER

First up today was a trip to the Victoria Market, where I was to launch *The Goods*, a directory of Melbourne specialist food shops by Melbourne foodies Allan Campion and Michele Curtis. Then a stopover at the Cafe to have lunch with Peter and Tony, who are in Melbourne to see to the costuming of a new production of *Phantom of the Opera*. They were delighted to be asked to arrange the still life on the front chiffonier at Stephanie's. Tony had done it so brilliantly every day in Italy that it was a very special pleasure for Maggie and me that he was able to do it once more.

I had ordered vegetables and fruits, and added embroidered cloths and handpainted pots from my own collection to decorate the Restaurant for the Tuscan dinner, not to mention the seventeen flags carried back from Siena. Anna and Sophie had created lovely menus decorated with strips of Florentine paper, and every place card was similarly styled. The flowers were wonderful. Lorrie had arranged terracotta tubs of bright-red petunias and geraniums on every ledge and windowsill, and on each table we had iron candelabra with fat candles and twining ivy.

The sheer volume of preparation is always the difficulty with dinners like this. Braising the legs of the rabbits, then cutting the muscles from the bone to toss with the braised vegetables took hours. Shelling peas and skinning broad beans for 140 was also an awesome task. Eventually we finished and Maggie and I dashed home to change, before turning around instantly to return and find our guests already gathering!

Each of the six rooms was entertained by singer Jessica Carrington and guitarist Jochim Schubert, and orchestrating the serving of courses to each room so as not to interrupt the singing and yet not to leave the diners starving was a bit like a military exercise.

I think the evening was a success. The food was certainly lovely.

19 NOVEMBER

*M*y earlier enthusiasm for the extra cooking classes organised before Italy has come home to roost. I would have to admit that the timing is less than wonderful! Six hours after hitting the pillow I am up and at it again, with fifteen students expected in an hour, and fifteen more this evening.

Former staff member Arnold is here to help me.

Of course, the classes went well, but as I crawled home at 10.30 p.m., I felt as if I had been crushed by a steamroller. Let those who are now clamouring for the Restaurant to remain open know that this is a young person's game. My body is sending me very clear signals, quite apart from any other reasons for having made the decision.

20 NOVEMBER

I am fighting panic.

'More staff!' is the cry – more cooks, more kitchen hands, more waiters, someone to deal with the phone!

So difficult to make sensible decisions when one is in panic mode. We have filled practically every seat in the Restaurant until the last minute; there are still some spaces available for lunch. Preparation hands and space in which to actually prepare have high priority. And then there is all the office stuff with which I should be concerning myself, not to mention the all-important final menu. I plan a testing day for tomorrow, when I will take over the upstairs kitchen and try to cook a few new dishes. But before that I have a two-hour interview with a journalist.

I am frightened at the way I lose track of my thoughts after a second –
I need a pencil and paper in my hand all the time. I cannot settle to one task
for more than ten minutes without interruption, and it is usually an
important question.

Why did I open this cupboard?

I have no idea.

What was I suddenly about to write as I sit with pen poised?

I have no idea.

Why am I heading down the stairs?

What did I need to ask Jeff?

No idea is the answer.

Off to a partners' meeting at the Cafe. Christmas preparations are well in
hand. Financial matters to mull over. Pricing decisions. Stock decisions.
Management pressure is getting to us all. Angie is tense, Anna is edgy. Lisa
seems fine, and Will is all smiles. New menu on Monday, new menu at
Stephanie's on Thursday, and the day after, another marathon double
cooking class.

I must say, the bright-yellow egg cups in their handknitted striped
beanies look very cheerful and are quite irresistible. I shall send one to Holly
in France. Lisa and I go out to dinner – still the best solution for me.
Mountadam chardonnay and some braised kid at Caffe Grossi, and an early
night.

21 NOVEMBER

$\mathcal{A}$ good day. An enjoyable interview with journalist Richard Yallop from
The Australian, then a constructive few hours cooking. I find the act of
cooking to be very therapeutic. A steady chop, then the reassuring sizzle of
vegetables in olive oil and soon the aromas of caramelised juices. Not only
do I feel excitement as the dish comes to life under my hands, but my
general confidence soars, and I feel relaxed and more able to concentrate.
People also have to come to me to ask questions so I am not being chased all
over the place. I keep a pen in my apron and a notebook on the bench, and
jot down anything I need to act upon.

A member of the public rings to ask if he can warm smoked salmon to have with his asparagus. Someone else rings to see if I might contemplate teaching secondary-school students how to cook. There is a letter of complaint from a customer who wanted steamed vegetables to be served on the side, no matter what dish she ordered. A cooking-class student feels a recipe is wrong as it has no milk. I am instantly sure I must have made a mistake and ring Nicky at the Cafe. Nonsense, she says, we have been making this cake for three months and have never needed milk. Phew!

But the 'rockpool' jelly (sea creatures in a light jelly) tastes lovely. The chicken in its red-wine sauce looks fabulous and tastes great. And the duck with a pear sauce and corn cakes will be a winner.

Home to make up the work lists that the staff must have by tomorrow.

22 NOVEMBER

*E*arly morning walk for Rosie, so my conscience is a little clearer.

She was to have had a bath, but for some reason I have no hot water. It will have to wait until Monday to be checked out! Very cheerful phone call from Holly, who assures me she will keep in touch and I should not worry about letter writing at the moment. What a gem she is.

Next, a book signing at The Vital Ingredient in South Melbourne. I combined the book signing with a little shopping – Nicky had been unable to find silver balls to put on the *zuccotto*, which is now on the menu at the Cafe, but here they were. Also, best-quality chocolate vermicelli for the chocolate and raspberry 'tartufo' at Stephanie's, and some dried wild mushrooms to add extra zing to the *rotolo*. It is such a good dish that we will have it on The Farewell Menu.

We have recruited one extra cook, one extra kitchen hand, and Valerie today met with a staffing agency who will send three waiters next week.

Melbourne is having one of its periodic heatwaves. It was 33°C today and tonight in the upstairs kitchen it was absolutely ghastly. The Restaurant was packed!

23 NOVEMBER

$\mathcal{A}$ day of complete leisure. I cannot quite believe it. I have been writing this diary for three hours in my lovely writing room. Last year I decided that as my writing is becoming more and more important, it should take place in a delightful environment. So I installed new bookshelves and a long work table and threw away some heavy curtains, replacing them with fine cotton Roman blinds. I can now see into the front garden and admire the rosy flowers of the crabapple tree and the apricot of the nearest roses, but I am hidden from the passers-by. Beautifully crafted blackwood bowls and boxes house paperclips and pencils, and a deep pottery bowl has business cards and invitations. The bowl was a very successful barter from potter John Dermer, offered in exchange for a copy of *Stephanie's Seasons* some time ago. I feel that I got the best end of the deal.

Writing done for the day, I will now do some domestic things and maybe pleasant social things later this evening, or I may go to bed at 8.00 with a book. I am stiff and sore from the week's exertions and now wish I'd had my hot water fixed so that I could have a bath.

24 NOVEMBER

$\mathcal{I}$ must give myself a day off more regularly. Today I feel revived and ready for the Cafe menu change. I stood at the pass and checked every dish, giving a running commentary to Nicky and Justin. 'Some more extra-virgin olive oil, please'; 'Can you move the salmon to leave a bit more space on the plate'; 'Please pass me the pepper grinder'; 'Let's toss the tomatoes once more with some chopped basil'; 'Great fish and chips'; 'More eggplant, please', and on and on until the main thrust of lunch service was over.

Julie arrived at 2.00 p.m., her arms filled with a huge bunch of fabulous orange flowers for me – the orange book, *The Cook's Companion*, has just sold its 100,000th copy! And there was a smart silver pen in a pale-blue Tiffany's box suitably inscribed to mark the occasion.

We celebrated with champagne, a prawn cocktail and the new platter of cured fish – smoked salmon, kippers, taramasalata and creamy eggs.

I ought not to rush past the moment without fully appreciating it. If it were not for the success of this book I would not have been able to contemplate my leap into freedom, to celebrate 'the lightness of being', as colleague Mietta puts it. Not only has it given me financial success, but it has pointed me in the new direction I shall take – that of the 'softly, softly' educator. I can sense my next major project, and I will be casting myself in the role of a foodie Pied Piper.

This afternoon, I treated myself to a pedicure and relaxed to the sheer bliss of a foot massage. Back to the Cafe to eat again with friends and try more dishes. The place was jumping and the noise was deafening. And people complain that Stephanie's is too quiet! I shared an olive pappardelle with my friend John and then I tried the grilled cuttlefish, Jean had the crumbed chicken and John had the minute steak. Pretty good, I thought, although a little tweaking here and there will be done in the next few days.

With one menu change achieved, some of the tightness eased from my shoulders. Now for the big one. My swan song at Stephanie's.

26 NOVEMBER

*A*nother double banger of a cookery class, morning and evening, this time devoted to vegetable cookery. Journalist Richard Yallop returned to sit in for a couple of hours. I was able to use fresh vegetables picked yesterday by George Biron and delivered last night. Very young kohlrabi, more artichokes, and a giant salsify plant, each root criss-crossed over the next in a very higgledy-piggledy manner. George has also grown and supplied *radicchio de Treviso*, which I oiled and cooked on the chargrill.

One of the very first dishes I prepared at Stephanie's in 1976 was radishes with unsalted butter, a simple bistro dish. I offered it again today with a plate of marinated goat's cheese and another of raw, double-peeled broad beans. I also cooked silver beet stalks in a blue cheese sauce and made an asparagus soup, which was a delicate apple-green colour. The temperature had reached 38°C and I was able to demonstrate the versatility of such vegetable soups by serving it chilled.

The students enjoyed the bitterness of the radicchio when served with an escalope of veal sharpened with caramelised lemon. And the stickiness of the combined vegetable braise.

27 NOVEMBER

The Farewell Menu is now a reality. And its first night was a great success.

On the menu I have included a sentence describing the origins of each dish and the year it first appeared. For posterity here is a copy.

~ *Appetiser* ~

SCALLOPS ON THE HALF-SHELL WITH
PONZU SAUCE AND CRUNCHIES

Devised a few years ago, after my introduction to the wonderful lemon and seaweed flavours of ponzu sauce. The crunchies are wisps of carefully cut carrot, leeks, ginger and nori seaweed. Each is separately deep-fried, dried and then mixed together most gently. A topknot of this on anything from the sea is wonderful. The salty tang of the seaweed and the hot, clean bite of the ginger is irresistible.

~ *Entrees* ~

ROASTED MARRON FROM MOUNT BARKER,
WITH SAUTÉD APPLES AND A KELLYBROOK
CHAMPAGNE BUTTER SAUCE

This has been a favorite entree since I was introduced to Warren Moore and his marron farm in 1990. The dish was a great hit at the week-long promotion Stephanie's Restaurant staged at The Regent Hotel in Sydney in 1991. Warren says I have picked the worst time of the year to put marron on the menu again, but together with one or two colleagues, he has pledged to do his best.

ROCKPOOL – SEA CREATURES IN A LIGHT AND TREMBLING JELLY

*A*gain, there have been many versions. The first rockpool appeared during Janni Kyritsis's time at the Restaurant, probably in 1978. Later versions incorporated the flavours of a Szechuan hot and sour soup. A wide soup plate is a necessity. Always oysters, with one shell upturned to resemble a rock. This time tiny school prawns, mussels, the tentacle of a rosy octopus and a pile of wasabi-flavoured flying fish roe floating on Tasmanian-farmed wakame seaweed.

BONED AND GLAZED BALLOTINE OF QUAIL WITH A FOIE GRAS AND DUCK LIVER STUFFING

*T*his was first served nestled in a small salad of leaves and violets. It was the starter at the fourteenth-birthday dinner of The Ladies' Wine & Food Society of Melbourne, 15 September 1981. This year I am able to buy excellent poached foie gras. We have included a big chunk in the stuffing and Michael has prepared slow-cooked tomatoes, which are served very cold with a flake or two of sea salt.

SWEETBREAD, PISTACHIO, TONGUE AND PIG'S EAR SALAD DRESSED WITH WALNUT OIL AND ORANGE ON SAFFRON ANGEL HAIR PASTA

A version of this salad was the first course at the very first dinner served at Stephanie's in Hawthorn, for *La chaine des rotisseurs* on 4 July 1980. This is a dish for the adventurous. The sweetbreads are from the calves that provide our sensational White Rocks veal chops from Western Australia. They are creamy and delicately flavoured. We flour and fry them, and they are then tossed with finely sliced ears and tongue. A delicious orange juice and walnut oil dressing adds piquancy and a slightly smoky flavour.

SMOKED SALMON CUSTARD WITH A RED WINE AND WATERCRESS SAUCE WITH A ROULADE OF SALMON IN A BUCKWHEAT CREPE

*I*n 1992 this was the first course at a luncheon hosted by the then premier of Tasmania, the Hon. Ray Groom. This menu's version is fancier and combines two or even three favourite combinations. Smoked salmon is rolled around lightly dressed salad leaves and encased in a hot buckwheat pancake. This is cut into three pieces and presented cut sides uppermost. The small but rich custard is sauced with red-wine butter sauce, and a few pearls of salmon roe are added.

TERRINE OF ROASTED SUMMER VEGETABLES
WITH OLIVE BREAD AND SAUCE AGRESTO
MADE FROM ALMONDS, PARSLEY, VERJUICE
AND EXTRA-VIRGIN OLIVE OIL

*T*he terrine was first cooked in 1991 and was inspired by a
similar dish from Marieke Brugman. I first tasted sauce agresto
prepared for me by Maggie Beer at a lunch we shared one day
in the Barossa while planning our 1997 Tuscan adventure.
The sauce agresto is a pesto-like assemblage of green leaves
(much of it parsley), nuts, verjuice and extra-virgin olive oil.
We had it on toast with fresh goat's curd.

ROTOLO – PASTA ROLLED WITH A STUFFING
OF SPINACH, MUSHROOM AND RICOTTA WITH
A SAUCE OF BROWNED BUTTER, PINE NUTS
AND CRISPED SAGE

*T*his dish was perfected by Maggie Beer at our memorable
schools in Tuscany in the European autumn (our spring) of
1997. Some of the mushrooms are wild porcini and they are
reconstituted in verjuice. I have donated ten new tea towels to
the kitchen to be reserved for the rolling and poaching of this
very popular entree.

~ *Main courses* ~

FARMED RABBIT FROM THE WEST, THE SADDLE
BONED AND STUFFED, THE LEGS BRAISED
WITH SUMMER VEGETABLES AND LIGHT JUICES

*T*hese rabbits were a sensation when I first served them in 1989
after a trip to the west to research *Stephanie's Australia*. No one

else had ever seen them at the time and they are still a little-
known delicacy. They are so tender that the legs are braised for
ten minutes only, then rested in a warm dish, where the
individual muscles are stripped, to be tossed with the juices, and
freshly shelled peas and double-peeled broad beans. In 1989
I also made a confit of the legs and served them shredded on
salad leaves tossed with chick peas.

THE GIANT VEAL CHOP

*A*nother magnificent product from the west. This has been
on the menu at Stephanie's almost without interruption since
1991. We have not dared remove it from the menu,
as someone else would snatch the supply! Some lucky person
will now take it over.

CRISP-SKIN SALMON ON GARLIC MASH WITH SLOWLY STEWED PEPPERS, CARAMELISED ONIONS AND PRESERVED LEMON

A signature dish since 1990. Stephanie's Restaurant was the
first establishment to prepare preserved lemons in commercial
quantities, and they have been a favourite ingredient in our
cooking since 1989. I have described each component of this
dish so often. It has even been a pin-up on a calendar I did one
year, and still it is a dish I never tire of.

ROASTED DUCKLING WITH ROASTED PEAR, CORN CAKES AND A CONFIT SALAD WITH PARSNIP CHIPS

*T*hese poultry salads have been important on the menu since the late 1980s – sometimes duck, sometimes pheasant, sometimes guinea fowl and sometimes squab pigeon. The salad component has varied and Steven Pallett and Simone Quinn made a special version of it for the Restaurant's twentieth-birthday dinner held on 1 December 1996. One of the secrets is that the sauce is thickened lightly with a separately made purée of pear and drops of sherry vinegar.

FILET À LA FICELLE WITH ROOT VEGETABLES AND CONDIMENTS, INCLUDING CREAMY HORSERADISH

*O*f all the dishes served, this is perhaps my favourite. Poached, tender rare meat; clear, flavoursome broth; simmered vegetables and the accompaniments of fine sea salt, mustard and horseradish. This was first served in 1979. It is a very restorative dish – the broth reminds me of the 'beef tea' Mum and I used to love drinking. With the very rare meat and all the vegetables and bits on the side, it is at once a sophisticated and simple dish. All the garnishes and the broth are vital in preparing its equally delicious but well-cooked cousin, *pot-au-feu*.

KING GEORGE WHITING FILLETS WITH YOUNG ZUCCHINI AND ZUCCHINI FLOWERS AND A LEMON THYME AND LEMON BUTTER SAUCE

*T*he most delicate of all our sea fish, and it has been a constant favourite since we moved to Hawthorn in 1980. The zucchini flowers in the sauce are a reminder of how ingredients have changed since those days. The combination of the young zucchini and currants suggest the flavours of Sicily or the Middle East.

COUNTRY CHICKEN SIMMERED IN A RED-WINE SAUCE, WITH SHALLOTS, BACON LARDONS, LITTLE POTATOES AND MUSHROOMS

*T*his was a rethink of *coq au vin*, the classic dinner party dish of the 1960s. It first appeared in 1988. The sauce combines previously reduced red wine and well-flavoured chicken stock. I have insisted that a heart-shaped fried crouton appear on the top of the dish.

~ *Desserts* ~

RASPBERRY TARTLET, RASPBERRY AND CHAMPAGNE JELLY, AND A CHOCOLATE, RASPBERRY AND ROSE-GERANIUM 'TARTUFO'

I have always enjoyed these threesome desserts that offer contrasting yet complementary textures and flavours. This one appeared in 1988. The trick is to capture the bubbles in the champagne so that as one eats the jelly they rush up one's nose in the same way as the drink.

POACHED PEACH, ALMOND ICE-CREAM AND A PLUM SAUCE

*T*his was inspired by a Chinese painting and was served at a dinner hosted by the Hong Kong Tourist Association in 1987. The original had jasmine tea ice-cream and that is still a delightful alternative. Our ice-cream is flavoured with one or two drops of pure bitter almond oil. Many people dislike the flavour, as they associate it with synthetic almond essence.

CHOCOLATE PUDDING WITH A SOFT CENTRE, AN ORANGE SAUCE AND A CANDIED ORANGE PEEL EUGENIE

*I*nspired by a similar dessert I ate at Jean Georges Vongerichten's restaurant, JoJo's, in New York, in the company of Geoff Lindsay, when we were there to cook for the New York media at the American launch of *Stephanie's Australia* in 1982. In our version, as one cuts into the pudding a rich chocolate lava oozes onto the plate to mingle with the sharp orange sauce.

PASSIONFRUIT SEVERAL WAYS ~ A SORBET, A BAVAROIS, A JELLY AND A BUTTERFLY CAKE FILLED WITH PASSIONFRUIT CREAM

A delicious tribute to the most intense of fruits. This has been a most successful dessert since 1990. The butterfly cake is a reminder of birthday parties years ago. I still find small cream-filled and iced cakes very exciting. A very 'girlie' dessert, says my friend Julie.

LEMON LAYER CAKE AND STRAWBERRIES

*T*his delicate combination of tender pancake and sharp lemon
curd was featured in *Stephanie's Feasts and Stories*, published in 1988,
and has been much copied since then. Its charm is in the
contrasting textures and the filling that is never tooth-achingly
sweet as many lemon tarts are.

DUCK EGG ON ITS NEST –
A MOULDED WHITE CHOCOLATE 'EGG'
FILLED WITH NOUGAT ICE-CREAM ON
BAKED KATAIFI PASTRY

*T*his is a variation of the dessert in our winning menu
in the Hyatt Gastronomic Competition in 1989.
The menu was titled 'A Feast of Pheasant', and commenced
with a feather on an empty plate and proceeded through the
barnyard to this finale.

AUSTRALIAN CHEESES AND
WALNUT BREAD AND OATCAKES

*A*nd how they have changed since we commenced operations
in 1976. In those days we made our own simple goat's milk
cheese as none existed in this country.

~ *Petits fours* ~

ANGELICA TARTS

*D*efinitely our signature, this one.

HONEY MADELEINES

*W*ith Proust, tonight we are remembering things past.

GATEAU OPERA

A toast to Paris, with this classic cake of thin sponge layers
sandwiched with butter creams.

~

Craig in the pastry room succeeded in making some of the best 'duck egg on
its nest' we have ever served and a champagne and raspberry jelly that
trembled and captured the fizz perfectly. Jeff made a delicious duck sauce,
lightly thickened with a purée of pears. The return of the cornmeal pancakes
stirred memories. And Leigh has taken over the making of the 'rockpool' and
the *rotolo*, Michael has produced stunning stuffed quail, Jody is now in
charge of the salmon custards, and Stuart is working with the farmed
rabbits. Stuart is also growing the very lovely zucchini flowers we are
serving with the whiting dish.

I had to teach most in the kitchen about male and female zucchini
flowers. In kitchen shorthand, we now shout for some 'girls' or 'boys'. Both
are used in this dish. The 'boys' are gently simmered with a little butter and
water and then have currants added; the 'girls' are steamed lightly and served
as the vegetable accompaniment. Torn marjoram goes very nicely with the
currants and the juices.

There is now not one seat left in the Restaurant any evening until we
close. I have booked four seats for the week after next – it is quite likely that
I will be put in the garden. I will hope for a warm evening.

Every day now I am experiencing moments of apprehension. My heart
squeezes, I feel panic, I feel tearful. There is a sense of 'last time' in
everything I do and touch. Have I eaten my last meal in the billiard room? It
seems likely. Where will I put my memories? On a more prosaic level, where
will I put the financial records? Have I absorbed everything I can from these

walls? How can I ever experience the pleasure of the calm and assurance that I have experienced over and over again in this place? What should I take and what should I leave behind?

For my birthday Lisa gave me a double CD of Ella Fitzgerald singing the songs of Cole Porter. Cole Porter seems to have a song for most of the BIG moments in my life. This time it will be 'Ev'ry Time We Say Goodbye'. 'Just One of Those Things' ended my first fine romance, and the 1930s classic by Herman Hupfield 'As Time Goes By' made me shiver at the twentieth-birthday party on 1 December last year. It was sung by Helen Noonan on that occasion, and Helen will be with us again on New Year's Eve.

28 NOVEMBER

I am having the kitchen storeroom cleaned out. Some treasures have been unearthed – a blender that has never been used, with a spare lid! Two electric waffle irons not used for several years, towers of French tinned charlotte moulds, with lids, bombe moulds and ceramic mussel dishes. Much of this had been stored inside boxes. Probably some chef in the past knew what was in the boxes, but not the current team. I am much happier now that they are sorted, cleaned and neatly arranged on open shelves. I even found the cherry stoner that had been asked for last week – I knew I had bought one a few years ago.

A great first night is often followed by a less than wonderful second night. And so it was tonight. We had two private functions as well as ninety other diners. The salmon custards let us down – in fact they fell down. Cooked too slowly, we think. By the time the next batch was ready, we had had to reinvent the dish for one of the functions, a wedding party. Once one thing goes wrong the rhythm is broken, and the systems collapse like a pack of cards. Another thing goes wrong, and so on. We all stumbled and cursed and sweated but eventually made up for the lost time. Very unsettling, though. Lunch had been huge and we were almost attempting the impossible in terms of people-power and endurance. But there was an incredible sense of satisfaction at the end of this night. Almost all of the anguish had remained within the kitchen walls – out there, the customers were relaxed and enjoying themselves.

Nothing will stop us now. After tonight we know the worst and can take action to ensure it never happens again.

29 NOVEMBER

*L*isa gave us all a fright by reporting that she could not see properly and was experiencing bright flashes of coloured light. She was whisked to the eye doctors across the road in Epworth Hospital, who found nothing wrong and suggested stress. She has gone home. I went home, too; somehow the thought of my darling daughter feeling unable to cope left me depressed and weepy. Am I to blame? Did she jump at this chance, or was she pushed? I cannot remember any more. She is a perfectionist (like her mother) and does not seem to be able to stop worrying, even when she is at home. The result is no sleep, no food, more worry and a sense of failure. The reality is that both Lisa and Angie are moving mountains daily. They are working with responsibilities that are new to them, acquiring new skills on the run, and having to make countless decisions without adequate discussion because there is no time. There is not even a spare table or chair at which to have a meeting. Nor is there privacy in the so-called office as staff are in and out all day long.

I am aware of my own drive to do things perfectly, which borders on obsessive behaviour. Especially when I am stressed. I might be in the kitchen, when I decide to put a coffee mug in the dishwasher. On the way, I notice that the breadknife is dirty – so I stop to wash it. Then I notice that the teapot needs emptying, and then … and so it goes, on and on. I have to give myself a talking-to and a list of priorities.

I will be more help to them both next year. But for now, we all have to hang in there until 1 January. I do feel much better in my head, though, since both menus have changed. More space for all the other things.

30 NOVEMBER

$\mathcal{A}$nother month gone. And there are just four weeks of Stephanie's Restaurant left.

Anna works with me three days a week now, and this is a wonderful relief. I still haven't found a dog-walker. Next week's extras include a speech to give to the Home Economics Association at a TAFE college, a planning meeting for a dinner to take place next March in the National Trust house, Como, and a *bollito misto* lunch to organise and cook for the Slow Food Movement this Sunday. And, of course, there is business as usual, now meaning a hundred for lunch every day and more than that each evening.

And I am still carrying the extra four kilos I put on in Italy. It is just not fair!

December

1 DECEMBER

*T*hirty-eight degrees! And serious bushfires near Lithgow. The start of a
long, hot summer and almost certainly a drought. I have decided to buy
Holly a plane ticket so that she can come to the final evening at the
Restaurant. So much of her life has been spent inside its walls, so many
special events celebrated there, that it does not seem right for her to be
absent. I rang and put the proposal and she was delighted – overwhelmed,
but delighted. I am leaving the arrangements to her. She told me it had just
started to snow in Lyon.

2 DECEMBER

*H*elen and Bruce are in residence for a few days until they fly out to the
States for a minimum of eight months. Looking at the extent of their
luggage, and listening to them organise the storage of all their possessions,
I am happy that I am staying put for the time being.

We had a cancellation at the Restaurant this evening, so Lisa and I snuck
in another dinner for two – this time to sample the very last menu. The
highlight of my dinner was the raspberry tartlet, a perfect combination of
crisp pastry, silky pastry cream and generous berries.

Servicing this huge restaurant full to capacity twice a day is a very big
task. Not just finding the hands to cook and carry plates, but dealing with
the ordering, the cleaning and dishwashing, the removal of the mounting
towers of cardboard, and crates of bottles, the extra correspondence, the
extra bills – absolutely everything escalates, and yet I cannot find enough
extra hands. There appears to be a shortage of skilled hospitality staff in
all areas. Colleagues ring me to offer jobs should any of my staff wish to
transfer to their establishments after our closure. All say that they, too,
are finding it difficult to recruit good staff. What is happening to all the
graduates from our hospitality courses? According to a report in *The Age*,
thirty per cent of cooking apprentices drop out of their training – at least
that has been the case in one of our major training institutes. There are
many stories of abuse and burn-out. I do not doubt these stories, but I do

question how realistic are the expectations of many new recruits to the cooking industry.

I have rung my friend and former head chef Steven Pallett. Steven is now a lecturer at the William Angliss Institute of TAFE, one of the largest training institutions for hospitality staff. In the past, Steven has recommended exceptional students to us, and he thinks he may be able to do the same again for these last few weeks.

This is an industry that still struggles to find an acceptable working structure, especially in the kitchen. When the pressure hits, the usual solution is for the same people to work longer without breaks. Employers cannot immediately double staff, especially if they have endured lean months over winter and kept everyone on, but no one can endure fifteen-hour days, five or six days a week with no time to rest or eat, for very long. It becomes difficult to retain one's enthusiasm for fine food. One of Melbourne's hotels has commenced its own culinary academy, hoping to provide high-quality training in the skills required in a good restaurant or a good hotel kitchen. A colleague of mine has successfully staffed his three restaurants, with no cook working longer than a straight eight-hour shift. I marvel at this, but have never managed to make the system work for me. Continuity of input is also very important. If one cook has the skill, experience and the patience to do the microsurgery necessary to bone a quail, and the determination to create the smoothest parfait to stuff it with, neither he/she nor I want to hand that job over to someone else just because his/her eight-hour shift is up. All my kitchen team are working like heroes, helped by as many casual staff as we can find.

We decorated the Christmas trees today and started putting bonbons on every plate!

4 DECEMBER

I had a most enjoyable afternoon amid the chaos starting the cooking for the Christmas party of Melbourne's Slow Food Movement, which will take place on Sunday. I remember the spectacular *bollito misto* I had at the Ristorante Ciccarelli at Madonna di Dossobuono, where the array of boiled meats – in all shades of cream, pink and brown – was wheeled to a table and carved to suit the whim of each diner. I want to offer a similar experience at this lunch. With nearly fifty guests, individual service will not be possible, but in all other respects I am aiming for a traditional *bollito misto*.

I spent the afternoon gently simmering beef ribs and baby veal shanks in a veal broth. I enhanced the broth with roasted onions, carrots and some scorched tomato skins, and as the flavours from the beef and the veal melded with the original liquid, a broth of great depth of flavour and subtlety was created.

A second batch of veal shanks, veal tongues and garlic sausage will be dealt with tomorrow. Corn-fed chickens have been boned and tomorrow Michael will make a traditional bread and onion stuffing for them. We will wrap each bird in muslin to keep it a lovely cream colour, and the birds will be poached in the broth on Sunday morning, as will the marrow bones and pigs' ears, which are still in their brine tub.

As I carefully arranged the cooked ribs and shanks in their juices and heaved the tubs into the coolroom, I felt calmed once more by the activity of cooking, and uplifted by the glow of virtue at being so well-prepared.

5 DECEMBER

I opened the paper this morning over breakfast and nearly choked on my cereal. My own face, twice life-size, stared at me. *Age* journalist Libby Lester has written a lovely piece and captured my mixed feelings of anticipation tempered with trepidation at what lies ahead. Sophie said it made her cry – so did Elena. I didn't find it sad. I was wearing my new rimless spectacles in the photo, and they are quite flattering!

6 DECEMBER

I am plunged into gloom again. The lists of things to do stretch before me, longer and longer. And there is still no sign of anyone willing to take over this establishment. An auction now seems likely. I shrink from this extra thing to organise. I suppose auctioneers are used to the flotsam and jetsam of people's lives; to me there are many treasures in these rooms, but I do acknowledge that there is some flotsam and jetsam as well.

Another sign that it is time to go. The Restaurant garden is bounded on its north side by a factory wall, on which we have ivy growing and a *Garrya elliptica* that has given me great pleasure over the years. We have been informed by our neighbours that the factory is to be demolished, and with it will go our wall of greenery. Fortunately, the wall stays until after our party on New Year's Eve, but as I looked out of my office window I saw men in masks removing the roof! I hope it is not sheets of asbestos that are being taken away.

A moment of pleasure this evening when I returned home to feed the dog. At 8.00 the sky was deepening from pale pink to rose-red. As I came into the garden, a rosy glow heightened all the colours. The green was greener. The blues were luminous. The rich pinks and purples of my snapdragons, and all the terracotta pots and paving, glowed with a special light.

A good service this evening at the Restaurant.

7 DECEMBER

*B*ollito *misto* day. What have I done to deserve the worst hours of my restaurant life so near to the end?

I was happily working away, making the rich bread and bone marrow sauce, *peara*, having finished the tomato and *salsa verde* sauces, when Jeff called me to his side of the bench. It was 10.00 a.m. and he had just discovered that our beef ribs set in their magnificent broth had all fermented. For ten minutes my brain was absolutely paralysed. What could I possibly do? I could not cancel the function. I didn't know how to contact the organiser on a Sunday morning. This and other equally feeble thoughts emerged from the glue in my brain.

The Slow Food Movement's luncheon was two and a half hours away, and there are no butchers open. Even if there were, I could not get these special ribs without notice and, more importantly, they take three hours to cook.

The second batch of tongues, shanks and sausages were all perfect. The chickens were yet to be cooked, as were the ears. The only problem, then, was the beef and the glorious broth. Jeff suggested that we poach fillets of beef instead. Thank goodness we had plenty of trimmed fillets ready for Tuesday morning!

And so we did. I had estimated very generous amounts of all the other things, so quantity was not in question. We started to build a new broth, using a few litres of the delicious beef broth from Saturday night's service, the existing perfect veal shank liquid, and some richly reduced chicken stock. All was combined, strained through double muslin, reduced and seasoned – and it tasted pretty good.

I was to describe the dish to the guests and I am afraid I told a lie. The beef ribs were unsatisfactory – too stringy, I said – so I had decided to substitute my own special favourite, poached fillet of beef. After all, I reasoned to myself and stated boldly, traditions can evolve and the spirit of the dish, of simmered unseasoned meats, was still correct.

My hope is that the first knowledge of this near-disaster for all the guests will be when someone reads this journal after publication. My story should give heart to all the young cooks out there. Mistakes happen to everyone – the important thing is how they are dealt with.

After such a black start, it turned out to be a good day and when I left the Restaurant, the Christmas pudding had been served and the guests looked very relaxed. By the time I got home, I felt shaky and very flat. I was in bed by 9.00 p.m., convinced that the sooner I left the industry the better for all concerned.

For the curious, the problem occurred through a combination of factors: Melbourne's 35°C temperature; and too many beef ribs stored in one large tub, which in turn meant that the cooling-down process took too long after the tub was refrigerated. I do know the principles, and it has never happened before. Coolrooms and refrigerators filled to capacity did not help, either.

The following two sauce recipes are delicious with any poached meats or poultry. Both are sharp and assertive in flavour and compensate for the lack of seasoning that is inevitable when meat or poultry is simmered in broth.

Peara

500 g sourdough bread with crusts
    removed
1 litre veal stock

1 cup chopped bone marrow
plenty of freshly ground black pepper
salt to taste

Simmer the chopped bread in the veal stock, stirring once or twice. The consistency should be like porridge. Add the bone marrow, the pepper and salt to taste. This bread sauce should be quite peppery. Serve it hot.

Serves at least 8–10

Salsa Verde

1 cup pickled cornichons (small
    pickling cucumbers preserved in
    vinegar), chopped
2 tablespoons capers, soaked and
    drained, roughly chopped

4 shallots, finely chopped
2 cups flat-leaf parsley, roughly chopped
½ cup extra-virgin olive oil

Mix all ingredients together. Add extra oil if it looks at all dry. There will almost certainly be sufficient vinegar from the cornichons. If not (and the sauce should be quite sharp), add some red-wine vinegar to taste.

Serves 8–10

8 DECEMBER

The Cafe is very busy. I enjoy doing the flowers there once a week. Green Irish bells, Christmas lilies, yellow canna lilies, long stems of seed pods from wild fennel, catmint, white lupins and opium poppies this week.

9 DECEMBER

Today is both Nicky's and Elena's birthday. I sent each of them a bunch of flowers. Presents will have to come later.

Back to the real world and preparation for tomorrow's second-last cooking class. Summer cooking this time, and I am demonstrating my summer favourites: white-cooked chicken with a Thai cucumber and rose-petal salad, and *vitello tonnato* with roasted peppers. This will be preceded by a rich gazpacho, emphasising the importance of the quality of the sherry vinegar used, and the luncheon class will finish with two fruit tarts, raspberry and peach.

Tonight's treat is to enjoy probably my penultimate dinner at Stephanie's, with Julie, Angie and Duffy. I have belated birthday presents for both women, framed drawings by Guy Mirabella, the talented artist and designer with whom I have worked on several projects and who has designed our labels and menus.

My last menu is headed:

Stephanie says Goodbye,
Twenty-one great years, 1976–1997.
Thank you, thank you, thank you.

Julie's eyes filled with tears as she opened her menu (I have already listed its offerings and the story that accompanied each dish). I started to panic when I saw her become emotional. It was a portent of what may happen on New Year's Eve. I made a decision to ask Anna to organise *A Book for Soppy Thoughts*, so that on the night, people who feel very emotional can write it down rather than weeping on me, which will have me completely undone and make my eyes puffy!

We had a superb dinner and as I looked around at this room, positively humming with goodwill, fear gripped my heart. I am giving this up. Duffy sensed this and said, 'Are you sure you want to close?'. We laughed and the moment disappeared. Yes, I am sure, but there will be grieving to go through.

When I was sulky or rude as a small child, my mother sometimes tried to jolly me from my mood by quoting the following nursery rhyme.

There was a little girl who had a little curl
Right down the middle of her forehead.
When she was good she was very, very good
But when she was bad she was horrid.

The Restaurant is a bit like the little girl.

I cannot go on and on about my impending loss, and yet there is this sense of inner meltdown. I know it will come, I know I cannot avoid it – and shouldn't even expect to avoid it – and yet I am afraid of its intensity. And how I will come out of it. The practical side of me takes over and reassures my emotional self that I will have so many nasty bits to cope with – solicitors, accountants and many others – that I will finally be pleased to walk out of the door. I am unconvinced.

10 DECEMBER

*J*eff and I had an excellent meeting sorting out the final ordering and planning for the three very important final services, Christmas Day, Saturday 27 December, and New Year's Eve. We will again need to hire some plates. Our former head chef Tom Milligan has offered to lend me thirty large *assiettes creuses* from the restaurant he is in charge of at the Casino. These wide, deep dishes are perfect for the poached fillet with its broth.

The very last of my bottled brandied cumquats will go into the duck stuffing for Christmas Day. They are two years old and look mummified in their jars, but taste sensational. I have part of a five-year-old cloth-wrapped cheddar – made by Jock Montgomery in Somerset, England – earmarked for the lunch, and it will be accompanied by cracked walnuts from northern Victoria, oatcakes from our kitchen, as well as sourdough fruit loaves.

On 27 December, our last regular service, Craig will produce 140 of his astonishing champagne and raspberry jellies.

I have ordered two kilograms of Russian caviar and one kilogram of French truffles to be flown in for the final extravaganza on New Year's Eve. Bit of an expensive joke, really. Such marvellous delicacies have never been part of my repertoire, but on this last night the very best of everything is to be available. (Besides, we have heard that it is almost certain there will be a world moratorium on caviar production in an effort to undo some of the damage done by rampant over-fishing in the Caspian Sea. This may be a last taste for a long time.) The tables will be decorated with ripe peaches picked from an orchard the day before. Forty kilos of just-picked strawberries will be the finale, while the guests dance the year away.

1 1 DECEMBER

I have just called Holly in France to wish her a happy birthday. I can't wait for her to arrive, and she, too, is eager to be here.

My sister, Diana, had her last lunch in the Restaurant today.

Anna has the New Year's Eve festivities well in hand. I hear snippets about organza bottle bags, and girls with Madame de Pompadour wigs, and drums, gold tassels, balloons and fairy lights. Sounds fun. I wish I were ten kilos lighter. The new dress I am planning is somehow not right on my solid body. Why do I even bother? I wondered about a Venetian mask, so that I might present an ever-smiling face on the night.

1 2 DECEMBER

𝓗olly received her birthday parcel exactly on her birthday.

The issues surrounding reconciliation of all Australians continue to dominate the news.

The contrast between the softly spoken, dignified leaders of the Aboriginal community and the defensive, hectoring tone of the government spokesmen is startling. It appears likely that there will be a double dissolution of parliament, as the Senate is refusing to endorse the government's ten-point plan aimed at resolving the issues surrounding the Wik decision. Many Australians rightly dread the prospect of an election where one of the main issues is race. We are back to the question of the 'haves' and the 'have-nots', to basic considerations of social justice and the need for this country to regain its honour as a mature nation by facing its obligations to all its citizens.

Of course there will be problems to resolve. In the business world it is seen as admirable to take on a challenge where there are significant problems to overcome. Why should the existence of problems be a reason for not proceeding in a social justice framework? Could it be that there is little monetary profit in social justice? Many Australians believe that there is enormous profit to be made by embracing reconciliation and, conversely, that the debts will continue to escalate the longer this process is delayed. Because it is inevitable.

1 3 DECEMBER

𝓣his morning I went to the Restaurant before anyone else was in and did a stocktake of the small equipment in the pastry room. So much stuff has been bought over the years. I had to check both kitchens, the coolrooms and cupboards, as well as the storeroom, and I felt a bit like Pooh Bear counting his honeypots. Thirty tinned French charlotte moulds with lids, 150 jelly moulds, 120 dariole moulds, 85 individual baba moulds (bought at Dehillerin in Paris on one visit when I was astounded to find myself standing next to Paul Bocuse at the counter – he was buying a whisk!), tartlet moulds in five sizes, and so on. The list ran to two pages. The same detail has to be put into listing kitchen pots and pans, but this is impossible at present with so much activity.

I have had a nibble of interest in the fixtures and fittings and the lease. But I will not allow myself to be excited yet. I have arranged a meeting with a firm of auctioneers tomorrow morning, so the final solution could still be either way. It may well be decided this coming week.

I spent the afternoon first at the Cafe, stopping in to pick up some pudding boxes, and then back at Stephanie's to wrap the puddings, sign some more copies of *The Cook's Companion*, and meet with Jeff again to plan strategies for the final two weeks.

It is interesting that although we have had many former members of staff who have come to say goodbye and to enjoy a last Stephanie's experience, not a single member of the food press, known as the 'food mafia', has bothered. It is fortunate that I have never believed my own publicity or I would now be crushed by the realisation that I am already *passé* as the food journalists continue their relentless hunt for the new.

Each day I am reading lovely letters from the public thanking me for happy times experienced at Stephanie's Restaurant.

I have not wanted to be part of the service these last two nights. As the team gears up for another workout, as the boards are cleaned and slapped on the benches, and the benches are swabbed and the set-up begins, for some reason my heart sinks to my boots and I want to go home. I am running away. And then once at home, as I cook and eat a simple meal, I am overwhelmed with guilt that I ought to be slipping and sliding through the action with the rest of the team. By 10.00 I am in bed, feeling very depressed.

Apart from reinforcing my decision to end my career as a hands-on restaurateur, it is likely that my reluctance to engage in these final nights is because I really have no role at this stage. The team is so well-organised, their responsibilities so well-grasped, their time so efficiently deployed that I would really be fluttering at the edges, possibly in the way. By contrast, on Christmas Day I will be part of the service team and part of the hustle and bustle.

Six lunch services to go, and then Christmas Day. Eight dinner services to go and then New Year's Eve.

19 DECEMBER

*A*nother week has passed.

Some decisions have been made. The landlady appears to intend to sell the building. She has had several inspections in the company of estate agents and would-be purchasers. I shall proceed with an auction of the contents on 9 February. I have agreed to help with the catalogue. The preceding weekend will be set aside for viewing, and a few days later I will fly off to New Zealand to carry out a teaching commitment, having finally closed the doors.

I rang Maggie to confess how miserable I was and she wondered if I was feeling 'cast out', a person without a role. I was inclined to agree, until I went to the Restaurant tonight to be part of the 'meet and greet' team. Rather than feeling cast out, I suspect I am subconsciously distancing myself from the energy that is so seductive as well as so exhausting. There is great humour in the kitchen and I love it. Tonight had all the signs of a ghastly service. When I left at 9.00 only a few small tables had ordered. The downstairs kitchen was inevitably going to be 'hit' with the orders from two functions at the same time. But there was no obvious tension or anxiety, just laughter, itself a great tension-breaker.

The countdown has really begun now. Tonight is the last Friday night service ever.

I am becoming obsessed with the peripherals.

I prowl about picking up dirty kitchen cloths, finding unwashed baking dishes, or towels incorrectly folded in the bathrooms, or protesting at piled-up cardboard boxes rather than flattened boxes, and so it goes on. Wild-eyed cooks dash past me with no time to respond to my tut-tutting. They treat me with affectionate tolerance. Mark plonks another mountain of cheques on my desk to be signed. Another odd thing about this industry is that one handles huge sums of money. Both in and out. The proportion left as profit is very small indeed, when expressed as a percentage, and a firm eye must be directed to the bottom line at all times. Only at times of full flood, such as now, can I afford to say to my managers 'Ring an agency, don't argue about the price – just get someone!'.

Tonight saw the return of Christoph as a wine waiter. For eleven years, Christoph ran the wine department. He is back to help out for these last few services and Brian is delighted to see him. Neither seems fussed about the role reversal.

A customer tonight presented me with a photograph of Lisa and me having a coffee at one of the *trattorie* on the piazza in Siena! She was somewhere nearby. Just as well I was not making a spectacle of myself. In fact, both Lisa and I seem a little worried in the photo – probably writing a shopping list for the extended family!

I have decided to put all the photographs of the building, the banner, the trophies and the framed awards into storage. I cannot bear the idea of turning a part of my house into some sort of trophy room, and yet there is history to be considered. Sooner or later someone will want to know how it happened, and what it all looked like. It is chilling to realise that soon very few will remember. I must be less casual about the memorabilia. I have been asked by the State Library for a menu collection. I have never been good about organising such things – there have just always been more where they came from, inside my head. And, by an extraordinary coincidence, I have now received Expressions of Interest in my manuscripts, menus and memorabilia from both the State Library and the National Library.

2 1 D E C E M B E R

Some day the full story of Stephen Downes and Stephanie's Restaurant will have to be told. I have a file of meticulously clipped paragraphs, and it would not take much for me to spill the beans. Today he published his comment on the passing of Stephanie's: 'Stephanie's closed because it was funereal and took itself too seriously. Its food, moreover, was Melbourne's most overrated'.

And this is from someone who has not set foot in the place for more than ten years.

If critics are permitted column space to comment on the collective work of a restaurant that they have not visited for more than ten years, it is little wonder that our food writers are held in such low regard by the experienced practitioners. I was supported by several more outraged calls and the knowledge that in the scheme of things this man is of no more significance than an annoying insect.

Rosie and I walked in the park this morning and it was deserted. It will be very hot later on. My own garden had a smarten-up yesterday, and gardener Richard and I decided that one could feel the plants' relief – they could now breathe more easily, freed of dead wood, dead heads and weeds. The agapanthus and plumbago are blooming with abandon, the tiny mauve flowers that make up each spray of lemon verbena move ever so slightly in the morning breeze. Richard has saved my Altissimo rose. It is triumphantly scarlet, each flattened flower magnificent against a silvery cedar shed. Last summer it almost died, but with a new position and some tender loving care it has gained strength and has put out two long, healthy water shoots, covered with buds. And, near the clothesline, the yellow-green dogwood still has a few of its open-faced, rounded flowers, each petal tipped with a trace of pink.

The Cafe staff have their Christmas party tonight and I am looking forward to a relaxed get-together, although I have been asked to make a short speech, stressing the need for a united team spirit and promising interest and excitement in 1998. Working to capacity for eight months has certainly emphasised the need to create a structure that allows for more communication. We all agree to set aside one afternoon per fortnight to hold meetings. For staff interested in owning their own business, it is smart to learn techniques of managing problems at our expense!

23 DECEMBER

Today I read an account by a colleague relating how he had researched crab salad via the Internet. It started me musing. I have nominated 1998 as The Year of Technology for me (starting with fixing the digital clock on the oven that is still registering pre-summer time), and I would be the first to admit that I am as an infant, yet to dip my toes in cyberspace. But the question needs to be asked: what point is being made? Certainly this chef is demonstrating how up-to-the-minute he is with technology. But then what?

This fine chef has at least ten years' experience of working with great ingredients. He has travelled widely, is intelligent and has a headful of ideas. So why does he need to surround himself with every possible permutation of crab salad before he can proceed? Probably his search largely confirmed what he already knew.

We are all stimulated by the ideas of others, but I believe the most meaningful influences are those that happen serendipitously. One travels to this place, not that place; speaks with this person, rather than that person; one tastes a dish here, rather than there; reads this book rather than that; one has spring onions in the refrigerator, but no shallots; one handles this type of crab, not that one.

The danger of becoming locked into the Internet as one's primary information source is that the search can become the end rather than the means. It is the infinite mass of undigested information that is available which worries me. The amount of time taken up by these seductive searches is also concerning to one who believes that life is best spent in the real world, rather than in any version of virtual reality. Of course, the technology is evolving faster than I can type, and the 'search engines' will become ever more discriminatory and so on. I still cling to my cautionary belief that the means must never be confused with the end.

Fancifully I wonder if, in another time, any cooks would have undertaken a full-scale literature search in the British Museum for how to prepare mashed potatoes? And once this search was completed, what about the Bibliothèque Nationale for French versions, not to mention the holders of numerous other collections?

Elizabeth David did spend a great deal of her last working years in the British Museum, researching everything to do with iced desserts, and produced an exhaustive, scholarly but largely impenetrable volume. Although by this time in her life, her interest had moved from the practical to the academic and historic, far from the clamour and adrenalin of the practising cook.

Were I to be thinking about mashed potatoes, I would use the more
serendipitous method I have suggested. My brain would wander from
mashed potatoes whipped with a cream made from slowly cooked garlic
(a classic Stephanie's accompaniment); to mashed potatoes whipped with
enormous quantities of butter (first tasted at Robuchon in Paris); to mashed
potatoes roughly crushed with very fine extra-virgin olive oil (south of
France); to mashed potatoes whipped with veal stock (to accompany *boeuf à
la mode* at Stephanie's twelve years ago); to potatoes puréed to almost runny
consistency with boiling milk (classic French *cuisine bourgeoise*); to mashed
potatoes with chopped green or black olives (can't remember); to mashed
potatoes mixed with spring onions and mounded around a well of melted
butter (Irish champ) – and this is just a five-minute mental reflection.

I am off to the kitchen to cook some potatoes!

24 DECEMBER, CHRISTMAS EVE

*B*oth Rosie the poodle and I have had a haircut today. She looks very sleek
and smart. My haircut is very short and a bit punk. I was even persuaded to
buy a pot of 'fudge' for the hair. Angie's youngest daughter uses it also, but
hers is blue. The kitchen staff all complimented me and Robyn said it made
me look twenty years younger! Flattery gets you everywhere. It does make
me feel very liberated.

I opened my Christmas present from Mark: a copy of Frances Mayes's
Under the Tuscan Sun. How apt. I was lent a copy for a few weeks before my
Italian sojourn and it now has extra significance. I opened it at random
and read:

Breakfast is one of my favourite times because the mornings are so fresh,
with no hint of the heat to come. I get up early and take my toast and coffee
out on the terrace for an hour with a book and the green-black rows of
cypresses against the soft sky, the hills pleated with olive terraces that
haven't changed since the seasons were depicted in medieval psalters.

The thought of such relaxed breakfasts made me shiver. For the first time I have an intimation that a new life may be around the corner, one I am able to choose, design as I wish, and enjoy.

We have worked so hard the last few days and tomorrow's Christmas Day lunch is the first of the three climaxes. I boiled and peeled 300 quail eggs today – they are to be part of an asparagus salad. I have always enjoyed the surprise of deep-fried boiled eggs. The yolks become very creamy, the crisp exterior a nice contrast to the softness within. In a Thai dish known as son-in-law eggs, a dressing of fish sauce, palm sugar and tamarind water is spooned over the eggs. I have decided to use these flavours with my asparagus and quail egg salad.

ASPARAGUS SALAD WITH SON-IN-LAW EGGS

6 handfuls of special salad leaves
12 quail eggs
24 spears of medium thickness asparagus
16 baby leeks, each no thicker than one's thumb

3 tablespoons crispy shallots (obtainable from Asian shops)
clean oil for deep-frying

SAUCE

4 tablespoons tamarind water
4 tablespoons palm sugar

2 tablespoons fish sauce
1 small hot chilli, seeded and finely sliced

Sauce   To make tamarind water, use 1 part tamarind pulp to 2 parts hot water. Squeeze together well and stand for 1 hour. Strain, pressing hard on solids.

Combine all ingredients and stir until sugar dissolves. Taste for balance, adjusting with fish sauce. Set aside until needed.

Wash and dry salad leaves, and set aside. Hardboil quail eggs for 4 minutes, and peel.

Trim asparagus and leeks and wash leeks well. Cook each vegetable separately till just tender in plenty of lightly salted water. Drain very well.

Arrange salad leaves on 6 plates. Divide asparagus and leeks and place on the leaves. Deep-fry the peeled hardboiled eggs until they are golden brown. Drain well. Add to salads and spoon over the sauce. Garnish with crispy shallots.
Serves 6

Today was the very last lunch served at Stephanie's Restaurant. I feel nothing at all. There is no time to reflect on *temps perdu*; we are all onto the next service. The duck dish tomorrow will require 300 turnips and 300 carrots to be peeled and simmered in a mixture of butter, water, stock and seasonings. Banqueting departments of big hotels can deal with these requirements without turning a hair. For us it is difficult. We do not have giant baking trays or huge convection/steam ovens. I did have a group in the back garden peeling turnips and carrots, though, and I had a flashback to Italy, remembering our courtyard teams of peelers and pluckers.

25 DECEMBER, CHRISTMAS DAY

A marvellous day.

I had T-shirts printed for everyone, with the message 'I survived Stephanie's last days, 1976–1997' on them.

The mood in the kitchen was relaxed and loving. The mammoth preparation paid off. Everything looked and tasted fantastic.

The warm, cheesy puffs that accompanied the small cup of gazpacho were as light as air.

The asparagus and son-in-law egg salad was delicious, and I had just the right amount of tamarind in my cupboard at home to make plenty of the savoury dressing without needing to go shopping.

The next course was a choice between the smoked salmon custard with its roulade of sliced salmon, seasoned greens and warm buckwheat crepe, or a caramelised tomato tart with a side salad of buffalo mozzarella, olives, torn parsley and caperberries.

One customer begged me for the smoked salmon custard recipe. I have resisted the request before, but at the end of Stephanie's, why not?

SMOKED SALMON CUSTARD WITH ITS ROULADE OF SALMON

SMOKED SALMON CUSTARD

neutral-flavoured oil or clarified butter for greasing moulds

175 g smoked salmon, without skin or bones (chilled at least one hour)

55 g beef bone marrow (chilled at least one hour)

½ clove garlic, chopped

1 tablespoon tomato purée

4 whole eggs

4 egg yolks

300 ml milk

300 ml cream

tabasco

salt to taste

Lightly grease 10–12 × 125 ml moulds and cut rounds of baking paper to fit the base of the moulds.

Blend or process salmon, bone marrow, garlic and tomato purée. When you have a smooth paste, add the eggs and egg yolks. Blend to mix well.

Bring milk and cream to scalding point and then add to salmon mix in the blender.

Settle a strainer over a deep bowl and line the strainer with a large, doubled piece of dampened muslin. Pour the salmon custard mix into the muslin and, with the help of a friend, gather up the muslin and twist the ends in opposite directions. This action will very quickly force the custard through into the bowl and will catch any little fish fibres and scrappy bits. Season with a few drops of tabasco and salt to taste.

Pour into moulds. Settle moulds in a baking dish two-thirds filled with hot water and bake at 160°C for 30–50 minutes until just set.

Allow to settle for 10 minutes before unmoulding. Serve hot or warm.

Note: We sauce this with a small quantity of *beurre rouge* (a variation on a classic *beurre blanc* but the reduction is made with red wine instead of white), and serve it with the smoked salmon roulade as described below. *Makes 10–12*

ROULADE OF SALMON
1 crepe per person
1 slice smoked salmon per person
a small handful of salad leaves,
    lightly dressed with extra-virgin
    olive oil and lemon juice

Warm the crepe in the oven and then lay on first the salmon and then the greens. Roll the crepe like a cigar and neaten the ends with a sharp knife. Cut into 2 or 3 pieces and stand these little logs on and around the plate.

Note: We substitute a few spoonfuls of buckwheat flour for plain flour in the crepe recipe, as the nuttiness of buckwheat is so good with salmon.

The main course was a choice between the stuffed ballotine of duck with its piquant brandied cumquat sauce, or fillets of rockling on a fondue of parsley with a ribbon of lemon butter.

Then the Jock Montgomery cheddar, and it was stunning – fabulous texture and flavour. The walnuts from Beechworth were sensational. They cracked so easily and sat pale and moist in their shells.

Then the pudding, or alternatively, a trifle. Craig and I had designed very pretty individual trifles, the bottom layer showing swirls of miniature jam rolls, then rich marsala custard, then our champagne jelly studded with raspberries. Everyone received a round of Scottish shortbread to take home with a signed menu.

I took home a bottle of Billecart-Salmon rosé champagne, which Lisa and I enjoyed together with smoked salmon on hot toast. We exchanged presents. I gave her a Le Creuset pot she coveted, she gave me the two-volume wine appreciation video by Jancis Robinson that I wanted. So we were both pleased!

26 DECEMBER, BOXING DAY

$\mathcal{M}$y Boxing Day family party has become an institution. This year the group was smaller – Helen and Bruce are in the States, Diana's son is in South Africa, some of the men went to the cricket, and Jenny, Graham and Jessica Little were in Canberra. We were still twenty for lunch, but it was a gentle day, without any obvious dramas. Jean and John have a new puppy that was much admired. The sun shone, but not too fiercely. Lunch was delicious. The stilton cheese from Colston Bassett was magnificent, as were the plum puddings with muscat ice-cream and rich vanilla custard.

I received several great books as presents and for once it seems likely that I may have time to read them. Tonight I have decided to go to bed very early with a P. D. James novel.

27 DECEMBER

$\mathcal{A}$ very good article in *The Australian* today written by Richard Yallop. It was a pleasure to be interviewed by someone whom I felt wanted to write a considered piece, one that set both the Restaurant and my work in a broad context. I am satisfied that his article did this.

Richard Yallop quotes me as saying (referring to my two divorces): 'You can't have it all and the sooner you realise that, the happier you'll be enjoying what you've got … I can't imagine what it would have been like if I'd fallen in love ten years ago in the middle of trying to run the restaurant: it would have been impossible'.

He concludes: 'In one sense, Alexander's heart was won long ago: her love of food has been a lifelong affair'.

And so it has.

I spent the afternoon cleaning out a cupboard in my office. First I discovered a pair of scarlet tap shoes, tucked away years before. I was reminded of William, a marvellous waiter who had attempted to teach me to tap dance. After our first few lessons I discovered I was tearing the ancient floorboards of the Restaurant with the tap shoes. From then on, we practised in regular footwear, which wasn't nearly as much fun. I don't remember conquering more than a few steps in our routine for 'Singing in the Rain' before I fell down the stairs, this time wearing kitchen clogs, and sprained my ankle. Lessons were suspended and sadly did not resume! William has sent me a postcard from London with warm wishes for the future.

Next, I found a carefully hemmed small square of Provençal patterned cotton and was reminded of chef Sally, who had prepared twenty-five of these napkins to line the bread baskets for The Grand Aioli Dinner, also several years ago.

I shall keep the pretty napkin, but I think the days of the tap shoes are over and they can go to the op shop!

The last Saturday night service – and it was not an easy one. The domino theory, of which one heard much during the Vietnam War, is a less talked about phenomenon in a restaurant kitchen. If one dish runs out, pressure on the next favourite causes it also to run out, and so on. The fallout can be disastrous. Worst of all is when one table has to be refused more than one thing. We hustled hard tonight to prevent this happening. Fish serves were counted and re-counted, salmon reserved for another use suddenly became an extra option, and the last three remaining saddles of Western Australian rabbit were offered with instantly designed garnishes of sweet and sour small onions, sultanas and crispy bacon.

Tonight's champagne jellies were the best ever, thanks to Craig's persistence. They positively strained to get out of the moulds, the expanding bubbles captured and set just as they were about to burst. Ice-cold champagne, ice-cold moulds, and just about setting gelatine is the answer.

THE BEST RASPBERRY AND CHAMPAGNE JELLY

1 cup light sugar syrup
12 leaves gelatine

30 ml raspberry liqueur (or raspberry syrup)
1 bottle champagne

LIGHT SUGAR SYRUP
Heat 2 parts water to 1 part sugar and stir until the sugar has dissolved. Cold syrup can be stored for weeks in a closed container in the fridge.

Chill 8 jelly moulds and a mixing bowl. Soak the gelatine in cold water for a few minutes. Bring measured quantity of sugar syrup to simmering point. Squeeze the gelatine and drop into the simmering sugar syrup. Swish to dissolve completely. Add the raspberry liqueur or syrup. Allow to cool, then tip into chilled mixing bowl. Gently pour the chilled champagne over the mixture, stirring carefully to combine but not to foam unnecessarily. Ladle the mix into the chilled moulds and refrigerate until set.

Serve with fresh berries.

Makes 8

As I walked to my car tonight I was acutely aware that this was the last Saturday night to be spent in this place. I found myself to be quite calm about it, even a bit relieved.

Holly is in the air and on her way home. I shall collect her early in the morning.

28 DECEMBER

We are all together again – just for a week. A perfect day spent in the garden. The sky is deep blue and there is the slightest breeze. It quickens the surface of the water in the pool, which then reflects as flickering light on the terracotta pots blazing with petunias. An unseen bird gives a throaty, liquid trill. The bronze foliage of the Penelope rose catches the light; the new blooms on my climbing Lorraine Lee suggest that it is settling into its trellis.

We lunched on Christmas ham, and mustard brought by Holly from Dijon. Lisa and I looked at her photos and caught up on her life. And then it was our turn. What a year for all of us this has turned out to be. Holly suggests that there is an unpleasant undercurrent to life in a large French town. Violence is a fact of life, as is overt racial hatred. Holly is not one to overreact, and walked the streets of New York without concern. But she will not use public transport after dark in Lyon, and said that this gritty edge to daily life has made her very appreciative of Melbourne. I am surprised, but interested.

Conversation moves to Australia's own unresolved racial issues. There seems to be no society free of negative responses when confronted by difference – of religion, politics or race.

Tomorrow I shall collect my new dress for the New Year's Eve party and do the flowers for the Cafe. The Cafe has collected several accolades as 'best new cafe' for 1997. It re-opens after a four-day break and I am excited by the challenge to make it bigger and better in 1998. Well, maybe not bigger, but there is scope for improvement and I will have energy to give.

2 9   DECEMBER

I am searching for the essence of what Stephanie's Restaurant has meant, to me and to the larger community. Some thoughts have been included in the menu booklet to be given on New Year's Eve. But I will still be expected to say something at the beginning of the evening.

This is where I have got to.

For twenty-one years I have had the privilege of being able to do exactly what I wanted to do most of all, and to make a living from doing it, and to have gathered affection and respect from many wonderful people while doing it.

There are many people to thank. My family, who have put up with me and my obsession. My staff, past and present. My former partner, Dur-é Dara. And many special friends, who have always been there for me. And Lorrie Lawrence, for her spectacular flowers created every week for the entire seventeen years the Restaurant has been here in Hawthorn.

I have found out that some of the young people I have worked with have never experienced the broadening influence of an exciting culinary background, as I did thanks to an enlightened and inspiring mother. My aim has been to provide a similar influence for these young cooks, and I know that for many it has been an important reference point for their subsequent careers. I am very proud of that.

Stephanie's Restaurant has also given me a significant public profile, of which I am also very proud. It can be inconvenient sometimes to be recognisable and I would certainly not want to eat a meat pie in the street – someone would notice. But I am very aware of the responsibility that comes with a public image. I have tried not to indulge in any mean or nasty personal abuse, no matter how tempting (and it has been very tempting at times). Rather, I have used my reputation for integrity, as a thinking 'foodie', as one who cares deeply for this country, to promote the cause of good food as an achievable and desirable goal for everyone, wherever possible.

Through my writing I have tried to bridge the gap that exists between practitioners and commentators. I believe it has been helpful – and even sometimes illuminating – for the general public to better understand the processes that are involved in restaurants, and it has certainly been helpful for restaurateurs to become more in tune with the farmers and producers who provide their raw materials. And, unlike most other food writers in the country, I truly understand what is involved in maintaining a quality restaurant.

There are those who believe that working with food is a very lightweight activity. Not so. Cooking is inextricably linked to the most important questions of our society. It involves an understanding of animal husbandry, of responsible agriculture, of personal independence, of pride in craft, and respect for and understanding of traditions from other places as well as our own. The shared table offers opportunities to learn and practise tolerance and to explore ideas, in addition to offering comfort and sensory delight.

As well as these lofty matters, I have loved the work. I have never been happier than when at my chopping board with a panful of something bubbling away at my side, or taking delivery of a crate of marvellous tomatoes, or talking through a dish with a new recruit, or else watching the team put out plate after plate of splendidly cooked, strong-flavoured dishes.

One does not go into restaurants to make a lot of money – or I don't know any who have achieved this. First and foremost, one must want to give. And one must have a genuine love of good food. Without these two things, it cannot be a good restaurant. Stephanie's Restaurant initiated discussion about the role of personal style. The current media attention devoted to the question of fine dining's continued existence seems to me to be missing the point. Good restaurants will always be there and they will reflect personal preferences of the owners. I just hope that in Melbourne there will still be restaurateurs who design dining rooms that permit conversation.

It is time to move on and move over. Roll on the next wave. It is inevitable the new young Turks will face the same challenges and experience the same heady mix of highs and lows. I have experienced love, pain, divorces, separations, births, deaths, accolades, axes, friendship, manipulation and greed. But I have not been bored for one minute of these twenty-one years. Depressed, exhausted, anxious, angry, exhilarated, excited, intoxicated – but never ever bored.

Happy New Year!

Or I shall say something to this effect!

30 DECEMBER

Such wonderful tributes in *The Age* today. Both my dear friend Graham Little and former colleague Geoff Lindsay have contributed articles that are generous, complimentary and glow with affection. What a lovely way to start the day. I feel hugged by their warmth.

And it is to be a very full day, preparing for the finale tomorrow. In the carpark there are banks of flowers in buckets. The marquee is being erected. Gift bottles of bubbly are being slipped into frothy organza bags and tied with satin ribbon. Shimmering gold and cream balloons arrive. 'I want the evening to have the smell and colour of ripe peaches', I had said to Anna.

In the kitchen, one hundred quail have been boned and filled with a foie gras stuffing. Two kilos of caviar arrive. The aroma of truffles suddenly fills the air as Michael slips a slice under each squab breast. He tucks one whole truffle into a bag of arborio rice for me and seals it up – a treat for 1998. The entire kitchen team tackles the mud crab: we have forty kilos of live crab to cook, cool and pick for the freshest crab salad. Faxes from colleagues begin to arrive.

Marvellous Anna is creating smaller and larger miracles – calmly, efficiently and creatively. A container for the oysters has been found.

The candelabra from our Tuscan evening have been borrowed again. Two hundred and fifty peaches arrive. Little gold-edged booklets are unpacked. These are the secret menus, and they are so beautiful. Inside are stories collected (again by Anna) from former staff members. I am glad to read them today, though they make me very teary. In fact, I have a big sob – the only one, as it turns out.

31 DECEMBER

*T*elevision cameras all morning, and we prepared a serve of every dish for Simon Griffiths to photograph. The band leader arrived to check his sound. I was thrilled to meet him – Mark Fitzgibbon is the son of one of Melbourne's jazz legends, 'Smacka' Fitzgibbon. It was already 30°C in the shade, and the sides of the marquee were rolled up to catch some breeze. All cars have been banished from the carpark, and tables and chairs are set out instead. Still some phone calls from the public, hopeful of finding a table. Lorrie is finishing off an absolutely spectacular floral extravaganza. Every table, every sideboard, every corner is bursting with flowers. There are roses everywhere, peachy and pink and yellow and cream, and every table has fresh peaches. The front foyer has a pyramid of peaches piled in a black urn. Simon snaps it all, so I can remember this amazing event. Flowers are delivered from Joan Kirner. A phone call from Elly in Venice and one from Helen in Florida.

The last big bash – and what a night it was.

I slipped into my long, silk dress, the colour of the stunning Salitage Pinot Noir I was to sip later on. Anna greeted me and handed me my crown for the night – a circlet of deep-red fragrant rosebuds and a Venetian mask adorned with the same scented rose petals, in case anything became too much! Anna looked gorgeous in peachy silk with ropes of pearls.

The oysters were served in the garden from a giant wok – the perfect receptacle for lots of ice and no drips. And Pol Roger in magnum. Plenty of it.

The Hunting Party arrived – two girls in high platform shoes, brilliant flounced dresses and towering velvet hats – to invite all the guests to the marquee for the formal part of the evening. Each guest was 'blessed' with a few grains of rice and the mystery speaker was introduced. It was Maggie! How appropriate. She spoke of our friendship and of how she used to be scared of me, but how she now knows that I am really 'a pussycat'. She talked of all the things we have shared; and of the time she spent in Stephanie's so long ago, when she felt isolated and dispirited at the Pheasant Farm Restaurant, and of how this experience had revived her spirits; and she spoke of how we have enjoyed each other's company … I responded with more or less the words I had planned.

And then I was presented with a magnificent antique copper stockpot, newly re-tinned, with sturdy, gleaming, brass-riveted handles – a gift from all my friends and the staff. This pot would not have been out of place in the kitchens of Escoffier. A perfect present, so beautiful and so workmanlike, and symbolising so exactly the soul of the kitchen.

We retreated to our beautiful tables and were presented with a platter of fabulous tastes.

The first dish of the evening was described as the extravaganza! Dollops of Osietra caviar, flying fish roe and salmon roe interspersed with carpaccio of salmon with sliced miniature peaches preserved in white truffle oil, gravlax of salmon with creamy scrambled eggs, smoked salmon rolled in a buckwheat crepe, all with Melba toast …

I shall not insist that readers follow our every mouthful, but it was a stunning meal. The wines were lovely and those listed on the menu were augmented all night by extras brought up from the cellar. After the main course, the band gave a few preliminary riffs and everyone rushed to the dance floor. Helen Noonan had joined us, leaving her understudy to sing her role in *Phantom of the Opera*. Her first song was 'They Can't Take That Away From Me' (including the great and appropriate line, 'The way you wear your hat'). And then my request was 'Ev'ry Time We Say Goodbye' ('I want to cry a little'), and I didn't – and, later in the evening, 'As Time Goes By'.

Midnight came with timely sparklers, poppers, hooters, and kisses and hugs and, for me, a huge welling of excitement for the possibilities in 1998.

Back at the table the cheese and bread had been cleared and in their place were baskets of berries – strawberries, raspberries, blueberries, redcurrants, white currants, blackberries – and bowls of clotted cream, with sugared puff-pastry biscuits and foaming flutes of sparkling shiraz.

The band left at 1.30 a.m. and then the jukebox took over, as former staff members poured in for the next wave of partying. More than sixty staff members and regular customers continued to bop and drink, and eventually eat (apparently supper was served at 4.00 a.m., by which time I was just hitting the pillow), until the last revellers left at 7.00 a.m.

The final bash was the party to end all parties.

My life will never be the same again. And I am so happy.

Billie Holiday says it best: 'So I say goodbye with no regrets'.

BIBLIOGRAPHY

Alexander, Stephanie. *Stephanie's Menus for Food Lovers*. Methuen Haynes, Sydney, 1985.

Alexander, Stephanie. *Stephanie's Feasts and Stories*. Allen & Unwin, Sydney, 1988.

Alexander, Stephanie. *Stephanie's Australia*. Allen & Unwin, Sydney, 1991.

Alexander, Stephanie. *Stephanie's Seasons*. Allen & Unwin, Sydney, 1993.

Alexander, Stephanie. *The Cook's Companion*. Viking, Ringwood, 1996.

Alexander, Stephanie. *Recipes My Mother Gave Me*. Viking, Ringwood, 1997.

Alexander, Stephanie and Beer, Maggie. *Stephanie Alexander and Maggie Beer's Tuscan Cookbook*. Viking, Ringwood, 1998.

Anderson, Burton. *Pleasures of the Italian Table*. Penguin, London, 1994.

Astley, Thea. *The Multiple Effects of Rainshadow*. Viking, Ringwood, 1996.

Babington, Moyra. *West Country Cooking* (New English Library edn). *Times Mirror* in association with TB Times, London, 1971.

Beer, Maggie. *Maggie's Orchard*. Viking, Ringwood, 1997.

Blanc, Raymond. *Recipes from Le Manoir aux Quat'Saisons*. Macdonald & Co., London, 1988.

Bruce, Mary Grant. *From Billabong to London* (rev. edn). Angus & Robertson, Pymble, 1992.

Burchett, Mary. *Through My Kitchen Door*. Georgian House, Melbourne, 1960.

Burchett, Winston. *The Timid Adventurer*. Unpublished.

Campion, Allan, and Curtis, Michele. *Chilli Jam*. Allen & Unwin, Sydney, 1997.

Campion, Allan, and Curtis, Michele. *The Goods*. Wakefield Press, Kent Town (SA), 1997.

Cassab, Judy. *Judy Cassab Diaries*. Random House Australia, Milsons Point, 1996.

Country Women's Association. *CWA Cookbook*. E. S. Wigg & Son, Sydney, 1936.

David, Elizabeth. *Italian Food* (2nd edn). Penguin, London, 1963.

David, Elizabeth. *French Provincial Cooking*. Penguin, London, 1970.

David, Elizabeth. *Spices, Salt and Aromatics in the English Kitchen*. Penguin, London, 1970.

David, Elizabeth. *An Omelette and a Glass of Wine*. Penguin, London, 1984.

Dessaix, Robert. *Night Letters*. Pan Macmillan, Sydney, 1996.

Drewe, Robert. *The Drowner*. Pan Macmillan, Sydney, 1996.

Dods, Mistress Margaret. *The Cook and Housewife's Manual* (6th edn). Oliver & Boyd, Edinburgh, 1837.

Douglas, Norman. *Old Calabria*. Penguin, Harmondsworth, 1962.

Douglas, Norman. *South Wind* (rev. edn). Secker and Warburg, London, 1979.

Douglas, Norman (ed.). *Venus in the Kitchen: Recipes for Seduction*. Halo Books, 1992.

Dowrick, Stephanie. *Forgiveness and Other Acts of Love*. Viking, Ringwood, 1997.

Erlich, Rita and Forell, Claude (eds). *The Age Good Food Guide*. Anne O'Donovan, Melbourne, 1997.

Freeman, Meera and Nhan, Le Van. *The Vietnamese Cookbook*. Viking, Ringwood, 1995.

Grizzuti Harrison, Barbara. *Italian Days*. Ticknor & Fidds, New York, 1990.

Glasse, Hannah. *The Art of Cookery* (8th edn). A. Millar et al., London, 1763.

Glowinski, Louis. *The Complete Book of Fruit Growing in Australia*. Lothian Books, Melbourne, 1991.

Hellenga, Robert. *The Sixteen Pleasures*. Hodder & Stoughton, London, 1994.

Jenkins, Sue. *21 Great Chefs of Australia*. Simon & Schuster, Sydney, 1991.

Kitzinger, Sheila. *Pregnancy and Childbirth* (rev. edn). Doubleday, Sydney, 1989.

Little, Graham. *Friendship: Being Ourselves With Others*. Text Publishing, Melbourne, 1993.

Maltby, Peg. *Peg's Fairy Book*. Murfetts, Melbourne, 1944.

Mayes, Frances. *Under the Tuscan Sun*. Broadway Books, New York, 1996.

Moodie, Ann-Maree. *Local Heroes: A Celebration of Success and Leadership in Australia*. Prentice Hall, Sydney, 1998.

Newton, John. *Wogfood*. Random House Australia, Milsons Point, 1996.

Santich, Barbara. *Looking for Flavour*. Wakefield Press, Kent Town (SA), 1996.

Shakespeare, William. *Julius Caesar*. Arden, UK, 1971.

Simetti, Mary Taylor. *Pomp and Sustenance*. Knopf, New York, 1989.

Süskind, Patrick. *Perfume: The Story of a Murderer*. Penguin, London, 1986.

Villaresi, Antonio. *Food and Drink in Florence*. Casa Editrice il Fiore di Aldo Capobianco, Firenze.

Walker, Barbara M. *The Little House Cookbook*. Harper & Row, New York, 1979.

Wilder, Laura Ingalls. *Little House in the Big Woods*. Penguin, London, 1963.

364

INDEX

INDEX TO RECIPES